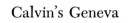

Calvin's Geneva

CALVIN'S
GENEVA

E. WILLIAM MONTER

ROBERT E. KRIEGER PUBLISHING COMPANY
HUNTINGTON, NEW YORK
1975

Original Edition 1967
Reprint 1975

Printed and Published by
ROBERT E. KRIEGER PUBLISHING CO., INC.
645 NEW YORK AVENUE
HUNTINGTON, NEW YORK 11743

Copyright © 1967 by
JOHN WILEY & SONS, INC.
Reprinted by Arrangement

Printed in the United States of America

Library of Congress Cataloging in Publication Data

Monter, E   William.
    Calvin's Geneva.

    Reprint of the ed. published by Wiley, New York, in
series: New dimensions in history: historical cities.
    Includes bibliographical references.
    1. Geneva--History. 2. Calvin, Jean, 1509-1564.
3. Geneva--Church history. I. Title. II. Series:
New dimensions in history : Historical cities.
[DQ449.5.M6 1975]   949.4'5   74-30258
ISBN 0-88275-227-8

For Barbara

PREFACE

Most libraries contain a shelf full of biographies of Calvin, but few or no works on Geneva. There is historical justification for this, of course, insofar as Calvin was greater and of more importance to western history than was his Geneva. Nevertheless, for students of the Puritan impulse, the city of Geneva has always been a fascinating place, attaining a certain secular importance far greater than her size would indicate. Ambiguous point of departure for Rousseau, home of the International Red Cross, seat of the League of Nations, Geneva has been, from the eighteenth to the twentieth century, a peculiarly important place. Her role in European history is secure, and her character —steady, serious, erudite, clannish, and proud—has remained substantially unchanged since she first became famous in the age of Calvin. It is this heroic age—Calvin's—to which this book is directed, as well as to the formation of a durable Genevan character.

The story of sixteenth-century Geneva is basically a success story. The city succeeded in maintaining a freshly won and very precarious independence against impressive odds. Her fame (or, conversely, her notoriety) spread rapidly over most of Europe soon after mid-century. Though her population grew sharply, her prosperity increased slowly from the dangerously low levels that prevailed when Calvin first arrived in 1536. In a single generation, however, starting from a virtual *tabula rasa,* Calvin's Geneva created a well-run state and a superbly run church.

This study will attempt to describe and explore Geneva's successes, partly by comparing her, where possible, with a few other European cities. What the study essentially presents is Genevan history occasionally rediscovered and sometimes rethought. It is a history whose emphasis is more political and ecclesiastical than economic (obviously, an unfair balance for any city), since we still have far too little knowledge of Genevan commerce and industry after 1540. It is Genevan history treated in somewhat the same manner as medieval men treated the ancients: by standing on the very solid shoulders of older Genevan historians. With this method one can sometimes see farther than they could—or, at other times, merely face in a different direction. In either case, this is purely and simply Genevan history, a subject far too interesting to be left to the Genevans.

This book is divided into three sections. The first four chapters outline the history of Geneva from the early sixteenth century to Calvin's death in 1564. They are chiefly concerned with showing the tumultuous environment in which Calvin worked, and the means by which his local opposition finally dissolved. The second section, consisting of three chapters, describes the principal institutions and social groups of Calvin's Geneva: the established church, the civil government, and the foreign refugee communities. The final section assesses Calvin's legacy to Geneva, and outlines the workings of Calvinism after its founder's death.

I will not attempt to portray Calvin directly, but through his environment—seen from underneath, if you prefer. I will try to outline the bases of Calvin's authority within Geneva, and the principal reasons for his success. His triumph, as I hope to show, was largely the result of his placing a brilliant mind and an undeviating will amidst the crude and confused surroundings of a revolutionary commune. I also hope to show the uniqueness of Calvin's environment, for he lived and worked in the only European city that both established and maintained her political independence during the age of the Reformation.

Perhaps the time is as ripe now as it will ever be to attempt a synthesis of the history of the Republic of Geneva in the age of Calvin. A sizable number of important historical monographs and documentary collections have been published since the semiofficial *Histoire de Genève des origines à 1798* appeared fifteen years ago. Three men in particular have enriched our knowledge of sixteenth-century Geneva: Robert M. Kingdon, whose *Geneva and the Coming of the Wars of Religion in France* appeared in 1956; Alain Dufour, whose study of *La guerre de 1589–1593* appeared two years later; and Jean-François Bergier (professor of economic and social history at the University of Geneva), whose *Genève et l'économie européene de la renaissance* began to appear in 1963. All three have helped me, in conversation as well as through their publications, to understand certain aspects of Calvin's Geneva.

Special help in preparing this book came from M. Louis Binz, assistant archivist at Geneva's Archives d'État. He established the text of Calvin's final address to the Company of Pastors from the previously unpublished version, which I have printed as an appendix. John A. Tedeschi of the Newberry Library read Chapter Seven, and suggested several corrections. My wife scrutinized the entire manuscript and ameliorated the more important translations. I wish I could say with the Venerable Bede that I have copied faithfully and that all the errors in this work have come from other men, but, unfortunately, I live in the twentieth century.

E. WILLIAM MONTER

Geneva
September, 1966

CONTENTS

List of Illustrations, *xiii*

Abbreviations, *xv*

One Cathedral and Market, *1*

Part A: Development of a City

Two The Genevan Revolution, *29*
Three The Tumult of Independence, 1536–1555, *64*
Four Calvin's Zenith, 1555–1564, *93*

Part B: Pillars of Calvin's Geneva

Five The Church of Geneva to 1564, *125*
Six The Secular Arm, *144*
Seven The Refugee Colonies, *165*

Part C: The Legacy of Calvinism

Eight Geneva after Calvin, *193*
Nine The Greatness of Geneva, *225*

Appendix: Calvin's Farewell Address to the Pastors, *239*

Bibliographical Note, *243*

Index, *247*

LIST OF ILLUSTRATIONS

Genevan coat-of-arms, 1540, *76*
François Favre and his wife, 1556, *77*
Genevan motto, 1547, *78*
Genevan coat-of-arms, 1558, *110*
Portrait of Calvin, *111*

MAPS

Pre-Reformation Geneva, the Episcopal City, *6*
Geneva in 1564, *116*
Possessions of the Republic of Geneva, *130*
Refugees to Geneva, 1549–1559, *168*
Rue des Chanoines and Place St. Pierre—1559, *175*
Geneva and her neighbors, 1536–1567, *195*

Maps by Russell H. Lenz

CHARTS

Genevan budgets, 1536–1566, *157*
Genevan wine prices, 1539–1568, *160*
The rise of Geneva's publishing industry, 1536–1572, *179*

Charts by John V. Morris

ABBREVIATIONS

G., on publications — Geneva.

AEG   Archives d'État, Geneva.

BPU   Bibliothèque publique et universitaire, Geneva.

MDG   *Mémoires et documents publiés par la Société d'histoire et d'archéologie de Genève.*

BHG   *Bulletin de la Société d'histoire et d'archéologie de Genève.*

MIG   *Memoires de l'Institut national genevois.*

BHR   *Bibliothèque d'humanisme et renaissance.*

ARG   *Archiv für Reformationsgeschichte.*

BSHPF   *Bulletin de la Société de l'histoire du protestantisme francais.*

R.C.   Rivoire and Van Berchem, eds., *Les Registres du Conseil de Genève,* 13 vols. (G., 1900–1940). Magnificent and painstaking piece of work which stops in May, 1536.

Sources du Droit Rivoire and Van Berchem, eds., *Les Sources du Droit du Canton de Genève,* 4 vols. (Aarau, 1920–1935).

R. C.   Registres du Conseil, mss. at AEG.

P.H.   Portefeuilles historiques, mss. at AEG.

L.H.   P.-F. Geisendorf, ed., *Le Livre des Habitants de Genève,* 2 vols. (G., 1957–64). We have used only vol. I, 1549–1560.

C.O.   Baum, Cunitz, and Reuss, eds., *Ioannes Calvini Opera quae supersunt omniae,* 59 vols. (Berlin-Brunswick, 1859–1900).

Herminjard   A. L. Herminjard, *Correspondance des réformateurs dans les pays de langue francaise,* 9 vols. (G.-Paris, 1866–1897).

R.C.P.   Kingdon and Bergier, eds., *Registres de la Compagnie des pasteurs de Genève au temps de Calvin,* 2 vols. (G., 1962–64).

Roget, *HPG*   Amédée Roget, *Histoire du peuple de Genève depuis la Réforme jusqu'à l'Escalade,* 7 vols. (G., 1870–87). Stops in 1568.

Studies   E. William Monter, *Studies in Genevan Government, 1536–1605* (G., 1964).

Babel, *HEG*   Antony Babel, *Histoire économique de Genève, des origines au début du XVIᵉ siècle,* 2 vols. (G., 1963).

ONE

Cathedral and Market

She is located at the end of Lake Leman, at the exit of the river Rhone which divides her, flowing from Bise (northerly) to Midi; the larger part is to the east, the smaller to the west. The river Arve borders the larger section on the side towards Midi, leaving a plain between the two rivers, which is called Plainpalais. Mountains encircle her like a crown. She once had handsome suburbs, churches, and monasteries. Now she is enclosed by walls, her suburbs pared away, her monasteries razed. She now has four main churches, namely St. Pierre and St. Germain in the Upper City, and St. Gervais and La Madeleine in the Lower City. The secondary school is located in what was formerly the [Franciscan] monastery at Rive. Her notable squares are the Bourg-de-Four near St. Pierre; the Fusterie; Molard; Longemalle; and St. Gervais. The city hall is in the Upper City, looking out in back on Plainpalais. There are three butchers' markets, two grain markets, few fountains but sufficient wells. There are two hospitals, one for paupers, the other outside the city in Plainpalais for plague victims.

Thus began the matter-of-fact chronicle composed in 1562 by one of Geneva's most famous magistrates, Michel Roset.[1] He is a sober and accurate guide, though he lacks the statistical thoroughness of a Villani or the eloquence of humanist historiography (Roset confines himself to a single simile, and a rather trite one at that). His very sobriety makes him a suitable figure to introduce us to a tiny and sober Alpine republic that was rapidly acquiring European fame — and infamy — as the seat of Calvin's experiments.

1

✝

Geneva was not an exceptionally large city, by comparison with the urban centers of Italy or south Germany, or by comparison with Lyon, her downstream neighbor on the Rhone.[2] But even with her suburbs destroyed, and despite some waves of emigration in the early sixteenth century, Geneva in 1536 was the largest city in a sizable region. She was far larger than any urban agglomeration in the large block of lands that belonged to the House of Savoy; and she was far larger than her other political neighbor, the city republic of Bern (whose rural territories were fourteen times as populous as the city herself) which defeated the Duke of Savoy in 1536.[3] Unless he were going to Lyon, a sixteenth-century Genevan had to travel for at least four days to reach another city as large as his own.

Geneva's population in the sixteenth century is a matter of approximation. The most reliable estimates give 10,300 inhabitants in 1537 (a slight decrease from the previous century, when Geneva's fairs had made her an international mercantile capital), with a sudden rise late in Calvin's lifetime, when religious refugees from France and elsewhere began to enter Geneva in truly impressive numbers. Despite a severe plague in the late 1560's, Geneva's population stood at about 13,000 when war broke out with the Duke of Savoy in 1589.[4] Such population estimates are based on the few available and exact Genevan statistics: the complete inventory of Genevan property of 1537, which showed 1000 buildings, 100 barns, and 12 mills inside the new city walls; the register of new Genevan residents, the *Livre des Habitants,* which lists about 5000 names between January 1549 and January 1560; and the census taken at the outbreak of war in 1589, which showed 2186 men fit for military service.[5]

These 10,000 native Genevans and the thousands of religious refugees living in Calvin's Geneva were confined within a relatively small space behind heavy and expensive fortifications. "Although the city is still handsome and enjoyable," said François Bonivard in the 1540's,

it is nothing by comparison with what it was in recent memory, before war broke out with the Duke [of Savoy], because not only were there suburbs longer in extent than the whole city is now, but also there were many pleasant buildings within the city which have been torn down, either to protect the city against her enemies or to remove Papist superstitions; in sum, her beauty has been diminished in order to augment her power.[6]

Refusing to build new suburbs for reasons of military security, Geneva remained crowded behind her walls until the end of the eighteenth century. She squeezed new buildings into the empty spaces (Calvin's new Academy of 1558 was the most spectacular example), she built houses where barns and stables had stood in 1537, and she added more stories to homes already built; but she did not expand her urban surface area. Geneva remained primarily a mighty fortress.

The style of architecture and the kind of house prevalent in Geneva when Calvin arrived in 1536 varied considerably according to the owner's wealth.[7] Rich merchants and Savoyard nobles (at least a dozen of them owned fine town houses in Geneva) preferred large, square, three-story stone houses with handsomely vaulted caves in the basement for storing wine and grain. Such houses often possessed a modest defensive apparatus, generally a tower, which permitted them to sustain a siege — hence their name of *maison-forte*. Such homes were built during the fourteenth and fifteenth centuries, probably in imitation of northern Italian cities whose prominent residents had similar military problems. The wealthy in Calvin's Geneva invariably possessed a courtyard or garden near their fortified home, and a barn or stable on some nearby street (there is still a rue des Granges in Geneva's Upper City).

Genevan artisans generally inhabited rectangular homes, narrow in facing the street but fairly long. These were usually two-story dwellings made of some non-flammable material such as tile; wood had been forbidden by municipal officials since the fourteenth century. On the ground floor were the artisan's shop and storeroom. At the back was a stairwell that led to the owner's bed-room, living-room, and kitchen on the second floor. Some of the more prosperous artisans added a third floor to lodge children and servants. Home furnishings were sturdy but simple — tables of oak or walnut; benches, stools, a storage cabinet, and usually a curtained bed for master and mistress. All lots — even the row houses in the parish of St. Gervais, east of the Rue de Coutances, that had been carved up into 20 x 50-foot lots in the fifteenth century — were large enough to provide a small garden in back, where the owner's family grew a few fresh vegetables.

The architecture of Calvin's Geneva changed but little from that of the episcopal city. Her narrow façades and Gothic windows were not replaced by Renaissance styles until the beginning of the seventeenth century; the Turrettini home on the rue de l'Hotel de Ville, built in 1618–1620, is the first pure example of the new trend. Calvin's Geneva was a poor and austere city which could not afford to construct vast new buildings in her crowded space. Indeed, about the only important change from the fifteenth century was that the ordinary Genevan inhabitant now had less fresh air and less living space. When Geneva began to be a rich city, in the seventeenth and eighteenth centuries, the buildings that had existed in the heroic but uncomfortable age of Calvin were generally replaced. Today's tourist, traveling around the "old city" of Geneva, is actually looking at the city of Rousseau and Voltaire, not of Calvin. No private homes built during the sixteenth century survive in Geneva today — the last one was torn down in 1911 — and very few traces of public buildings, apart from the spiral ramp of the old *Maison de Ville* and some fragments of Calvin's Academy, remain from Calvin's century. Physically, except for its churches, Calvin's Geneva has almost entirely disappeared, and reconstructing it is a job for one's historical imagination.

A city, however, is not an agglomeration of buildings but a collection of men. What sort of men inhabited Geneva in 1536, where did they come from, what trades did they ply, and what were their religious sentiments? These questions can all be answered with some degree of accuracy. Between 1501 and 1536, a total of 1112 men were admitted to Genevan citizenship, and over 90% of them listed both their place of origin and their profession.[8] Geographically, over three-fifths (612 in all) came from the lands of the Duke of Savoy, including 43 from the Pays de Vaud, and 28 from Piedmont. Geneva received 174 citizens from France, 124 of them from the Duchy of Burgundy. About one-sixth (162) of Geneva's new citizens were born in the city, or in nearby lands belonging to the Bishop or Chapter of Geneva. Twenty *bourgeois* came from Germany, including the Swiss League; 3 came from north Italy; 7 from the Free County of Burgundy; and 3 from the Netherlands. Professionally, one-eighth (127) of these new citizens were cobblers, and the rest practiced a wide variety of trades. There were 58 tailors; 55 pastry cooks; 47 carpenters; 39 merchants; 37 day-laborers; 32 butchers; 26 notaries; 25 barbers; 20 stone-masons; 16 apothecaries; 12 furriers; and at least 20 more professions were represented among this thousand.[9]

The professional structure of Calvin's Geneva was to be altered radically by the arrival of religious refugees in the 1550's. About half of these newcomers (2247) listed their professions.[10] Here again, the great majority (1536) were artisans, including 181 cobblers, 67 goldsmiths, and 672 immigrants connected in some fashion with textile production. But this list also includes 180 merchants, 113 printers and booksellers, and 70 noblemen — three figures that compare eloquently with the Geneva of 1536, which contained about 50 merchants, only 3 printers, and probably no noblemen.[11]

The localization of crafts within Calvin's Geneva was haphazard. Some trades, such as the furriers, cauldron-makers (*peyroliers*), and *rôtisseurs*, who gave their names to Genevan streets, were sharply concentrated. Some, like the tanners, were confined to a small area near the Rhone, because the odors of their shops would be less offending there, or because they needed water. The bridge over the river was lined on both sides by a cluster of shops and mills. Notaries lived mostly in the upper part of the city, around the cathedral or in the parish of St. Germain, whereas the apothecaries and merchants inhabited the chain of broad downtown streets, *les rues-basses,* which extended from the Rhone bridge to the gate at Rive near the Franciscan convent.[12]

The only vital division in Calvin's Geneva separated the area within the walls into the Upper and Lower City. This distinction probably extended back to late Roman times, and was embedded in Genevan political life; from the fourteenth century until 1603, two of Geneva's four chief magistrates or Syndics were annually elected from each half of the city. Nature and history had com-

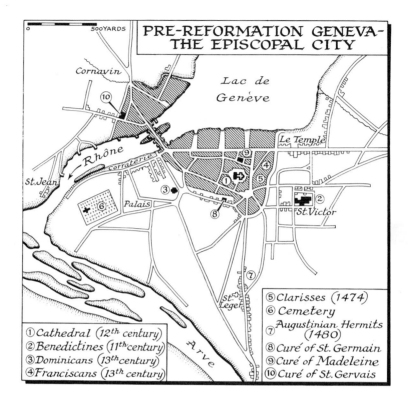

PRE-REFORMATION GENEVA—
THE EPISCOPAL CITY

0   500 YARDS

Cornavin

Lac de
Genève

Rhône

Corraterie

St. Jean

Le Temple

Palais

St. Victor

St. Léger

Arve

① Cathedral (12th century)
② Benedictines (11th century)
③ Dominicans (13th century)
④ Franciscans (13th century)
⑤ Clarisses (1474)
⑥ Cemetery
⑦ Augustinian Hermits (1480)
⑧ Curé of St. Germain
⑨ Curé of Madeleine
⑩ Curé of St. Gervais

bined to bisect Geneva into a small but steep hill and a long
arc of plain beneath this hill, bordered on the west by the Rhone
and on the north by Lake Geneva. Atop the hill, in the Upper
City, the Helvetic tribes had built their citadel. There the bishops of Geneva built their cathedral in the sixth century, and there
the civil government of Geneva built its town hall in the fifteenth
century. Along the plain, sheltered by the hill and in close contact with the natural trade routes formed by the lake and the
river, the Lower City grew. It has been the center of Genevan
commercial activity from Roman times through the period of the
great fifteenth-century fairs, down to today's great cluster of
banks and department stores. (It seems only fitting that the last
sixteenth-century home on the *rues-basses* should have been de-
molished to make way for Geneva's largest department store).
Men of letters, men of justice, clerks, and officials always lived

6

in the Upper City; businessmen lived in the Lower City. Government was concentrated on Geneva's hill, with commerce beneath it, thereby providing a world view that encapsulates the history of many of Geneva's prominent families as they struggled socially upward from commerce to the liberal professions.

With this division in mind, let us look briefly at each half of Geneva, and at one typical representative of the Upper and Lower City as they existed when Calvin arrived in 1536. Both our examples happen to be Genevan citizen-chroniclers, and both (for very different reasons) happened to be in the Genevan spotlight in 1536.

✝

The *rues-basses,* heart of the Lower City, were divided by three great public squares (Fusterie, Molard, and Longemalle), all of which extended down to the edge of the lake. The main thoroughfare went by a different name each block: from the Rhone to the Fusterie ran the rue des Allemands; from the Fusterie to Molard came la Rivière; from Molard to Longemalle, the Poissonerie; and beyond Longemalle came the rue de Rive. The most interesting sight along these busy streets was an almost continuous chain of tiny wooden shops (only 7 x 8 feet) called *hauts-bancs,* which were sheltered from the elements by tall roofs called *dômes.* These *hauts-bancs,* which the city rented to artisans and merchants, attracted the curiosity of Geneva's new schoolmaster in 1538, who described them in a brochure:[13]

The most crowded, the longest, and most mercantile street of all is very spacious and wide and has very long and high special roofs on both sides. These roofs are well supported by traverse beams and by pillars for horizontal support. They serve to protect merchandise and to provide a sheltered path for pedestrians in case of rain, wind, or excessive heat.

Between the rows of *hauts-bancs* was an open space through which carriages could pass. These stalls for merchandise had been erected for the convenience of foreign merchants during the fifteenth-century fairs; they continued in use as the fairs declined, and were rented to immigrant and native merchants and notaries throughout the sixteenth century.

The best-known and most luxurious of Geneva's two dozen inns were also to be found on or near the *rues-basses*, because they too had been erected for the convenience of foreign merchants in the fifteenth century.[14] In the late 1530's, two of these inn-keepers were Genevan magistrates, members of the Small Council: François Rosset of the *Tête Noire* in the Poissonerie, and François Lullin of the *Tour Perse* near the rue des Allemands. Most Genevan inns took their names from commonplace heraldic symbols, such as crosses, suns, stars, crowns, keys, towers, or shields. The most interesting and symptomatic change to occur among them during Calvin's lifetime was the decline of the three inns called the White Cross (symbol of the House of Savoy), and the growing fame of Jean Lullin's Bear (the Bernese symbol), which coincided with Geneva's shift from Savoyard to Bernese protectorate. The inns of Calvin's Geneva continued to host foreign visitors on a reduced scale, lodging frequent embassies from the Swiss and other foreign visitors of a less official nature, among whom Michael Servetus was the most notorious.

A few foreign merchants, for whom the *hauts-bancs* and the inns had been built, still lived in Geneva when Calvin arrived. Four of them can be identified from the 1537 inventory, all living on the well-named rue des Allemands. They are Henri Embler, or "Sr Henri l'allemant"; Jacques Manlich; George des Clefs; and Johann Kléberger.[15] They form an interesting group. Kléberger (1486–1544), born at Nürnberg, was a financier who acquired Bernese citizenship in 1521 and exchanged it for French citizenship in 1536. He had extensive urban properties in Lyon and Paris, as well as his little-used two houses, mill, and garden in Geneva. He was an internationally known figure whose portrait was done in 1526 by Dürer and whose statute stood in Lyon, where he was known as the "good German."[16] No other merchant-financier of his stature was to be found in Geneva, and Kléberger himself was seldom to be found there. The only other representative of an important German trading firm was Manlich, whose Augsburg business weathered many storms before finally going bankrupt in 1574.[17] Jacques, the nephew of the firm's director, had been trading in Geneva since 1516 and became a Genevan citizen in 1517. His brother Matthew, who became a Genevan citizen in 1538, founded a family that produced a sixteenth-century Genevan magistrate.[18] Embler was a Bernese merchant of modest wealth, whose relatives had acquired Genevan citizenship in 1494, and whose descendants ran Geneva's mint in the 1550's.[19] Des Clefs, whose origins are obscure, was strongly committed to the Bernese and anti-Calvin faction. He perished in the tumult of June 1540.[20]

The rue des Allemands was not only the home of Geneva's principal merchants, but also the cradle of the Genevan reformation. The evangelical groups, formed with Farel's help after 1532, met in private homes in this street, and the preachers themselves generally stayed in downtown homes such as Jean Lambert's. The government of Bern even sold a home in the rue des Allemands to a rebellious Savoyard nobleman in 1533 in order to use it as a "front" for the Genevan evangelical community.[21] But if the *rues-basses* were the cradle of the Reformation and the bastion of Bernese influence in Geneva, they were, for these very reasons, to be the center of opposition to Calvin and to the French immigrants in the 1550's. Jean Philippe, leader of the first-anti-Calvin faction in 1540, lived near the Fusterie. Ami Perrin, leader of the second such faction, lived on la Rivière. Their supporters came partly from these downtown streets (witness George des Clefs) but probably even more from the right-bank suburb of St. Gervais, Geneva's artisan quarter, which preserved a certain *frondeur* spirit throughout Calvin's lifetime.[22]

†

Our representative from the Lower City lived not on the rue des Allemands but on the eastern extremity of the *rues-basses* — the rue de Rive — only six houses away from the city's eastern gate. Jean Balard (ca. 1488–1555), son of a Savoyard admitted to Genevan citizenship in 1487, was a merchant specializing in ironware.[23] Balard was a prudent and honorable burgher who adjusted his opinions to the rapidly changing circumstances of Geneva's civic revolution in the 1520's and 1530's. He had been active in civic councils since 1515, participating in 40 of 149 sessions over the next decade. He was suddenly raised to political prominence in 1525 as one of Geneva's four Syndics or chief magistrates; the portion of his diary that has survived also begins in that year. Balard apparently belonged to neither of Geneva's political factions of the mid-1520's, the pro-Savoyard Mammelukes or the pro-Swiss Eidguenots. He displayed consistent moderation and caution, which enabled him to remain afloat throughout this stormy decade of Genevan politics. He served as municipal treasurer from 1527 to 1529, was again made Syndic in 1530, and constantly remained a member of Geneva's Small Council, the two dozen men who ran the city's daily business, until 1536. (Balard's diary stops in October 1531.)[24]

Balard spoke no German and was a lukewarm adherent to the Swiss alliance of 1526. Apparently he also disliked the Protestantism that Bern began to promote within Geneva after 1532, but, characteristically, he never spoke out against these religious novelties until January 1536. Then he quarrelled with Farel after the abolition of the Mass in Geneva. Balard publicly remarked that "if the Mass is worthless, then the death and Passion of Jesus Christ are worthless"; whereupon several of his colleagues dubbed him a heretic, ordered him to go hear the word of God as expounded by their preachers, and Balard soon absented himself from meetings of the Small Council.[25] His colleagues made half-hearted attempts to force Balard to conform. He was ordered to attend sermons, but he refused to go. He was then ordered banished for a year, but he refused to leave. His shop was ordered closed, but apparently it didn't stay closed for long. Questioned about his religious beliefs on July 24, he replied on a small piece of paper that he "wished to live by the Gospel and not to follow it through the interpretation of private persons, but according to the interpretation of the Holy Ghost through the Holy Universal Church in which I believe." Asked whether he would attend the sermons, Balard replied that his conscience would not permit it and that he didn't want to go against his conscience.[26] Six months later, in December, Jean Balard contributed the sizable sum of 50 écus to help the new Republic of Geneva pay to the Bernese the enormous debt from her war of independence.[27]

In 1537, Balard refuted an accusation of treason made against him by a locksmith; his innocence was obvious and his reputation, except in religious questions, unblemished. He was even promoted to the Small Council once again in 1539, after having been dropped from it in 1537. However, at Christmas 1539, he was once again interrogated about his religious beliefs by the Republic's prosecuting attorney, Thomas Genod (formerly parish priest at St. Gervais, now married to the only Genevan nun who had accepted the Reformation). Balard responded that he was "entirely ready to believe all the articles of faith that the whole city believes, and that he wishes his body to be united with the body of the city, as a loyal citizen should do," but his interrogators were unsatisfied. A second interrogation on Christmas Eve ended when Balard answered that "he couldn't judge things which he didn't know or understand; but since it pleases the government that he say the Mass is evil, he will say that the Mass is evil." He added at once that "no one could judge of a man's heart, and the Gospel says that those who are godly shall live and those who are ungodly shall perish." "Afterwards he confessed the Mass to be evil," calmly remarks the official register, and no doubt Balard took communion that Christmas.[28]

After this episode, however, Balard was dropped from the Small Council, and he never returned. Suspected, as the Consistory put it in January 1542, of being "still an idolater,"[29] Balard lived out his Genevan existence quietly. He continued to sit on the Council of Two Hundred after 1541, and he was even promoted to the Council of Sixty in 1546. Balard participated in none of the factional quarrels between Calvin's allies and Ami Perrin's *enfants de Genève* that filled Genevan political history during the last decade of his long life. Balard took part in no important public business at all, partly because he was old and sick, and partly because he had no sympathy for either of the factions then struggling for power. His son Jean, whose marriage in 1541 was celebrated with dances, sonnets, and mummeries that drew the wrath of the newly formed Genevan Consistory, also sat on the Council of Two Hundred after 1549; but he too was apparently not connected with Perrin's faction. The younger Balard was dropped from the Council in 1557 for interfering with the election of Syndics, and died in 1558, only three years after his father.[30]

Jean Balard is an interesting man, a Genevan deeply imbued with the spirit of the old commune, who in 1539 "wishes his body to be united with the body of the city, as a good citizen should do." Balard was not especially rich; he owned only one house in the city while some of his colleagues owned half a dozen, and he had only a modest bit of vineyard and pasture south of the city at Bossey.[31] But he gave liberally whenever Geneva needed to raise money quickly; forty écus to help pay the rapacious Swiss after their military aid in 1530, and fifty écus for a similar purpose in 1536.[32] As a chronicler, he was dry, factual, and surprisingly impersonal, never mentioning his personal role. He was a prudent man, moderate but resolute, who defended both the *civitas genebennsis* and the *corpus christianorum*. He was the only Genevan magistrate who served continuously on the Small Council from 1525 through 1536. Balard's sentiments are probably most clearly expressed by a passage from his diary in November 1530:[33]

Because I have seen the cause of good and of evil in the city [of Geneva] I wish to give warning. The cause of evil is pride. The cause of good is humility, having your principal trust in God rather than in men. For in doing good, one should never fear that things will not turn out favorably for the city of Geneva, which may it please God in his great pity to inspire with his grace and preserve from all mischance. Amen.

✝

Geneva's Upper City was dominated by the cathedral of St. Pierre. Considering that she was the capital of a very large diocese, which contained 443 parishes in 1447, Geneva did not possess a grandiose cathedral.[34] Neither was St. Pierre an impressive work of medieval architecture. In Calvin's age it stood as a bewildering hodgepodge of various Romanesque and Gothic styles, for it had been repaired several times by different architects after its foundations were laid in the mid-twelfth century. Geneva's internecine struggles of the fourteenth century did much damage to the building; there was a severe fire in 1430, and another disaster in 1441 when one wall of the nave collapsed onto the cloister. Geneva's chapter, who were required to keep the cathedral repaired, were still trying to efface this damage in 1529, but their task had not been completed when the Reformation came to Geneva and contributed its share towards ravaging the interior of St. Pierre. Perhaps the most impressive adjunct to Geneva's cathedral was the great bell which had been installed in the north tower in 1407; *La Clémence* has survived the centuries and still rings in Geneva today. Her rich, deep tones must have been audible for many miles in the sixteenth century, far outside the narrow boundaries of the new Republic. A Gothic inscription around the base of *La Clémence* proclaimed her mission: "I praise the true God, I summon the people, I assemble the clergy, I weep for the dead, I chase the plague away, I embellish feast days. My voice is the terror of all devils."

Geneva's cathedral suffered from secularization in 1535 and 1536, when the chasubles and silver plate were melted down. However, a large cross atop the main (west) façade remained shamefully intact, "as a mark or insignia of Papal deviltry," noted the Genevan secretary, until it was providentially struck by lightning in August 1556.[35] Only then was the St. Peter's of this reformed Rome a fit arena for Calvin's sermons.

Adjoining the north side of the cathedral was the cloister, once the property of the Venerable Chapter of Geneva. Here Geneva's general citizen assembly met, both before and after the Reformation, in order to elect the city's four Syndics each February and to elect Geneva's principal judicial officer, the Lieutenant, each November. Before the Reformation, the cathedral square had been surrounded by a wall with a single gate, and the open space within occupied by small wooden benches, used principally by notaries and by the legal proletariat attached to the ecclesiastical courts. After the Reformation, this wall was removed, but the benches remained to be used by Genevan printers and booksellers in the 1550's.

The square surrounding the cathedral included not only the cloister, but also the official residence of Geneva's Bishop, which the Republic converted into its public prison. Scattered around this square, and extending westward along the rue des Chanoines, were the homes of episcopal officials and many of Geneva's 32 canons. This was the quarter of Geneva most devastated by the decade of war and revolution that preceded Calvin's arrival in Geneva in 1536. The inventory of 1537 showed that the three wards or *dizaines* in this area were the only ones where over half the buildings had been owned by fugitives or absentees.[36] Here, in a cluster of well-furnished vacant houses, the reformed preachers serving the new state replaced the old inhabitants of the rue des Chanoines. But reformed Geneva required fewer preachers than the old regime required canons, and many of these homes remained vacant until the arrival of wealthy Frenchmen in the 1550's (see the reconstruction of the Place St. Pierre and the rue des Chanoines, p. 175).

The second center of life in the Upper City was the *Maison de Ville*.[37] Begun in the fifteenth century, this town hall was greatly improved by the construction of the Tour Baudet in 1455. This fortress and seat of government still survives today, and continues to fill some of its sixteenth-century functions. A chapel was added to the building in 1504, in the basement, which the reformed Republic soon turned into a depository for her public archives. Above this grotto were some none-too-comfortable rooms, equipped only with walnut benches (not even covered with cloth until after Calvin's death) where the regular sessions of Geneva's governing councils were held. Adjoining the Tour Baudet were the public stables and a few small houses where the magistrates stored public armaments and supplies. The only major change to Geneva's town hall during Calvin's lifetime was the construction of a handsome spiral pathway in front of the Tour Baudet — a major enterprise that required almost twenty years to complete.

Apart from these capitals of church and state in Calvin's Geneva, there were few major landmarks in the Upper City. East of the cathedral stood the former nunnery, now converted into an almshouse, the *hôpital général*. There were a few small churches in the Upper City, which the new state used to store grain or, in the 1550's, to provide for the foreign refugee churches. Two of them still serve a similar function today: the Scottish Presbyterian church on the site of the old *auditoire* on the cathedral square, and the Old Catholics in the former parish church of St. Germain. Otherwise, there was little of importance in this part of Geneva, and very little commercial activity in the Upper City. This had once been the home of the lawyers, the *gens de longue robbe,* whose departure had been sadly noted by the nun Jeanne de Jussie as early as 1526;[38] this would later be the home of "men of letters and justice, of foreigners and book-sellers," as the French cosmographer Pierre Davity described it in 1637.[39] But Geneva in 1536 was deprived of these classes. It would be Calvin's special contribution to the history of Geneva to attract men of learning and piety to live near him on the rue des Chanoines in the Upper City, and to restore the balance between commerce and erudition in Geneva, a balance which had been temporarily broken after the defeat of her Bishop by her citizens.

†

Among the very few traditional inhabitants of the Upper City who were residing there when Calvin arrived in 1536, one is fairly well known. François de Bonivard (1493–1570), ex-abbot of the Benedictine monastery of St. Victor just outside Geneva's walls, ex-canon of Geneva, poet, chronicler, and littérateur of Renaissance tastes, had recently been released after six years of imprisonment in the fortress of Chillon.[40]

Born at the river town of Seyssel into a noble clan who had served the House of Savoy since the thirteenth century, François — a second son — received an excellent education designed to prepare him for an ecclesiastical career. He matriculated at the University of Freiburg-in-Breisgau in 1513, partly to learn German and partly to study law. Bonivard soon migrated to Italy, that Mecca of sixteenth-century scholars, and in 1515 acquired the title of *juris utrisque doctoris* from the University of Turin. He also acquired a taste for humanistic studies from his principal professor, the well-known political theorist and translator of Polybius, Claude de Seyssel. After completing his studies, Bonivard settled in Geneva, where in 1514 he had inherited the abbey of St. Victor from his uncle. The young man was soon ordained, and assumed his duties as a canon of Geneva, a rank automatically entailed by his possession of St. Victor. He soon got embroiled in local politics, and made a reputation for himself as an ardent partisan of a Swiss alliance; Bonivard's name appears at the head of 86 Genevans who signed a *combourgeoisie* with the canton of Fribourg in 1519. Duke Charles III of Savoy was incensed by Bonivard's act, which was most probably inspired by motives of revenge, for the Bishop of Geneva, a cousin to Charles III, had recently seized a rich abbey which had also belonged to Bonivard's uncle.[41] Bonivard repulsed the Duke's attempts to win him back through "flatterbo" and expiated his rash deed by a year's imprisonment and by the loss of St. Victor. Pope Leo X deprived Bonivard of the abbey's revenues in 1521, in favor of his Florentine friend Leonardo Tornabuoni.[42]

We know little of Bonivard's life in Geneva in the 1520's. Much of his time was apparently spent in literary activities, and even more on vain attempts to win back his abbey by diplomacy or once by armed attack. In 1530, while on a prolonged visit to his parents, Bonivard was taken prisoner by ducal officials near Lausanne. This time, he spent six long years — which he tersely described as his "second Passion" — in confinement, whiling away the time by composing poems.

Liberated, Bonivard returned to Geneva in April 1536. He emerged like Rip van Winkle into a city completely independent of its Prince-Bishop and newly converted to the Reformation, and apparently it took him some time to adjust to this new state of affairs. The Republic provided him with the vacant home of a former episcopal officer, but denied Bonivard the revenues of St. Victor, which the new government claimed by right of war (the abbey itself had been destroyed along with the rest of the city's suburbs, but the taxes which supported it were still regularly collected). Geneva granted Bonivard a pension of two hundred écus, which amounted to about a third of the abbey's old revenues. He said he could not live in such circumstances, and left the next year for Lausanne, where he became a Bernese citizen and soon acquired a German-speaking wife. After more than five years abroad, Bonivard returned to Geneva permanently in 1543; the Republic had invited him to write its official history and again offered him a pension, slightly smaller than in 1536.

This time, Bonivard lived in Geneva for twenty-seven years, and not in luxury. He repeatedly fell into debt, and the government repeatedly bailed him out. He got into many quarrels with the new Consistory, which summoned him in 1543 for gambling with dice and playing "trique-trac" with the poet Clément Marot, and which excommunicated him as late as 1564 for writing seditious poetry after Calvin's death. Bonivard had an especially turbulent married life. His second wife, a widow whom he married in 1544 to the amusement of Calvin, soon deserted him and even sold their furniture. She died in 1552, and Bonivard married a much quieter woman with whom he lived for six years. Finally, in 1562, he was compelled by the Consistory and the magistrates to marry a fourth wife, an ex-nun who had been his housekeeper — despite his sexual impotence (which the Council minutes faithfully record). This farce soon became a tragedy when the young nun was drowned and a servant of Bonivard's beheaded in 1565 for their adultery.[43]

Bonivard's literary production, nearly all of it in a vigorous vernacular, is surprisingly diverse. He was an incurable versifier, prolific producer of quatrains and rondels, which were partially gathered into a small collection of *menus pensées* but which also lie strewn through his prose works. He had the ingenuity to produce a unique French-German-Latin lexicon, arranged by alphabetical order in parallel columns (such as "jugent=aetatis juvenilis=jeunesse") and totaling about 3000 entries, which occupied much of his time in the 1540's. Although this work was "not only profitable, but even more, necessary," as Bonivard remarked in his preface, it remained in manuscript along with the rest of his works. (No trilingual dictionary was printed at Geneva until 1611).[44] Bonivard's principal and official task at Geneva, however, was the compilation of an official history. He worked diligently at this for about three years and finally completed his account through the year of his own imprisonment, 1530. He submitted this manuscript to the Small Council in 1551. Geneva's government, however, refused to permit its publication because their Swiss allies were not treated with sufficient gentleness and because the language was "crude". The manuscript was kicked from pillar to post — a councilman's widow admitted in 1556 that her husband had lost it — and it remained unpublished, like all other Genevan chronicles of this century, until the nineteenth century.

Bonivard also found time to undertake some French translations from Latin and German. One of them, an anti-clerical hor-

ror story, which he adapted from Stumpf's *Schwyzerchronik* in
1549, was the only work he ever published. Above all, however,
Bonivard liked to compose treatises or digressions, which he
labelled *advis et devis,* on any number of subjects. His treatises
were generally based upon some extant Latin work, which
Bonivard translated while adding his own opinions and information to those of the original author. He composed at least eight
such treatises in the 1550's and 1560's on such topics as Degrees
of Nobility, Language, the Origin of Sin, the Three Political
Estates and Their Corruptions, the Source of Idolatry and Papal
Tyranny, the Different Kinds of Reformations, True and False
Miracles, or the Old and New Government of Geneva.[45]

Bonivard was a literary intellectual, perhaps the only man of
this type to be subsidized by the new Republic. Geneva protected him, as his biographer noted, for his learning and his
loyalty. They observed in 1558 that he was "not sufficiently industrious to run his own affairs properly," but also observed
both in 1551 and 1561 that he "has always been well disposed
towards us."[46] His will, drawn up in 1557 and never substantially modified, stipulated that his entire estate should go to public charity, which it eventually did. Bonivard was vehemently
opposed to Luther, who, he claimed, preached a gospel of pillage as Mohammed had done, and he was even more vehemently opposed to Papal tyranny. Nevertheless, he was no enthusiastic Calvinist. Bonivard's writings illustrate this point well.
His syntax was virtually identical with that of Marot or Rabelais;
his orthography phonetically betrays his Savoyard origins; he
very seldom mentions Calvin by name in his writings, and his
biographer is probably correct in calling him the last Genevan
author whose style remained unmodified by Calvin.[47] Bonivard
had many favorites among modern authors, including Erasmus
and Ramus, but there was no modern writer whom he cited
more frequently than Rabelais — and Bonivard apparently read
and cited him only *after* Calvin's scathing denunciation of this
"atheist" in his *De Scandalis* of 1550.

Bonivard's remarks about the character of pre-Reformation
Geneva could be applied to himself with considerable justice:
"gentle, benign, courteous and liberal, more magnanimous than
prudent. For the most part they were carefree; but war, neces-

sarily, and the reformation of religion, voluntarily, have made them a good deal more withdrawn."[48]

✝

Describing the hinterlands of Geneva, Michel Roset observed in 1562 that the city was "surrounded by the territories of MM. of Bern, after which the lands of the Duke of Savoy are nearest"; formerly, the lands of Savoy had entirely surrounded Geneva, or as Bonivard put it, in the old days you could hardly spit over the walls without reaching Savoyard soil.[49] The watershed between Savoyard and Bernese occupation of Geneva's environs falls exactly in 1536, the year of Calvin's arrival. And it is an odd coincidence that these lands were returned to Catholic Savoy through the Treaty of Lausanne, signed in the year of Calvin's death, 1564. The importance of these dates is crucial. Only a few enclaves near Geneva had belonged to the Bishop and chapter, and were thus to be governed directly by the new Republic after 1536. In fact, Geneva lost part of the Bishop's dominions, for the large *mandement* of Thiez, which lay within territory occupied by the French in 1536, was taken away from Geneva by Francis I in 1539.[50] Like most free cities, Geneva controlled only a very small fraction of her economic hinterland, even if we include about thirty rural communes where Calvin's Republic collected tithes, introduced the Reformation, and dispensed low justice. However, the problem of who *did* have political control of her hinterland was of vital importance to this city state. And the interesting fact is that only during Calvin's residence in Geneva, from 1536 to 1564, were these lands in the legal possession of Geneva's religious and political allies, the Bernese. Both before and afterwards, Geneva was surrounded by Savoy, whose princes had been mortal enemies to the city since 1526 and who remained so for centuries. (Today, many of Geneva's bus routes extend far into what were once Savoyard lands). In other words, only during Calvin's lifetime was Geneva surrounded by a political and religious cushion.

But Geneva's relations with Bern, as we shall soon see, were often tense and difficult. Quarrels were frequent and pacification was slow. Bern especially disliked the somewhat different religious establishment which Calvin so energetically promoted within Geneva. Nevertheless, the government of Bern was certainly the lesser of two evils as neighbors; for they had vowed, a few months before Calvin arrived in Geneva, to keep their conquered territories, "with the aid of God who has given them these lands, so that the inhabitants may enjoy the benefits of order and justice, and of the Word of God." They did exactly that. Bern abolished canon law, ordered all notaries to draw up their acts in *romant* instead of Latin, and arranged a series of public disputes in each commune in order to adopt the Reformation through popular votes.[51] It was against this rural background, the Bernese *baillages* of Gex, Ternier, and Thonon, that Calvin's Geneva acted out her daily existence.

Because sixteenth-century Geneva controlled only a small part of her hinterland, making her a "city without a country," we should not overlook the numerous ties connecting the city to this hinterland. Economically, Geneva and Savoy were interdependent. Geneva herself was semirural and had to legislate against keeping pigs and goats inside the walls even after 1536. Every Genevan homeowner had his garden and every prosperous homeowner his stable within the walls. Nearly every Genevan citizen also owned some rural property outside the walls where he grew his grain and prepared his wine; wealthier Genevans also had a sizable piece of pasture where their own cows grazed. All the necessities of life — bread, wine, and dairy products — were produced in Geneva's hinterland, frequently on lands outside Genevan political control, and transported to the burgher's town house, where they were stockpiled in the basement. Furthermore, a sizable portion of Geneva's commercial activity was directed towards the surrounding peasantry. Shrewd old traders made sizable profits from the *renève,* a cash loan which peasants repaid in grain or wine after the annual harvest, often at rates that were highly usurious.[52] Others, like Ami Perrin's father who sold wooden plates and glassware, traveled about the neighboring *baillages* with their wares strapped to their back, beginning as peddlars and ending as sedentary merchants.[53] After 1546, Calvin's Geneva held four annual fairs for rural merchants, peddlars, and horse traders, just south of the Porte Neuve in Plainpalais.[54] Geneva's connections with her rural neighbors were daily and intimate — necessarily so, since any city is primarily an economic unit and to some extent a parasite feeding upon the local peasantry. Even as far as her population was concerned, sixteenth-century Geneva was totally dependent on her rural environs. (Recall that three-fifths of her new citizens from 1501–1536 came from Savoy, and one-sixth from lands of Geneva's own Prince-Bishop, while only about one-fifth came from lands more than eighty miles distant.) All in all, the division between city and country in Calvin's Geneva was nowhere near as sharp as many authors have supposed.

In concluding this introduction to the city of Geneva in 1536, one should underline two points about her peculiar character. First, Geneva was a city that thrived on commerce but was virtually devoid of any type of manufacturing (as the sixteenth century understood the term).[55] In the fifteenth century, Geneva's fairs had raised her to European fame as an entrepot, and a branch of the great Medici Bank had been established there for almost forty years. Yet Geneva herself never produced any bankers. Worse yet, she established no industry, not even that great medieval staple, the textile industry, which flourished nearby at Fribourg. The Genevan merchant of the sixteenth century was an industrious retailer, as Ami Perrin's father had been. But the typical Genevan artisan produced only for local consumption, not for export. Perhaps it was for these reasons that Geneva had more than fifty religious and social fraternities (confréries) before 1536, but no craft guilds (jurandes) until late in Calvin's lifetime (the first craft regulations in Geneva date from 1557).[56] The first products manufactured in Geneva for export date from the 1550's, along with the thousands of religious refugees who carried both money and skills with them when they abandoned France and Italy. The French installed Geneva's first export industry, publishing. The Italians introduced silk-weaving, which gradually replaced books as Geneva's basic export by the end of the sixteenth century. But when Calvin died in 1564, this process of Genevan "manufacturing" had only begun; and the only exportable product which his Geneva produced — the printed book — was a religious as well as an economic enterprise.[57]

Second, Calvin's Geneva was very much a frontier city

religiously, politically, and even culturally. In Calvin's lifetime, she stood at the southwestern extremity of organized Protestantism, which explains some of the city's attraction for Frenchmen and Italians fleeing from the harsh policies of Henri II or the Roman Inquisition. (Refugees from northern France could and often did go to Strasbourg, and the Marian exiles generally stopped at points much nearer England than Geneva.) Geneva acquired her huge refugee population partly through Calvin and partly through geography.

Politically, Calvin's Geneva was an independent city, though she neither desired nor acquired the official title of an Imperial Free City. Geneva was also something of a political orphan. In the long and dangerous process of establishing her independence, a process just completed when Calvin first arrived, Geneva had definitely thrown off any allegiance to her *de facto* sovereigns of the fifteenth century, the House of Savoy. But the intriguing part of Genevan history is that the city developed no dynastic or national loyalties to replace Savoy. Calvin's city was neither Swiss nor French, either politically or culturally. This is not to deny the obvious fact that residents of Geneva flagrantly displayed their sympathies for one country or the other, especially during Calvin's lifetime. But it should be emphasized that the entire history of the independent Republic of Geneva is precisely that of a buffer state between the Swiss — then known in Geneva as *les allemands* — and the equally foreign French, whose laws and language were very different from the Savoyard customs and *patois* which prevailed in sixteenth-century Geneva.[58] Ultimately, Geneva's destiny was determined by influences such as Calvin and the French Revolution, and her fate was to be culturally French and (since 1815) politically Swiss.

Genevan patriotism was and still is intensely local. The road along the north side of the lake, towards Lausanne, is still known as *la route suisse,* and roads are usually named after their destinations. The word *national* in a Genevan title often does not mean "Swiss," but "Genevan." This is true both of the *Église nationale protestante* and of the chair of *histoire nationale* at the University of Geneva. Such is the character of a small but free state.

NOTES

1. Like all sixteenth-century Genevan chronicles, Roset's work was published in the nineteenth century: *Les Chroniques de Genève*, ed. H. Fazy (G., 1894).

2. In the mid-sixteenth century, Lyon had about 50,000 inhabitants and was the second city of France (estimates based on 8500 able-bodied men mustered in 1544, and 7400 men mustered in 1557): see A. Kleinelausz, *Histoire de Lyon* (Lyon, 1939), I, pp. 486–87; R. Mols, *Introduction à la demographie historique des villes d'Europe du XIVe au XVIIIe siècle* (Louvain, 1954), II, pp. 515–17.

3. Sixteenth-century Bern had between 4000 and 5000 inhabitants, but ruled over 70,000 inhabitants in her Oberland: Richard Feller, *Geschichte Berns* (Bern, 1954), II, pp. 23–24. No Swiss city, with the exception of Basel or Zurich, was as large as Geneva, and none was larger.

4. Louis Blondel, *Le Développement urbain de Genève à travers les siècles* (Geneva-Nyon, 1946), pp. 115–17.

5. AEG, Recensement A 2; P.–F. Geisendorf, ed., *Le Livre des Habitants de Genève, Tome I: 1549–1560* (G., 1957); A. Dufour, *La Guerre de 1589–1593* (G., 1958), p. 22.

6. Bonivard, *Les Chroniques de Genève*, I, p. 35, quoted by H. Naef, *Les Origines de la Réforme à Genève* (Geneva-Paris, 1936), p. 7.

7. See Antony Babel, *Histoire économique de Genève des origines au début du XVIe siècle* [hereafter *HEG*] (G., 1963), I, pp. 514–21; Blondel, *Developpement urbain de Genève*, pp. 52–54, 65–66; Emile Doumergue, *Jean Calvin; les hommes et les choses de son temps* (Lausanne, 1905), III, pp. 408–48.

8. Analysis and tables in Babel, *HEG*, II, pp. 610–11.

9. Babel, *HEG*, II, pp. 620–23 gives a broadly similar range of occupations from a Genevan tax-roll of 1464. Compare Kleinclausz, *Lyon*, I, 277 ff., for a similar distribution of trades in 1446.

10. R. Mandrou, "Les Français hors de France au XVIe siècle," in *Annales: Histoire, économies, civilisations*, 14 (1959), pp. 665–66.

11. Geneva's Council of 200 contained 46 merchants in 1536; see my *Studies in Genevan Government 1536–1605* (G., 1964), p. 92 f.

12. Babel, *HEG*, II, pp. 83–85, 616–19.

13. Doumergue, *Calvin*, III, pp. 187–90 (quote, p. 188).

14. Babel, *HEG*, II, pp. 428–36.

15. AEG, Recensement A 2, fols. 43–44.

16. Major studies on Kléberger: Th. Heyer, "Jean Kléberger le bon allemand," in *MDG*, 9 (1855), pp. 421–53; R. Ehrenburg, "Hans Kleberg, der 'Gute Deutsche'," in *Mitt. des Vereins für Gesch. der Stadt Nürnberg*, 10 (1893), pp. 1–51; E. Vial, "Jean Kléberger," in *Revue d'hist. de Lyon*, 11 (1912), pp. 81–102.

17. A summary of the business activities of the Manlichs in R. Ehrenburg, *Le siècle des Fugger* (Paris, 1955), pp. 105–06.

18. Matthew's son Jacques was elected to Geneva's Small Council in 1578

and served five times as Syndic before his death in 1602. This history of the Genevan Manlichs is rich and complex; many documents concerning them are dispersed throughout Geneva's Archives d'Etat.

19. Babel, *HEG,* II, p. 333; *Dict. hist. et biographique de la Suisse,* II, 772.
20. Bonivard, *Advis et devis sur l'ancienne et nouvelle police de Genève,* ed. G. Revillod (G., 1865), p. 49.
21. AEG, P. H. 1666; Herminjard, *Corr. des Reformateurs,* II, pp. 461–62; Doumergue, *Calvin,* III, pp. 198–99.
22. Doumergue, *Calvin,* III, pp. 48–50.
23. See the richly annotated hundred-page introduction by J.-J. Chaponnière to the *Journal du Syndic Balard, 1525–1531* (G., 1854).
24. P.-F. Geisendorf, *Les Annalistes genevois du début du XVIIᵉ siècle* (G., 1942), pp. 156–70, indicates that Balard continued his diary until 1545.
25. Chaponnière, *Balard,* pp. lxiv–lxvi and notes.
26. *Ibid.,* pp. lxvii–lxviii and notes.
27. *Ibid.,* p. lxviii n. 1, confirmed by AEG, Finances T 1.
28. Chaponnière, pp. lxxiv–lxxv and notes.
29. *Ibid.,* p. lxxxi n. 1.
30. *Ibid.,* pp. lxxxvii, xciii–xcvi.
31. *Ibid.,* pp. xcii–xciii.
32. *Ibid.,* p. xxxix n. 1; *supra,* n. 27.
33. *Journal du Syndic Balard,* p. 309.
34. Doumergue, *Calvin,* III, pp. 263–92; H. Naef, *Les Origines de la Réforme à Genève,* pp. 10–12.
35. Doumergue, *Calvin,* III, pp. 269–71; Roset, *Les Chroniques de Genève,* Bk. VI, Ch. 9 (pp. 386–88).
36. AEG, Recensement A 2, fols. 5ᵛ–8, 8ᵛ–11, 26–28. These *dizaines*—Notre-Dame-la-Nove, St. Pierre, and Boulangerie—had 91 of 155 houses in these conditions, including (fol. 11) one string of 11 consecutive houses. Geneva had 27 *dizaines* in all.
37. Doumergue, *Calvin,* III, pp. 314–24; Ch. Martin, "La Maison de Ville de Genève," in *MDG* in 4⁰, v. 3 (1906).
38. *Le Levain du Calvinisme,* ed. G. Revillod (G., 1856), p. 2.
39. Quoted in Doumergue, *Calvin,* III, p. 399.
40. See Joseph-E. Berghoff, *François de Bonivard, Sein Leben und Seine Schriften* (Heidelberg, 1922). Bonivard's life in Geneva is amply documented by J.-J. Chaponnière, "Notice sur François Bonivard," in *MDG,* 4 (1856), pp. 137–304, about half of which is *pièces justificatives.*
41. Berghoff, pp. 49–61, discusses Bonivard's probable motives.
42. *Ibid.,* pp. 72–73. The revenues of St. Victor were farmed for Tornabuoni by a famous Genevan, Besançon Hugues (cf. *infra,* p. 48) for 640 écus per year.
43. Full documents in Chaponnière, pp. 191–99, 206–11.
44. Berghoff, pp. 143, 150–65. It was based on Robert Estienne's French-Latin dictionary of 1539 and on Petrus Dasypodius' German-Latin lexicon of 1537.

45. *Ibid.*, pp. 191, 207, 167ff, 237ff, 263ff, 272ff, 284ff, 312ff, 314.

46. *Ibid.*, pp. 119–20.

47. *Ibid.*, pp. 285–95, 332–47 (quote, p. 337).

48. *Les Chroniques de Genève*, I, p. 35, quoted by Naef, *Origines de la Réforme à Genève*, pp. 29–30.

49. Roset, *Chroniques de Genève*, Bk. I, Ch. 1; Bonivard quoted by A. Roget, *Les suisses et Genève* (G., 1864), I, p. 52.

50. See my *Studies in Genevan Government*, pp. 76–80, and references there.

51. Chas. Gilliard, *La Conquête du Pays de Vaud par les Bernois* (Lausanne, 1935), pp. 245–75 (quote, p. 255).

52. Jean-François Bergier, *Genève et l'économie européene de la Renaissance* (Paris, 1963), p. 84 n. 6, and his fine description of Louis Bec (+1520) on pp. 88–89. The whole third chapter, "Ville et campagne," is fundamental for an understanding of Genevan rural history.

53. Bonivard, *Advis et devis sur l'ancienne et nouvelle police de Genève*, ed. G. Revillod (G., 1865), p. 55.

54. Bergier, *Genève et l'écon. européene*, pp. 96–97.

55. *Ibid.*, pp. 244–48; see also Babel, *HEG*, II, pp. 145–73.

56. Babel, *HEG*, II, pp. 240–71.

57. *Infra*, pp. 179–183.

58. The French used in the official history of Calvin's Geneva was in many ways as artificial a language as the Latin it replaced in 1536. However, very few documents in the rich, everyday dialect of Geneva have survived, except for one lengthy popular song and a few nasty threats directed against Calvin: for the former, see A. Burger, ed., *Cé qu'è lainô* (Geneva-Lille, 1952: Soc. des publ. romanes et françaises, #37); for the latter, see Roget, *HPG*, II, p. 323.

PART A

Development of a City

TWO

The Genevan Revolution

Une ville est assise és champs savoisiens
qui par fraude a chassé ses seigneurs anciens . . .
—Ronsard, 1562

When Calvin arrived in September 1536, Geneva was a new-born city state that had just shaken off the yoke of tyranny. She was freed from episcopal control, but as yet provided with no political substitute; she was liberated from Papistry, but as yet provided with no religious substitute. Geneva was virtually a *tabula rasa*, freshly emerged from the culmination of a dual revolution. During the decades that preceded Calvin's arrival, the citizens of Geneva had accomplished an unusual feat. They had successfully breasted the tides of their age by establishing their civic independence at a time when most princes were rapidly increasing their control over formerly autonomous cities. Very few cities as small as Geneva preserved any real independence in the sixteenth century, and no other city of her size succeeded in permanently establishing her independence. Yet on August 8, 1536, when Genevans heard that their treaty with their Bernese protectors had been signed, Geneva's Council minutes noted jubilantly that "we will remain as princes in our city."[1] Princes they were to remain until 1798.

How did the Genevans do it? At first glance, the history of medieval Geneva appears to furnish few clues toward understanding the brave stubbornness and the surge of civic patriotism that affected her citizens early in the sixteenth century. In fact, the strongest single impression one receives from medieval

Genevan history is one of civic retardation.[2] There are no traces
of political privileges given to Geneva's citizens before the mid-
thirteenth century. The city's first commune was sworn in 1285,
about sixty years after the peak of the communal movement in
France and eighty years after Lyon, her downstream neighbor
on the Rhone.[3] The bishops admitted the legal existence of
Geneva's commune only in 1308. The oldest letter of citizenship
dates from 1339. The Bishop granted Geneva her charter of liberties (*les franchises*) in 1387 — after nineteen smaller villages in
the diocese of Geneva already had such charters, four of them
for over a century.[4] (The reason was partly because the Bishop
of Geneva was in a better financial situation than the Counts
of Savoy and thus didn't need to sell such charters.) The records
of Geneva's municipal council begin only in 1409, and the
council acquired a properly embellished home for itself only in
1455.

Though she was the center of a very large diocese, Geneva
was not an archbishopric. Though the Emperor granted her
bishop a charter for a university in 1365, Geneva possessed no
institution of higher learning. Though medieval Geneva was a
good-sized commercial city, she manufactured virtually nothing
for export and had no craft guilds. The city's prosperity was due
almost exclusively to her four annual fairs, which attracted merchants from many parts of Christendom in the mid-fifteenth century.[5] But after the end of the Hundred Years War, Louis XI
of France attempted to restore the prosperity of his kingdom
at the expense of Geneva (and of Savoy, which had fallen into
the camp of his Burgundian enemies) by establishing privileged
fairs at Lyon in 1462; he made their dates coincide exactly with
Geneva's fairs. The Florentines, led by the powerful Medici
Bank, soon transferred their operations to Lyon, and by 1475
there was only one Italian banker left in Geneva.

Although the international aspect of Geneva's fairs was
crippled by Louis XI and the fairs of Lyon, the regional aspect
of Geneva's fairs persisted. The city was still a commercial mag-
net for the lands of Savoy, for the Free County of Burgundy,
and for the cities of the Swiss League.[6] Deprived of the wealth
and glamor of the Florentines, Geneva's fairs continued well
into the sixteenth century on this regional scale. Many edicts

were passed concerning these annual fairs even after the Reformation, in 1536, 1539, 1541, 1544, and 1545.[7] But their great days had clearly passed, and Geneva's importance as a commercial entrepot gradually diminished. By the 1530's, many of Geneva's own leading merchants regularly attended the rival— fairs at Lyon; in the age of Calvin and for much of the rest of the sixteenth century, they also regularly attended the international fairs at Frankfurt. In the early sixteenth century, while Geneva struggled with her political and religious revolutions, the city was not as prosperous as she had been two generations before. Her economic decline was mild but noticeable.

Politically, the municipality of Geneva had not taken many great strides towards autonomy by the early sixteenth century. The Prince-Bishop permitted the citizens to try criminals, but not to arrest or to execute them, nor to try civil cases between laymen. Most of the sources of revenue within the city were in the Bishop's hands. He received two-thirds of the tariffs levied at Geneva's public market, as well as the revenues of justice. The ordinary budget of Geneva's commune was quite small, although the records are too fragmentary to draw up absolutely accurate figures.[8] The general citizen assembly, the physical incarnation of the commune, was still summoned regularly in fifteenth-century Geneva, when it was already a moribund curiosity at Lyon or in the more advanced cities of the Swiss League such as Basel, Zurich, or Bern.[9] The commune of Geneva was sometimes summoned to the Estates of Savoy, as in 1484, but she never attended;[10] Geneva's bishop apparently represented the city's interests. Geneva scarcely benefited from this exemption from the Estates, for the House of Savoy levied a series of "voluntary" donations on her. Such subsidies were collected at least twenty times in the fifteenth century.[11]

The only important conflict in medieval Geneva had been between the House of Savoy and the Prince-Bishop, who, together with his Cathedral chapter, claimed to hold Geneva directly from the Emperor. The House of Savoy had established a foothold within Geneva in the thirteenth century, when the Bishop in 1265 granted them as a fief the office of *vidomne*, entailing the execution of justice and the prosecution of criminals within the city. The Count of Savoy next acquired the best

Genevan stronghold, the old episcopal castle on the island in the Rhone, in 1287. Such encroachments by the House of Savoy finally led the Bishops of Geneva to make peace with the citizen commune early in the fourteenth century, in order to preserve their independence.

But this rivalry between the Prince-Bishop of Geneva and the House of Savoy, which had acquired all the lands around the city, ended in the fifteenth century. Savoy's power grew until she was made a Duchy in 1424. Her first Duke, Amadeus VIII, later became a hermit and was created Pope by the Council of Basel, taking the title of Felix V. When this Duke-Pope abandoned his papal title in 1449, he retained the title of administrator of the See of Geneva. After his death in 1451, his eight-year-old grandson was named Bishop of Geneva. The see passed from one member of the House of Savoy to another, generally to nephews, almost without interruption. From the time when "Felix V" reserved the See of Geneva for himself in 1444, until the installation of the Savoyard courtier Pierre de la Baume in 1522, six members of the Savoyard dynasty occupied this bishopric for seventy of these seventy-eight years. Nearly all these prelates were absentees, following the Court of Savoy; none of them lived a canonical life, and some were not even ordained. However, these details made no difference. As a contemporary Swiss historian has observed, "Geneva had been able to increase her civic and communal prerogatives more than her neighbor Lausanne, but she knew that she too belonged, for better or for worse, to that constellation of vassalages that rotated about the Savoyard sun. She neither sought nor felt the need to escape from it."[12]

About 1500, Geneva was the largest city and head of the largest diocese within the extensive lands of the House of Savoy. She was still a prosperous city, if no longer as wealthy as she had formerly been. She had added two new convents, for the nuns of Ste.-Claire and for the Augustinian Hermits, to her four older convents in the last quarter of the fifteenth century. She had redecorated many of her seven parish churches. Her first printer, a Swabian wanderer named Adam Steinschaber, had come to Geneva in 1478. A second printer appeared in 1480, a third in 1493; work for the large dioceses of Lausanne and

Geneva kept them busy. Geneva had purified herself by expelling her Jewish colony in 1490 and by burning her first witch in 1495 (about a dozen more witches suffered the same fate before 1531).[13]

†

If thus far Genevan history offers few clues to the rise of a revolutionary movement in the early sixteenth century, it is partly because we have not examined the city's geographical position with sufficient care. Geneva was one of the outposts on the arc of westward expansion undertaken by the Swiss cantons, especially Bern and Fribourg, after their defeat of Charles the Bold and his Burgundians in 1477. The political activities of the Swiss extended as far west as Neuchâtel, which they seized from its hereditary count, the French Duke of Orléans, in 1512. Six years later, they concluded a short-lived civic alliance (*combourgeoisie*) with the Imperial Free City of Besançon in Burgundy. Bern had been casting covetous eyes at the Savoyard pays de Vaud, which covered a broad territory north of Lake Geneva, ever since 1477.[14] The city of Geneva, a political enclave at the west end of the pays de Vaud, had first felt the presence of the Swiss in 1475. Unfortunately allied with the Burgundians, Geneva was menaced by a Swiss army which extorted a huge ransom of 28,000 écus from her — 2000 to be paid in a week, 10,000 in a month, and the balance within a year. To meet this ultimatum, Geneva had to impose a tax of 6% on the entire wealth of the city; borrow heavily from Strasbourg and from the Medici Bank at Lyon; and, finally, introduce a tax on all wine brought into the city. The Swiss, as a nineteenth-century Genevan historian noted, "did not display a particularly admirable conduct after the Burgundian wars. They began conflicts for frivolous reasons, were quite rapacious, and often trampled humanity and the rights of peoples beneath their feet in a revolting manner."[15]

Yet Geneva rapidly resumed her contacts with these rude mountaineers on more friendly terms. The explanation lies in the peculiar nature of Geneva's political constitution. The city was always regarded as a single body whose head was the

Prince-Bishop and whose two "members" were the Cathedral chapter, composed of thirty-two canons, and the citizens.[16] The Bishops, as we have seen, were closely attached to the House of Savoy. But the chapter (which in theory had the right to elect the Bishop) and the citizens were not so tightly attached to a dynasty which could assure neither Geneva's commercial prosperity nor her military security. The rather low degree of loyalty to Savoy among Genevan citizens is dramatically illustrated by the fact that only 13 Genevan families acquired Savoyard nobility in the fifteenth and early sixteenth centuries (a total of 263 families were ennobled in Savoy during this period, including 42 from the small town of Chambéry).[17] Geneva's Cathedral chapter, seeking some external support to buttress their precarious independence from Savoy, sometimes looked with favor upon the Swiss.

The chapter, whose power grew during an episcopal interregnum that extended from 1482 to 1490, encouraged the civic consciousness of Geneva's citizens. A *Treatise on the Liberties, Franchises, Pre-Eminences and Exemptions . . . belonging to the eminent, rich, and gentle City of Geneva* was published in 1493, dedicated to the prominent canon Malvenda. This canon also reinvigorated the citizen militia, the *Abbey of Our Lord St. Peter of Geneva,* in 1491, with its motto "what touches one touches all." This organization was Geneva's first true civic guard, and its commander (later transformed into a Captain-General) exercised his functions until the moment of Calvin's triumph in 1555. A so-called "Golden Bull" was even forged in 1483 to demonstrate Geneva's complete independence of Savoy. It later disappeared, to the annoyance of the commune and the embarrassment of the chapter. An advisory citizen Council of Fifty, comparable to other medium-sized councils in Swiss cities, was established in Geneva in 1502.[18]

Nevertheless, the links connecting Geneva's chapter and many of her prominent families to the court of Savoy should not be overlooked. Feudal dynasties, seconded by learned dynasties of ducal and episcopal secretaries, apostolic protonotaries, and appellate judges, filled the upper ranks of the Genevan clerical and political structure. Nepotism was as rife here as on the episcopal chair.[19] Almost the only prominent Genevan canon whose family

interests led him away from Savoy and toward the Swiss was
Aymon de Gingins (ca. 1455–1537).[20] Scion of the oldest noble
house in the pays de Vaud, pluralist on a grand scale, he was
addicted to all the forms of gracious living, including a dwarf-
jester and a well-dressed mistress who bore him a son and a
daughter. His social prestige was no doubt responsible for his
election as Bishop by the chapter in 1513, for the citizens of
Geneva had observed seven years before that he "ignored the
rudiments of both civil and canon law." His election was calmly
by-passed by Pope Leo X, who duly consecrated a Savoyard
prince. Aymon de Gingins was a notorious *Eidguenot*, partisan
of a Swiss alliance, and it is something of a mystery why he was
at last made episcopal vicar in 1527. This canon, who willed his
entire estate to the Reformed government of Bern, never showed
the slightest trace of his clerical profession except in his belated
and utterly ineffective opposition to the introduction of the
Reformation in Geneva.

In general, Geneva's merchants were more zealous supporters
of a Swiss alliance than were the canons. Their reasons were
partly economic; after the departure of the Italian bankers,
Geneva's prosperity rested almost exclusively on the continued
participation of Swiss and German merchants at her fairs. Furthermore, many Genevan merchants had family as well as business connections with some of the Swiss cities, especially with
Fribourg.[21] But even among her merchants, Geneva's impulse
toward an overt alliance with the Swiss was small at first. The
new Duke of Savoy, Charles III (1504–1544), successfully persuaded Geneva to loan him her artillery for a campaign against
Valais in 1506. He also persuaded her to build a wall around
the right-bank suburb of St.-Gervais in expectation of a Swiss
attack against Geneva. However, when a cousin of the Duke
was installed on the episcopal throne in 1513 over the canonical
election of Aymon de Gingins, half a dozen prominent Genevan
merchants took the precaution of acquiring citizenship at Fribourg in order to escape the wrath of the House of Savoy. (This
precaution had already protected a Genevan syndic six years
earlier.)

A number of Genevan citizens were arrested for various insults
to their Bishop or to the House of Savoy in 1517. The growing

estrangement between the citizens and their Bishop, and the rapid eclipse of the chapter, soon led to a factional division within Geneva. The arrested citizens were now tried as part of a great conspiracy to kill the Bishop; finally, two relatively obscure Genevans named Navis and Blanchet were beheaded. Tension mounted inside the city. A delegation of 86 Genevans, headed by François Bonivard, traveled to Fribourg where they were made citizens on January 7, 1519.[22] Their deed was instantly denounced by the episcopal and ducal party within Geneva, and the factions that appeared in Geneva's Council minutes in May 1520 as *eyguenots* and *mamellus* began to acquire their definitive shape.[23]

Following rapidly after this January maneuver, the whole city of Geneva signed a pact of alliance (*combourgeoisie*) with Fribourg in February 1519. This pact, however, was of brief duration, since (as Bonivard explained) the Savoyard faction held the majority of seats on Geneva's council, and also because there were many Savoyard pensioners in Fribourg and other Swiss cities.[24] Savoyard diplomacy had in fact persuaded the Swiss Diet to annul the Fribourg-Geneva pact in March. This prepared the way for Charles III's triumphant entry into Geneva, armed from head to foot, surrounded by dozens of gentlemen and hundreds of soldiers, on April 5. Four days later, the Duke issued letters-patent confirming all episcopal privileges in Geneva and promising a general amnesty. Next, on April 11, a general citizen assembly was summoned, which solemnly renounced the Fribourg alliance. The eighteen Swiss delegates present at this meeting accepted this renunciation, on condition that they be paid 6000 écus at once, to permit them to disband an army that they had raised for the relief of Geneva.

Many Genevan citizens who had been heavily compromised by the Fribourg pact followed Bonivard's example and prudently left Geneva when Charles III entered, but returned after the general amnesty had been proclaimed. Then, in late August, after Charles V had been elected Emperor, Geneva's Bishop Jean de Savoie made his solemn entry into Geneva, accompanied by 500 men. He seized and executed the ringleader of the Fribourg alliance, Philibert Berthelier, two days later. Within a week, the Bishop held another general citizen assembly at which he listed the citizens' rebellion and infractions of their privileges and then punished them by dismissing Geneva's four syndics and naming four others to replace them. He also decreed that henceforth no Genevan syndic could be elected without episcopal consent.

"The pigeon has fallen," exulted one Genevan magistrate when Berthelier was summarily executed. For the next few years, no comparable pigeon appeared publicly among Geneva's citizenry to replace him. A somewhat suspicious quiet reigned for the next two years. A pact between the rival civic factions was arranged at the 1521 elections, and the Bishop was also inclined to moderation. He even struck from the list of men proposed for syndics one man who was too violently anti-Swiss.[25] The overt marks of factionalism briefly declined; Eidguenots refrained from wearing their Swiss-style cock feathers, and Mammelukes ceased wearing their holly. This new harmony among Geneva's citizens, and their rapprochement with the House of Savoy, reached its peak during Charles III's prolonged residence in Geneva from August 1523 to March 1524. Preparing for the joyous entry of the Duke and his bride, Beatrice of Portugal, the citizens adopted a true carnival spirit, replete with masques, dramas, and a public fountain flowing with wine. On such an occasion, even the most vigorous Eidguenots vied with each other to see who would wear the more handsome costume. Besançon Hugues, later leader of the *combourgeoisie* of 1526, led the civic guard of honor.[26] During his residence in Geneva, Duke Charles ran a "grand and ample court," and was "as well or better obeyed at Geneva as at Chambéry. He spent much money in the city and he had drawn both large and small to love him by the prospect of gain. There were no more Bertheliers who scorned death."[27] The Duke presided, in approved Renaissance style, over the election of Geneva's syndics in 1524.

Much of the credit for the success of these anti-Swiss and pro-Savoyard policies in Geneva of the early 1520's is due to the activities of Eustache Chapuys.[28] This clever and ambitious Savoyard, future Imperial Ambassador in England during the divorce trial of Catherine of Aragon, had been named *official* (chancellor and alter ego) to the Bishop of Geneva in 1517. Chapuys spent much of the next eight years at Geneva, playing an important role at the councils that renounced the Swiss alliance in 1519 and in the capture and execution of Berthelier. This friend and classmate of Bonivard at Turin did a great deal to reinforce episcopal authority and to restore civic harmony in Geneva while serving under both Jean de Savoie and his successor.

This successor, who became Bishop in 1522, prudently left his episcopal city when Charles III made his triumphant entry the following year. Pierre de la Baume (1477–1544), former coadjutor to Jean de Savoie, was the last bishop to exercise temporal jurisdiction in Geneva or to reside there. He was in some ways a curious choice for a Savoyard Bishop of Geneva, for he, like his predecessor, had been confirmed by the Pope over the canonical election of Aymon de Gingins. De la Baume came from an international family who were vassals of Burgundy, France, and Savoy.[29] His father had belonged to the Burgundian Order of the Golden Fleece. His elder brother became a Lieutenant-General with the French army, and his younger brother was created Marshal of Burgundy by the Emperor Charles V. Pierre de la Baume was not related to the House of Savoy; but Charles III had been impressed by his "remarkable qualities" as early as 1513, and had sent him as an observer to the Lateran Council in 1515. De la Baume undoubtedly used the See of Genev primarily as a stepping-stone to greater honors, which he eventually received. He became a cardinal in 1539 and Archbishop of Besançon in 1542.

Despite his "remarkable qualities" and his subsequent honors, however, Pierre de la Baume was to prove a catastrophic choice both to the House of Savoy and to the See of Geneva. As Bishop of Geneva, he would not faithfully execute the Duke's policies, and could not effectively oppose them. Pierre de la Baume was a very clever man, and a typical Renaissance prelate. The harness on his mule was trimmed with gold; he wore a green rosary "like the Bishops of Rome"; he spoke fluent Italian. Bonivard, his good friend, reported that he was "a great spender on all sorts of superfluous things, and thought it the sovereign virtue of a prelate to keep a sumptuous table with lots of good wine — up to thirty-one different kinds per meal. He was liberal to his servants, and very proud — not of his virtues, but of his noble family." A woman of mystery, Mme. de Gruyère, often inhabited his town house.

In addition to this suitably furnished train of life, the Bishop of Geneva prided himself on his political finesse and on his eloquence. He attempted to arrange all matters to suit his personal convenience. His principal aim in life was merely to enjoy the honors and revenues of as many benefices as he could possibly accumulate. To achieve this, he had to balance and conciliate several potentially hostile elements, on both local and international levels. Relying on his considerable skills, he began his intricate political games in Geneva, playing factions off against one another: city against Duke, then Duke against Swiss, then city against his own chapter. But de la Baume's very unwillingness to defend consistently either the independence of Geneva or the privileges of Savoy, coupled with his lack of armed followers, left him helpless in the next decade's struggle between them.

†

In 1524, two more episodes disturbed Geneva's public tranquality. An episcopal judge, Aimé Levrier, had made himself obnoxious to the Duke by defending episcopal and civic privileges during Charles' residence; he was seized and executed shortly before the Duke's departure.[30] Later that autumn, Geneva's public treasurer fled to Savoy after serious charges of embezzlement had been made against him during a quarrel in the town hall. Much of the following year was spent in fruitless harangues between Geneva and the ducal court at Chambéry, which had pronounced an unjust sentence clearing the ex-treasurer of all charges and condemning Geneva to pay him a heavy indemnity. Geneva seized his property, and threatened, on Pierre de la Baume's suggestion, to appeal the whole case to Rome. A public assembly in September 1525 finally decided against this latter course by a close vote of 53 to 42.[31]

Charles III, worried by such signs of restlessness and disobedience, again prepared to turn his attention to the business of Geneva. While he prepared another solemn entrance in the autumn of 1525, the most compromised among Geneva's Eidguenots, who had learned from the case of Levrier the truth of the old adage *indignatio princeps mors est,* became increasingly nervous. Finally, a week before the Duke's official entrance, twenty of them fled the city. "This was no game," as their leader said afterwards; they were pursued as far as the Bishop's lands in Burgundy by Savoyard agents, and some traveled through forests for a whole week before reaching Fribourg. The struggle for control of Geneva between the imperialistic Swiss and the ambitious House of Savoy now reached its climax, with the city's hapless "sovereign," the Prince-Bishop, squirming between them.

Charles III struck first. He entered Geneva, as he said, "to punish evil-doers and reward the deserving." He promised to repeal the unjust sentence against Geneva, but demanded in return the confirmation of the 1519 edict that gave Savoy a veto over the election of Genevan syndics. His negotiations with the Swiss were proceeding slowly, and there was a serious constitutional hitch at Geneva: one of the fugitives was the new city treasurer, who had apparently taken the official public seal with him. But these were after all minor impediments to Charles' preparations to extend his authority within Geneva. Finally, on December 10, 1525, he summoned a general citizen assembly which has become famous in Genevan history as the *Conseil des Hallebardes.* (In theory, only the Bishop had the right to summon such an assembly, but his vicar protested in vain against this meeting.) The Duke, accompanied by his armed retainers, demanded that Geneva's citizens make no alliance with the Swiss, that none of his or the bishop's privileges be abrogated, and that the election of syndics be subject to his veto. In return, he agreed to revoke all fines levied against Geneva by his council at Chambéry. "Everybody present answered 'Yea, Yea,' without taking time to think," as one eyewitness, Jean Balard, reported. Thus having apparently completed his coup d'état, the Duke rode out of Geneva two days afterwards to rejoin his wife and pursue more important political matters.[32]

Letters were immediately dispatched to the fugitives and to the governments of Bern and Fribourg announcing this news. Geneva's syndics decreed on December 16 that no Genevan be allowed to acquire foreign citizenship or make any public alliance without episcopal permission. Meanwhile, the fugitives had been negotiating for several months to conclude a general pact of alliance with the Swiss similar to the one which had been annulled in 1519. This was a delicate piece of business. On the one hand, Charles III kept up an intensive diplomatic offensive against them, especially at Bern where he had several pensioners among the leading members of the government. On the other hand, the legal rights of these Genevan émigrés to conclude such an alliance in the absence of their bishop were none too certain. The rupture of the alliance with Fribourg in 1519 had been confirmed by the Swiss Diet on strictly legal grounds. But legality had apparently changed in seven years. Bern and Fribourg signed a pact of *combourgeoisie* with the independent episcopal city of Lausanne (also an enclave in the pays de Vaud) on December 4, 1525. News of these negotiations had contributed heavily to Charles III's decision to enter Geneva that month. Geneva's fugitives were enthusiastically supported by Fribourg, as in 1519, but quite reluctantly by Bern. Only after two months of political maneuvering did Bern finally yield and agree to the *combourgeoisie* with Geneva on February 7, 1526. Perhaps the news of the election of one of Geneva's émigrés to the honor of syndic *in absentia* helped crystallize this decision. Pierre de la Baume sent two messengers to Bern on February 5, the day of Geneva's election, bearing diametrically opposed letters, one favoring and one opposing the alliance. This curious policy did him no good in the moment of crisis. His next message, which firmly denounced the alliance, arrived at Bern after the matter had been decided on February 7, and was disregarded.[33]

Beyond this point, the decline and fall of Bishop de la Baume was rapid. He had already badly undermined his position by subtly sabotaging the plans of Charles III earlier that winter. Then, after hurriedly entering Geneva on February 1, 1526, he had failed to prevent or annul the election of an émigré as syndic. As soon as he heard the news of Bern's ratification, he vetoed the entire pact on February 9. "We are unhappy that our prince doesn't favor us, but we'll do the best we can," wrote the Genevan liaison to the émigré leaders, adding à propos of the Prince-Bishop, "I'm never sure of him."[34] Despite many frantic exchanges of messages between Geneva, Charles III, Bern, and

Fribourg, nothing more was done before the fugitives triumphantly re-entered Geneva on February 21. Greeted by civic artillery, and with each principal fugitive flanked by two of his new
Swiss allies, this procession was welcomed by the citizenry with
jubilation.

Events now moved with impressive speed. Several Genevan
magistrates and the city secretary were replaced two days later
by Eidguenots. Then Besançon Hugues, recognized leader of the
fugitives, called for an "almost general" citizen assembly, where
he translated and interpreted the new Swiss treaty which he
carried with him. Hugues demanded a full citizen assembly on
February 25, but the Bishop refused. Next morning, Geneva's
canons attempted unsuccessfully to stop the Eidguenots from
ringing the great cathedral bell in order to summon the citizens;
once again, episcopal opposition could not prevent such a meeting. La Clémence tolled, a huge crowd assembled, and the Swiss
ambassadors were introduced. Then, quite unexpectedly, Pierre
de la Baume appeared and sat on the highest chair, but the
meeting continued according to the fugitives' plan. Besançon
Hugues spoke eloquently about the fugitives' mission and the
difficulties they had encountered during their months of exile.
He once again translated the parchment treaty into French. The
chief syndic then called for a vote on its ratification. The pact
was approved with five or six dissenting voices. One man who
attempted to speak against the treaty was checked by the swords
of his neighbors. The Bishop then protested against this hasty
ratification and requested a second general assembly to decide
the question after everybody had thought it over carefully.
Hugues answered brusquely that any delay would risk troubles
and bring down two or three thousand Swiss into Geneva.
Whereupon the Bishop appealed to Rome and to the Emperor,
and had notarized letters to this effect drawn up. Then — perhaps the worst of his compromises — de la Baume declared that
if Geneva's citizens truly had the legal right to contract such
alliances without the consent of their prince, he would make no
further opposition. (These remarks were eagerly copied down
verbatim by the new city secretary, and inserted in French into
the Latin of the official minutes under the title of "Occult Ratification or its Equivalent.") Hugues reassured his Bishop that

the citizens did in fact possess such rights, and cited a few specious examples to prove his point. The rest of the meeting continued anticlimactically, with the Bishop complimenting himself for having made enemies neither of the Swiss nor of Charles III.[35]

This stormy ratification of the Swiss pact was at least as illegal and as much a *tour de force* as the Duke's rigged assembly of December 1525. Balard, no friend to Charles III, noted that the adherents of Hugues at the preparatory assembly of February 24, 1526, were mostly young men and that no one dared to speak publicly against the pact in the presence of the Swiss.[36] It should be noted that the Swiss did their best to avoid provoking armed quarrels during the actual ratification. But the important fact is that Geneva's Prince-Bishop was opposed to both rigged assemblies, and unable to prevent either. And the second important fact is that the Swiss alliance held at Geneva uninterruptedly after 1526, while Savoyard influence within the city declined steadily. Geneva's second pact of *combourgeoisie* proved sturdier and more durable than the first, primarily because Bern, much larger though less aggressive than Fribourg, was now included. The Eidguenots quickly consolidated their victory. A new seal was engraved to be used on the treaty. Geneva's government created a new advisory Council of Two Hundred, modeled in name and function after similar councils in Swiss cities. A fortnight after the ratification, a dozen of Geneva's more prominent Mammelukes fled, never to return. The defeated Bishop followed them out of the city on March 12, riding for the Duke's court. "This is a noteworthy and memorable thing," said Balard; "whether it signifies good or evil, I'll have to leave the judgment to God."[37]

What best explains this triumph of Geneva's Eidguenots over her Mammelukes? First, there is the blunt truth that the Swiss were a major military power and that Savoy was not. Second, there is the factor of superior leadership. Besançon Hugues, who emerged as the Eidguenot leader after Berthelier's execution in 1519, was far abler and cleverer than anyone promoting the interests of Savoy (except for Eustache Chapuys, who was present in Geneva only intermittently and who had no roots there). Third, there is the Janus-faced nature of the Duchy of Savoy, a bilingual block of lands straddling the Alps, deeply involved in both French and Italian politics; its prince and his councillors were clearly unable to devote enough of their united energies to solving the problem of Geneva to their advantage.[38]

The social composition of Geneva's rival factions in the 1520's has never been adequately studied. A rapid investigation by Henri Naef into the rival syndical families of 1519 brought few concrete results, except that "in the beginning, families were divided by principle alone."[39] And it does seem clear that though both factions were supporting the claims of their Prince-Bishop against foreign enemies, they differed radically over just who these enemies were. By the moment of crisis in 1525–1526, it is possible to discern a different class background and a different "style" between these factions. In comparing the fugitives of November 1525[40] with the fugitives of September 1526,[41] it becomes apparent that the Eidguenot leadership was composed primarily of wholesale merchants from newer Genevan families. These merchants had matured after the great age of Geneva's fairs, and their leading commercial contacts were with Swiss and south German merchants. Many of their complaints against Duke and Bishop are economic in nature.[42] In 1526, they decisively wrested power from a cluster of slightly older Genevan families — Versonnay, de Pesmes, d'Orsières — who had acquired their wealth in the fifteenth century and who had held the balance of Genevan political power ever since. Young wealth — and young men, as Balard noted — successfully overturned such honor-laden older families. Their most persistent enemies were to be found by 1526 among the vast majority of Geneva's canons and her small army of episcopal and ducal officials, the lawyers and judges of the Upper City.

✝

Geneva's Eidguenots spent the next few years implementing their triumph of 1526.[43] Their principal victim was Pierre de la Baume. Unable to annul the alliance, Geneva's Bishop attempted a clever maneuver in July 1527. He asked the citizens of Geneva to grant him citizenship and thus (he thought) automatic participation in the Swiss *combourgeoisie*. In return, he offered to confirm the alliance and to concede the right to exercise civil justice to the syndics. Bern and Fribourg, however, refused to consider Geneva's Bishop as included in the alliance; he, in turn, attempted to revoke the concessions he had just granted, but to no avail. To make matters worse, Charles III had deprived de la Baume of the revenues of two rich benefices in Savoy and had even tried to kidnap him. The harried Bishop fled by night to his family stronghold in Burgundy in August 1527.

Geneva's citizens rapidly took over more episcopal prerogatives. Appeals from their sentences to the court of Geneva's Archbishop were forbidden. The authority of the *vidomne*, the secular arm of Genevan justice which had belonged for centuries to the House of Savoy, was chiseled away and the office itself was virtually abolished in July 1528. Only after prolonged negotiations was de la Baume able to retain the right to judge churchmen. Culminating this legal revolution in November 1529 was the creation by the citizens of Geneva of a new civil tribunal, presided over by a new popularly elected official, the Lieutenant. This last innovation, which the Bishop correctly considered an act of overt rebellion, virtually annihilated the remnants of episcopal justice in Geneva.[44]

Meanwhile, Geneva's citizens successfully attacked another citadel of episcopal authority and episcopal government. The canons of the Venerable Chapter of Geneva had tried, almost unanimously, to prevent the ratification of the 1526 alliance. Worse yet, a series of show trials of their servants had heavily implicated them in the July 1527 plot to kidnap the Bishop; after the failure of this attempt, many canons had left Geneva, and their homes were pillaged by irate patriots. Geneva's magistrates locked up the canons' titles that September with the consent of the new episcopal vicar, Aymon de Gingins. The final step was taken in April 1528. The Bishop, trying to salvage some of his authority in Geneva, agreed to a scheme that had probably been concocted by Besançon Hugues: to nationalize the chapter by appointing only Genevan citizens (including her Bernese or Fribourgeois allies) and thus to eliminate all Savoyard influence within it. Geneva's Venerable Chapter continued to exist as an institution until 1535 (its last records date from April 1530), but it too was now effectively a tool of the Eidguenots.[45]

Pierre de la Baume fought a delaying action against these acts of insubordination against his judicial powers, and Charles III did not accept the loss of his influence within Geneva tamely. But Savoy's means of action were limited. Diplomatic negotiations with the Swiss led nowhere and were very expensive. An appeal to Pope Clement VIII was more successful, and Geneva was placed under an Interdict in April 1528. Charles' most effective means of action was through the petty nobility living in the vicinity of Geneva. The local gentry, loyal to the white cross of Savoy and reinforced by Mammeluke fugitives from the city, formed a Fraternity of the Spoon in the summer of 1528. This fraternity, aided by Ducal edicts and after August 1530 by a mandate from the Bishop to punish rebels and conspirators,[46] blockaded Geneva. They carried on incessant guerrilla warfare by pillaging the rural properties of Genevan citizens and by ambushing merchants on the highway. The death of the fraternity's commander in January 1529 — he was skewered while boldly attempting to ride through Geneva under cover of darkness — failed to discourage them. Within two months, they mounted a night attack on the city; but the alarm was given at the last moment and the attempt failed.

For her part, Geneva could ward off the harassments of this fraternity, although the most serious incidents in January 1529 and in October 1530 led them to appeal to their redoubtable Swiss allies for military help. And on both occasions the Swiss responded, sending a few hundred men for a fortnight the first time, and assembling a huge relief army of 12,000 which marched into Geneva the second time. This army was quartered in the city for ten days, while Balard observed that Geneva was "pillaged outside by her enemies, while her food and money were eaten up inside by her friends."[47] The maxim of Voltaire, *"point d'argent, point de suisses,"* surely applies to Geneva after the 1526 alliance. Bern and Fribourg collaborated to help her, at Genevan expense (as the pact stipulated). Swiss arbitration in December 1530 to end this guerrilla war officially reconfirmed the 1526 *combourgeoisie,* but also restored the office of *vidomne* to Charles III. The Swiss convicted the Duke of Savoy of the responsibility for the recent conflict and ordered him to pay the three allies a very large sum. Bern and Fribourg, however, levied an even larger sum upon the commune of Geneva for their military aid: 15,000 écus, more than twice the war damages charged to Savoy. Neither Charles III nor Geneva could pay these debts in full, although both made strenuous efforts to do so in 1531. Geneva decided to raise most of her money by borrowing 8000 écus at Basel in January 1531, thereby starting a public debt which they would eradicate exactly 123 years later.[48]

Geneva's alliance with Bern and Fribourg had survived some severe strains. The continuation of their alliance is even more perplexing when one considers the religious situation within the Swiss League from 1526 to 1531. The multiple tensions within the alliance caused by the spread of the Reformation built up steadily after the Diet of Baden in 1526 and culminated with the first Swiss war of religion and with the death of Zwingli on the battlefield. Fribourg and Bern found themselves in sharp religious opposition within two years after signing their joint alliance with Geneva. Fribourg's Catholic orthodoxy remained absolutely unshakeable, and her persecution of heretics was swift and rigorous. A public profession of faith, whose text has survived, was imposed on her citizens and on servants within the city in 1527; Fribourg was the first city in Europe to require such a Catholic loyalty oath.[49] The last suspected "Lutherans" were expelled from Fribourg's chapter by Christmas 1530, and the Catholic victory at Kappel definitively ended all attempts to implant Reformed doctrines in the city or territories of Fribourg.[50]

Bern, however, became a Reformed city in January 1528, after the usual long series of public disputations.[51] The city's principal preacher had been converted to Zwinglianism for many years, and he quickly won a sympathetic audience among Bernese guilds. Opposition to the Reformation centered in Bern's patriciate and in the vast majority of her rural population. The political breakthrough at Bern occurred during the annual elections at Easter 1527, when five of the six magistrates most hostile to the new doctrines were removed from the governing council by vote of the guilds. After the Mass had been abolished within the city, an edict extended the Reformation to Bern's rural possessions. This provoked a terrible peasant uprising in her Oberland in the summer of 1528, but the magistrates of Bern (still aided at this point by Fribourg) crushed this revolt with impressive speed. "I would never have imagined their power to be so great," reported a Genevan observer that October.[52]

The first six years of Geneva's Swiss alliance saw the city take many important steps to eliminate the local power of the Duke of Savoy and to undermine the power of her Prince-Bishop. Such steps were taken carefully, by a commune testing the limits of her practical authority against a vacillating and often absentee sovereign. Geneva's successful erosion of episcopal and ducal power in this period was to a large degree the work of a single citizen: Besançon Hugues (ca. 1480–1532).[53] The son of a rich furrier from Strasbourg who acquired Genevan citizenship in 1478, Hugues was connected by marriage to several of Geneva's most prominent families. He also had numerous friends at Fribourg, where he purchased citizenship in 1513 and later even purchased the small fief of Pérolle. Bonivard, who had no great love for Hugues, described him as a rich merchant with lots of credit among Geneva's artisans; it seems clear that Hugues' finest skills were exploited in political rather than commercial ventures. He was primarily responsible for the short-lived reconciliation between Eidguenots and Mammelukes in 1521. He was clearly the leader of the Eidguenot fugitives of 1525, and it was his influence at Fribourg and his eloquence at Bern that enabled these émigrés to win the support of those two powerful governments that winter. It was Hugues who decisively outmaneuvered the clever de la Baume in the assembly of February 25, 1526. And it was Hugues who persuaded the Bishop to confirm him as the city's military commander, to nationalize the Venerable Chapter and to name a notorious Eidguenot as episcopal vicar a year later. Besançon Hugues became the virtual dictator of Geneva in 1528, when he combined the offices of First Syndic and Captain-General. He seems to have kept his predominant influence among Genevan citizens intact to the moment of his death in October 1532. It is probable also that he deserves part of the credit for preserving the smoothness of Geneva's alliance with Catholic Fribourg and Protestant Bern during the difficult period after 1528. As a careful Genevan historian noted long ago, Hugues' death coincides precisely "with the moment when the current of the Reformation came in brusque fashion to mingle its waters with those of the movement for political emancipation."[54]

✝

It should not be forgotten that the Genevan revolution, in its origins and development, was political rather than religious. The first overt signs of "Lutheranism" appeared at Geneva in the summer of 1532. Small printed placards, that favorite weapon of the Reformers, mysteriously appeared one morning at several places including the Cathedral. Soon afterwards, the famous itinerant missionary, Guillaume Farel, paid his first visit to Geneva under a Bernese safe-conduct. But before 1532, signs of Protestantism at Geneva are few and scattered. Levrier, the obstreperous Genevan official executed by agents of Charles III in the spring of 1524, admitted to owning books by Luther. Levrier respected him as a doctor of great authority who spoke eloquently against modern Popes.[55] No doubt there were other Genevans who had sampled Lutheran literature and who were ripe to be shaped into an Evangelical congregation by Farel after his visit of 1532. But the surprising thing about Protestantism in Geneva in the 1520's is its weakness. Thomas von Hofen, a minor Bernese official, lamented to Zwingli in January 1527 that it would be futile to propagandize the Gospel in Geneva because of the hundreds of monks who would oppose themselves "feet and hands" to any such activity.[56] Balard's chronicle first notices the existence of "Lutheranism" (abroad, not at Geneva) and attempts a curious definition of it only in December 1529.[57]

A small nucleus of Protestants existed in Geneva before 1532. It is doubtful whether the humanistic circle of 1521–1523, which centered about the wandering alchemist Cornelius Agrippa, contained anything more than a few Erasmians, and direct connections between this circle and Geneva's Evangelical congregation are impossible to trace. Genevan merchants such as Baudichon de la Maisonneuve, who were in frequent contact with such hotbeds of Lutheranism as Augsburg and Nuremburg, really were affected by the new doctrines, at least to the point of violent anti-clericalism. Baudichon himself ate meat during

Lent as early as 1526.[58] However, the religious revolution in
Geneva was to be accomplished only as her political revolution
was nearing completion. And in both revolutions, the decisive
impetus was to come from Bern.

Without the Bernese safe-conducts for Farel and for the
Protestant printer Pierre de Vingle, Geneva would not have
organized a Reformed congregation. Without the constant mixture of threats and encouragement from Bern, it is hard to tell
whether Geneva would have been Reformed or not by 1536;
just as, without Bernese adherence to the *combourgeoisie* of
1526, it is hard to tell if the burghers could have overcome their
Duke and their Prince-Bishop. It is also very important to note
that the history of the Genevan Reformation between 1532 and
1536 is in large measure the story of how Bernese influence came
to triumph in Geneva at the expense *not* of the Prince-Bishop,
who had already been reduced to a fraction of his former authority, but of the other *combourgeois* of 1526, Fribourg.

Immediately upon hearing of Geneva's "Lutheran" placards,
Fribourg informed an embarrassed Genevan embassy in July
1532 that if Geneva fell into Lutheranism, they would send a
large embassy to Geneva (at Genevan expense, of course) to cut
Fribourg's seal right off the pact of alliance and leave them for-
ever.[59] They did so exactly twenty-two months later. Handi-
capped severely by the inopportune death of Besançon Hugues,
Fribourg was unable to counterbalance the influence of Bern,
and the heresy promoted by Farel spread rapidly within Geneva.
A French immigrant hatmaker established Geneva's first Evangelical community in October 1532. A Protestant schoolmaster arrived from France a month later, and a Protestant printer, also
from France, joined them in February 1533. Relying on Bernese
support, Geneva's Evangelical faction now took the offensive,
and the city's magistrates were unable to prevent frequent quarrels in which several people were wounded and at least one
killed. On Good Friday 1533, Geneva's Reformed held their first
public service in a garden, where the French hatmaker and a
transient preacher distributed Communion. The hatmaker was
banished for his boldness.

But the street fighting between rival factions continued. A
huge riot broke out on May 4, 1533, when the Reformers were

deprived of the presence of some of the city's leading merchants, who had gone to the fair at Lyon. The tocsin rang. A large contingent, led by one of Geneva's new canons, a Fribourg citizen named Werly who kept shouting "All Christians, follow me!", charged down from the Upper City into the Place du Molard. Among the hundreds of men involved in this riot, several — most of them Reformers — were wounded. A syndic, trying to establish order, received a hard blow on the head from an unidentified party. Werly, separated from the rest of his faction in the mêlée, was wounded and attempted to flee; but he was pursued and killed by a second assault while the confusion was at its height.[60]

The consequences of Werly's death were serious. Geneva arrested a dozen men, including two priests, charged with fomenting the riot, but the murderers of Werly were impossible to find. News of this incident caused a Milanese diplomat in Lucerne to exclaim excitedly that the "Lutherans" were beginning to prevail in Geneva, and that if God didn't intervene, the government of Bern certainly would, thereby making the city wholly "Lutheran."[61] Actually, however, it was Fribourg whose wrath was most aroused. Her government determined on this occasion to purge Geneva of Lutheranism once and for all. They persuaded Pierre de la Baume to return to Geneva for the first time in five years in order to try the culprits; they even escorted him into Geneva on July 1. Bern, meanwhile, vainly demanded that one Genevan church be given to the Protestants so that they could worship freely. Geneva's bishop immediately arrested most of the Evangelical ringleaders, but the city's magistrates successfully protested that an episcopal court had no jurisdiction over murder cases in Geneva. De la Baume conceded this point, demanding only that judges from Bern and Fribourg be added to the traditional court for this case. Within a fortnight of his arrival, Geneva's Bishop, fuming with indignation, took leave of his episcopal city for the last time. Anticlimactically, the murderers of Werly were caught and executed a month later.

The delicate equilibrium between Catholic and Reformed parties, between Fribourg and Bern, continued for many months after this episode. Farel, accompanied by a Bernese herald, delivered an official complaint from Bern about the preaching of a

Sorbonne Dominican in Geneva in December 1533. Fribourg countered with a request for the immediate expulsion of Farel from Geneva. Neither request was explicitly honored. Instead, a great public dispute was held between Farel and the Dominican before Geneva's Council of Two Hundred on January 27, 1534. The climax of the debate came when the Dominican accused his opponents of being stooges for the Swiss. A riot broke out, and the Dominican was ordered to retract his charges. At the appointed time and place, he duly appeared but refused to retract a single word. This provoked a greater riot and another death. Finally, the Dominican was hauled off to Geneva's prison until such time as he changed his mind (he spent two full years there before being released in exchange for a Protestant school-teacher).[62]

Beyond this point, the balance turned steadily in favor of the Reformers. Meeting in a private, Bernese-owned home in the rue des Allemands, Farel celebrated a few baptisms and a marriage. On March 1, under cover of another riot, which was apparently instigated by Baudichon de la Maisonneuve, the Reformers seized a wing of the Franciscan convent and literally thrust Farel into its chair to preach. Even more serious was the arrest and trial of an episcopal notary who had been sheltering a murder suspect. The judicial inquest discovered among his papers some undated legal forms, signed by the Prince-Bishop, which instituted an unnamed military governor from Fribourg for the city.[63] This was the last straw. Geneva's government refused to receive a Fribourg deputation that arrived in April to renew the pact of alliance. Further negotiations between them proved futile, although the Genevans insisted to the very end that their quarrel was only with the Bishop, not with Fribourg.[64] Nevertheless, the official seal of Fribourg was removed from the pact of *combourgeoisie* on May 15.

Since Protestant Bern was now Geneva's lone protector, there could be no more political opposition to the Reformation. And the Reformation, in turn, became more closely identified with the struggle for complete political independence from the Prince-Bishop. Serious attacks of iconoclasm began to occur with monotonous regularity within Geneva. Even more serious was a surprise attack against the city on the night of July 30, 1534, by troops gathered by the Bishop and by Charles III, aided by a few accomplices within the walls. Thanks to alert watchmen, the attack failed. Forty compromised episcopal partisans fled to a nearby castle at Peney. This wave of fugitives, which even included a few prominent Eidguenots, now allied with the local gentry to carry on a series of guerrilla campaigns against the citizens of Geneva.[65] The whole affair was very similar to the activities of the Mammeluke exiles and the Fraternity of the Spoon; and these new fugitives, called Peneysans, were to continue their program of sporadic terrorization of Geneva until the moment of Bernese conquest.

The consolidation of the Reformers' triumph within Geneva took longer than might have been expected, mainly because of the persistent neutrality displayed by Geneva's ruling magistrates. Most of these magistrates were religious conservatives or else religious moderates. As late as January 6, 1535, they menaced a shopkeeper with banishment for refusing to close his shutters during Epiphany; they had punished iconoclasts and warned Farel about his intemperance as late as October 1534.[66] But these same magistrates resolutely battled the Peneysans and decided on September 13, 1534, to destroy all Genevan suburbs east of the Rhone, meanwhile constructing a new and greatly improved wall to cover the entire city including the remaining suburb of St.-Gervais. Most important of all, these cautious magistrates took the radical step of declaring the office of Prince-Bishop vacant in October 1534.

Another spectacular incident came to aid the extreme Evangelical party in March 1535. Pierre Viret, Farel's chief collaborator and like him a subject of Bern, was poisoned, though not fatally, after eating a plate of spinach. The case was sensational, and the servant who had done the poisoning confessed that she had acted in collaboration with a Genevan canon; however, a clever defense by a good lawyer got the canon acquitted.[67] The reformers used this episode to promote a second great public disputation, and the government agreed to hold it in June. Aided by the freshly converted guardian of the Franciscan convent, and opposed by no men of any great skill (the Sorbonne Dominican refused to emerge from prison on this occasion to champion the cause of the Church), Farel and Viret

argued for a full month. Eight judges, four from each side, presided over the assembly, and four secretaries took down its
minutes. But when the dispute at last ended, Geneva's eternally
prudent government refused to draw any immediate conclusions
from it, despite strong pressure by Farel. Only a month later,
after an outbreak of iconoclasm at the Cathedral, did he win
from the Two Hundred a decree that the Mass should be "provisionally" suspended. The same decree also forbade further
outbreaks of iconoclasm, but its important consequence, of
course, was the long-expected suspension of the Mass. Immediately afterwards, Geneva's canons and all but one of the twenty-
five nuns of Ste.-Claire left Geneva for their new homes at
Annecy. Geneva's Franciscan and Dominican monks were ordered
on December 5 to attend the new sermons or else to leave the
city; apparently only seven of twenty Franciscans chose exile.[68]
By this act, the entire Genevan clergy was either converted or
expelled. Meanwhile, an inventory of all ecclesiastical property
was taken, and old revenues were diverted to the support of a
new public almshouse, located in the former nunnery. The last
prerogative of episcopal sovereignty crumbled on November 26,
1535, when Geneva's magistrates established their own mint.

The winter of 1535–1536 witnessed the crisis and conclusion of
Geneva's long struggle for independence. Charles III had at last
managed to assemble 500 Italian mercenaries to reinforce the
Peneysans and the local gentry, and Savoy now began to be-
siege Geneva in earnest. Genevan appeals for help to Bern produced no response. A volunteer succeeded in raising 500 men at
Neuchâtel, all Bernese subjects, and marched them to the relief
of Geneva in October 1535. They fought a successful skirmish
with Savoyard militia, but just as the road to Geneva lay open
before them, they were disbanded on orders from the government of Bern. Geneva's leading magistrates had also been negotiating with a mysterious minor court official of Francis I of
France, a man with the odd name of *le magnifique* Meigret who
was then a refugee in Geneva for religious reasons. Meigret
promised French help, and succeeded in persuading a Savoyard
nobleman in French service to raise a cavalry force of 200 for
the city's relief. This army, attempting to cross the Alps to
Geneva in mid-winter, was ambushed by a force of Savoyard

peasants. Most of the horsemen fled, and only seven of them and their commander succeeded in reaching Geneva, which was promptly claimed for the crown of France.[69]

Futile as it was, this French adventure nonetheless threw a healthy scare into the hearts of the Bernese. Fearing that a considerable plum might escape her grasp, and encouraged by the international situation, Bern finally decided to act against Savoy. She quickly raised a formidable contingent of 6000 men and 16 cannon in January 1536.[70] Bern neglected to inform her Genevan allies of these preparations until hostilities against Savoy had actually begun. A Genevan magistrate, François Favre, was writing to his brother in Lausanne in January 1536 that "we are given over to the king [of France], who has accepted us, and has promised to maintain us in our liberties and franchises, to let us live according to the new Reformation, and who besides will pay all the loans we have made in Germany." He did not mention the possibility of Bernese aid.[71] The Bernese army, soon assisted by a French army that independently attacked Charles III, paraded triumphantly through the northern territories of Savoy against token opposition.

This army officially liberated Geneva on February 2, 1536. Bern "liberated" Geneva in the twentieth-century sense of the word, intending to turn her erstwhile allies into Bernese subjects. On February 5, the Bernese commander formally requested from Geneva's Syndics and Council the old authority, jurisdiction, and preeminence of the Bishop, together with the old judicial office of *vidomne*. Geneva's magistrates were given ten days to ponder this demand, while Bern completed her conquests around the south side of Lake Geneva. Then Geneva replied that "we have endured war against both the Duke of Savoy and the Bishop for seventeen or twenty years . . . not because we intended to make this city subject to any power, but because we wished that a poor city which had warred and suffered so much should have her liberty." Geneva's secretary reported in a considerable understatement that the Bernese were unhappy with that response. They requested a meeting of the Council of Two Hundred, feeling that they would react with more generosity toward the city's military saviors. The Two Hundred reported on February 17 that "they supposed that our *combourgeois* had come not to put us in subjection but to deliver us from captivity and to give us our liberty, just as we once used to possess it."[72] This was a bold response to give to a conquering army, but it succeeded. Geneva avoided the fate of Bern's other civic ally, Lausanne, which lost her independence in this same campaign. Perhaps Geneva preserved her independence because of the presence of Swiss deputies who accompanied the Bernese army, and who had often been told by Bern's commanders that they were fighting only to aid Geneva; perhaps it was because of the nearby French army, whose king sent in *his* demand for sovereignty three days later. (Francis had less success than the Bernese; Geneva's magistrates refused even to hear his request).[73]

While the French army continued its southward progress to Milan, and while Bern was busily engaged in organizing her new conquests, Geneva's magistrates concluded their Reformation and revolution. Well before their negotiations with Bern were concluded, the Genevans held a general citizen assembly on May 25, 1536, which unanimously voted to "live henceforth according to the Law of the Gospel and the Word of God, and to abolish all Papal abuses."[74] A new church had to be constructed inside the old episcopal city. Three months later, Farel successfully persuaded a brilliant young theologian named John Calvin to help him build it.

†

Since her attempted alliance with Fribourg in 1519, Geneva had undergone a complete revolution in her political and ecclesiastical constitution. At the moment in August 1536 when they could legitimately call themselves princes, Geneva's magistrates completed their assumption of the honors and privileges of their city's independent Prince-Bishop. The process was certainly neither smooth nor easy, especially since the Genevans always had to rely on outside aid to sustain their cause. In retrospect, one can see that the political future of Geneva was at stake, and the outcome genuinely in doubt, on three occasions within a single decade. From December 1525 to February 1526, Charles III of Savoy battled the Swiss for hegemony in Geneva. From June 1532 to April 1534, Geneva's Swiss allies

struggled bitterly over the city's religious future, with the larger
of them, Bern, eventually winning. Then, from October 1535 to ₃.
February 1536, Bern disputed her control of Geneva with
Francis I. On each of these three occasions, Geneva ran a serious
risk of being conquered militarily by one side or the other. Yet
she emerged as an independent buffer state.

The reasons for Genevan success, apart from the stubbornness
and skill of her political leaders and a bit of pure luck at the
critical moments, are hard to discover. Genevan historians seem
oblivious to the extent to which Geneva's future was in jeopardy
during this decade, and thus seem unaware of the genuine greatness of her achievement. Nevertheless, this triumph of 1536
inaugurated the 250-year history of the Republic of Geneva, a
state far different from the independent Prince-Bishopric of 1519.
In the course of this revolution, Geneva's citizens had usurped
one by one the various prerogatives of their Bishop: the right
to summon the citizens together, the right to judge civil cases
and to execute judgments in criminal cases, the right to regulate
the form of religion, and last of all, the right to coin money.
Geneva's Bishop, the greedy but hapless Pierre de la Baume,
failed to preserve his position, partly because he never built a
core of citizen support around himself. Even an originally well-
intentioned magistrate like Balard was led to remark in 1528,
"note that princes can't be trusted, because he has turned his
back on his city and subjects of Geneva from fear of losing two
of his benefices."[75] In a sense, the citizens were correct in declaring the episcopal seat vacant in October 1534, for their
Bishop had in fact deserted them.

The most remarkable thing about this Genevan revolution is
that in the official records of Geneva it doesn't seem to have been
the least bit revolutionary. Nothing was more repulsive to the
sixteenth-century mind than the thought of rebellion against a
lawful prince. Consequently, Geneva's citizens had to dust off
all the ancient charters they could find, and usually had to
stretch their meaning a good deal, in order to prove those "ancient liberties" which the Two Hundred invoked in replying to
Bern in February 1536. As Pascal once remarked, we must
never sense the fact of usurpation. Geneva could never afford
to admit that she had undergone a decade of revolution. Ge-

nevan historians, following the lead of her official sources, echoed this opinion. A century ago, one of the finest among them observed that "we are forced to admire the spirit of moderation and the respect for legality, from which the Genevans of that epoch never departed. How little do men like this, so devoted to liberty, resemble *revolutionaries!*"[76] Until well into the twentieth century, Genevan historians continued to deny the existence of a revolution in their tidy little patrimony: the earliest such admission dates from 1926, but the official history of 1951 still refers to the decade after 1526 under the euphemism of "political emancipation."[77]

The Bishops of Geneva knew better. Pierre de la Baume sent a furious letter to the dying Besançon Hughes in October 1532:

I think that you covet the role of princes. But be content to live in the customary fashion of your forefathers, who were good merchants, and who aimed at no higher honors than befitted their station. You'll have a hard time turning the Rhone from her path, and you'll have just as hard a time trying to destroy the Church.[78]

Any court, he said, even Lucifer's, would find the Genevans guilty of the most radical disobedience. The most famous among Pierre de la Baume's successors, St. Francis de Sales, once prepared a memorandum for a trip to the court of Henry IV in 1601. He declared that the Bishop of Geneva was the sole legitimate prince of Geneva and her dependencies, notwithstanding the pretensions of the Dukes of Savoy, as successors to the Counts of Geneva, on the one hand, and of the citizens of Geneva on the other. St. Francis continued by listing all the privileges exercised by the Bishops as immediate vassals of the Emperor. He admitted that the Bishops had granted a few nonessential prerogatives to the House of Savoy, but insisted that the claims of the citizens of Geneva were based only on usurpation.[79]

This legal summary, coming from a doctor of civil and canon law from the University of Padua, was hard to refute. Genevan statesmen throughout the sixteenth century were hard put to defend the strict legality of their actions from 1526 to 1536. Sometimes they had a difficult time justifying their sovereignty to their powerful allies in France or Switzerland. James VI and I of England expressed doubts about Geneva's right to sovereignty in 1603, and Genevan magistrates fought a pamphlet war with Savoyard officials (though not with St. Francis) over this issue in 1605 and 1606.[80]

The crowning touch of the Genevan revolution, the most daring step which her magistrates took after long hesitation in 1535, was the destruction of the established church in Geneva and the seizure of her extensive properties. This was justified as a "reformation," a restoration of the pure Gospel and of primitive Christianity. It was the ecclesiastical counterpart to the city's "ancient liberties." Nothing could better illustrate the program or the logic of these conservative revolutionaries, who always expressed genuine, unfeigned annoyance whenever their opponents accused them of revolutionary activities.

Notes

1. Quoted by Amédée Roget, Les Suisses et Genève . . . au XVIe siècle, 2 vols. (G., 1864), II, p. 238.
2. The basic account of medieval Geneva is in the cooperative Histoire de Genève des Origines à 1798 (G., 1951), especially the chapters by Henri Grandjean, "De la féodalité à la communauté," pp. 91–137, and by Fréd. Gardy, "Genève au XVe siècle," pp. 139–69.
3. See A. Kleinclausz, ed., Histoire de Lyon des Origines à 1595 (Lyon, 1939), p. 155 f.; Chas. Petit-Dutaillis, Les Communes françaises (Paris, 1947), p. 132.
4. Babel, HEG, I, p. 479. For a similar case in a nearby diocese, see Kleinclausz, Lyon, I, p. 174 n. 1.
5. Jean-Francois Bergier, Genève et l'économie européene de la Renaissance (Paris, 1963), pp. 217–431, gives a large-scale treatment of the fairs which stops in 1480. Babel, HEG, II, pp. 345–427, gives a summary that extends well into the sixteenth century.
6. A summary based on Bergier's still unpublished researches in Babel, HEG, II, pp. 413–27.
7. Ibid., II, p. 423.
8. Ibid., II, pp. 19–28. See also L. Micheli, Les institutions municipales de Genève au XVe siècle (G., 1912), pp. 144–72.
9. L. von Muralt, "Reformation und Stadtgemeinde in der Schweiz," in Zeitschrift für Schweizerische Geschichte, 10 (1930), p. 356; Kleinclausz,

Lyon, I, pp. 291, 318 f. and especially the important remarks of René Fedou, *Les Hommes de Loi Lyonnais à la Fin du Moyen Age* (Paris, 1964), pp. 381–92. Petit-Dutaillis, *Les Communes françaises,* pp. 253–54, notes that the oath of citizenship had disappeared almost everywhere in France by 1500.

10. Roget, *Suisses et Genève,* I, p. 64 n. 2
11. Complete list in Babel, *HEG,* II, pp. 9–13.
12. Henri Naef, *Les Origines de la Réforme à Genève* (Geneva-Paris, 1936), p. 101 [hereafter Naef, *Origines*].
13. *Ibid.,* pp. 12–13, 16–19, 299–306, 216–18.
14. Feller, *Geschichte Berns,* II, p. 350 f.
15. Roget, *Suisses et Genève,* I, p. 41. See Babel, *HEG,* II, pp. 32–35, for a list of financial measures taken then.
16. Naef, *Origines,* p. 31.
17. A. Dufour, "De la bourgeoisie de Genève à la noblesse de Savoie, XVᵉ-XVIᵉ siècles," in *Mélanges . . . Antony Babel* (G., 1963), I, pp. 228–38, esp. 235.
18. Naef, *Origines,* pp. 106–23.
19. *Ibid.,* pp. 28–29, 45–46.
20. *Ibid.,* pp. 75–81.
21. For an exhaustive study of one such set of connections (doubtless the most important among them), see Henri Naef, "Besançon Hugues, son ascendance et sa posterité, ses amis fribourgeois," in *BHG,* 5 (1933), pp. 355–585.
22. Complete list in *Registres du Conseil,* VIII, p. 290 n. 1.
23. Henri Naef, *Fribourg au secours de Genève, 1525–1526* (Fribourg, 1927), p. 22 n. 4 [hereafter Naef, *Fribourg*].
24. Henri Naef, "L'occupation militaire de Genève et la combourgeoisie manquée de 1519," in *Zeitschrift für Schweizerische Kirchengeschichte,* 52 (1958), pp. 48–86.
25. *Reg. du Conseil,* IX, pp. 41–42.
26. Naef, *Origines,* p. 126.
27. Bonivard, *Chroniques de Genève,* II, pp. 215–25.
28. See Garrett Mattingly, "Eustache Chapuys" (unpub. Ph. D. diss., Harvard University, 1927), pp. 11–91.
29. Naef, *Origines,* pp. 64–72.
30. *Ibid.,* pp. 462–64.
31. Naef, *Fribourg,* pp. 28–36: Mattingly, "Eustache Chapuys," pp. 80 f., 82–85.
32. *Ibid.,* pp. 99–130 *passim.* Compare Ed. Favre, *Combourgeois: Genève-Fribourg-Berne, 1526* (G., 1926), pp. 59–74, which is an official and highly patriotic work commemorating the 400th anniversary of this alliance. Favre pays far less attention to Swiss politics and especially to the key role of Fribourg in these negotiations. The phrase *conseil des hallebardes* is of contemporary origin, as Naef demonstrated (*Fribourg,* p. 130 n. 3). Geneva's official council minutes leave a large blank space in lieu of reporting this session. See *R.C.,* X, p. 170 n. 1.

33. Naef, *Fribourg*, pp. 139–218 *passim*.
34. Quoted *ibid.*, pp. 220, 226.
35. Basic accounts of this crucial assembly are in *Journal du Syndic Balard*, pp. 51–52, and *R.C.*, X, pp. 207–10, 593–94. Modern narratives in Naef, *Fribourg*, pp. 243–45, and Favre, *Combourgeois*, pp. 107–09.
36. *Journal du Syndic Balard*, p. 51 (this passage has escaped the attention of most modern Genevan historians).
37. *Ibid.*, p. 54.
38. This fact is brilliantly demonstrated by Lino Marini, *Savoiardi e piemontesi nella state Sabaude, I: 1418–1536* (Rome, 1962), pp. 312–96 *passim*, esp. 356 ff.
39. Naef, *Origines*, pp. 129–30.
40. Complete list in *R.C.*, X, p. 106 n. 1.
41. *Ibid.*, p. 418 n. 2; compare *Journal du Syndic Balard*, p. 72.
42. See Jean-Francois Bergier, "Recherches sur les foires et sur le commerce international de Genève de 1480 à 1540" (unpub. thèse de l'Ecole des Chartes, 1956), pp. 225 ff.
43. This account of Genevan history from 1526 to 1536 is based primarily on the excellent narrative by Henri Naef in the *Histoire de Genève des Origines à 1798*, pp. 187–217. There is an old but intelligent account by H. D. Foster, "Geneva before Calvin," in *American Hist. Rev.*, 8 (1903), pp. 217–40; and a newer account by Chas. Borgeaud, "La conquête religieuse de Genève," in *Guillaume Farel, 1489–1565* (Neuchatel-Paris, 1930), pp. 298–342. The fullest account of these years is still A. Roget, *Les suisses et Genève*.
44. G. Werner, "Les institutions politiques de Genève de 1519 à 1536," in *Etrennes genevoises* (1926), p. 34, considers this the most important political change in this whole turbulent age; I agree.
45. Henri Naef, "La conquête du Vénérable Chapître de St.-Pierre par les bourgeois," in *BHG*, 9 (1939), pp. 36–126.
46. *R. C.*, XI, p. 620.
47. *Journal du Syndic Balard*, p. 303.
48. *Ibid.*, p. 315; *R. C.*, XI, pp. 525–26. Geneva's obligations to Basel are filed in 20 volumes at AEG, Finances L.
49. Bernd Moeller, *Reichstadt und Reformation* (Gutersloh, 1962), p. 26 n. 34.
50. Naef, *Origines*, pp. 352–59.
51. See Feller, *Geschichte Berns*, II, pp. 147–66; Naef, *Origines*, pp. 359–72.
52. Quoted in L. Marini, *Savoiardi e piemontesi*, p. 386.
53. A classic biography of him, suffused with pardonable Genevan patriotism, by J.-B.-G. Galiffe in *MDG*, 11 (1859), pp. 197–451; numerous corrections and additions by Henri Naef, in 1933 (cited *supra*, n. 21).
54. Roget, *Suisses et Genève*, I, p. 390.
55. Naef, *Origines*, pp. 462–63. Luther's works were known at Lyon and Avignon in 1520, at Tournai and Besançon by 1523; see W. G. Moore, *La Réforme allemande et la littérature française* (Strasbourg, 1930), pp. 61 ff.

56. Herminjard, II, pp. 9–11.
57. *Journal du Syndic Balard*, pp. 268–69.
58. Naef's arguments in *Origines*, pp. 309–41 and 405–70, linking the Genevan Reformation to humanism, are neatly summarized in his chapter in the *Histoire de Genève . . . à 1798*, pp. 193–94. Their fragility was demonstrated by Hektor Ammann, "Oberdeutsche Kaufleute und die Anfänge der Reformation in Genf," in *Zeitschrift für Württemburgische Landesgechichte*, 13 (1954), pp. 150–93; Ammann's thesis is implied by his title.

    The political origins of the Reformation in the episcopal city of Lausanne, where systematic preaching was simply one aspect of Bernese imperialism, provides an interesting comparison to Geneva: see Chas. Gilliard, "Les débuts de la Réforme à Lausanne," in *Etudes et documents inédits sur la Réformation en Suisse Romande* (Lausanne, 1936), pp. 5–29.
59. Herminjard, II, pp. 421–24.
60. Contemporary accounts (for Bern's benefit) in Herminjard, III, pp. 46–51; in *R. C.*, XII, pp. 264–65, 599–600; and the religiously committed eyewitnesses, Antoine Froment, *Les actes et gestes merveilleuses de Geneve*, pp. 57–59; Jeanne de Jussie, *Le levain du Calvinisme*, pp. 64–67.
61. *R. C.*, XII, p. 604.
62. Herminjard, III, pp. 119–24, 132–36; *R. C.*, XII, pp. 437–42, 447–49, 474, 623–28.
63. *R. C.*, XII, pp. 613–14.
64. *Ibid.*, pp. 510–12, 523–24, 629–30.
65. No work has yet been done to determine the basic composition of Geneva's Evangelical and Episcopal factions of the early 1530's; the problem is as interesting and as obscure as the composition of the Eidguenots and Mammelukes of the preceding decade. See Herminjard, II, pp. 459–62, for the names of the Evangelical nucleus of 1532, and *R. C.*, XII, p. 600, for the twenty signers of the May 1533 report to Bern on the Werly riot. A list of the Peneysan fugitives of August 1534 is in *R.C.*, XIII, pp. 639–42.
66. Naef, in *Histoire de Genève . . . à 1798*, p. 201.
67. J.-F. Bergier, "L'empoisonneuse de Pierre Viret," in *Revue de Théologie et de Philosophie* (1961), pp. 236–50.
68. Naef, *Origines*, pp. 23, 256. Compare Moeller, *Reichstadt und Reformation*, p. 35 n. 2, for other examples elsewhere.
69. *Histoire de Genève . . . à 1798*, pp. 204–06; Chas. Gilliard, "Les combats de Gingins et la Faucille," in *BHG*, 9 (1939), pp. 3–27; Alexis François, *Le Magnifique Meigret* (G., 1947), pp. 27–52; and J. Freymond, *La politique de François Ier à l'égard de la Savoie* (Lausanne, 1939), chap. 5.
70. Chas. Gilliard, *La Conquête du Pays de Vaud par les Bernois* (Lausanne, 1935), pp. 32–77.
71. *Ibid.*, p. 45 n. 3.

72. *R.C.*, XIII, pp. 433, 444–47; Gilliard, *Conquête*, pp. 97–99, 149–50.
73. Gilliard, *Conquête*, pp. 150–51; M. Roset, *Les Chroniques de Genève*, Bk. III, ch. 64–65 (pp. 230–31). Compare Gilliard, *Conquête*, pp. 251–53, on the Bernese takeover at Lausanne.
74. Bern had adopted the Reformation through a similar *Gemeinschworung;* see Feller, II, p. 163f. Compare Moeller, *Reichstadt und Reformation*, p. 28 n. 45, for other examples.
75. *Journal du Syndic Balard*, p. 164.
76. Roget, *Suisses et Genève*, I, p. 391 (his italics).
77. See Georges Werner, "Les institutions politiques de Genève de 1519 à 1536," in *Etrennes genevoises* (1926), p. 25: "En réalité, la conclusion de l'alliance de 1526 est un acte audacieux, un véritable révolution." Compare the title of Naef's chapter in the *Histoire de Genève . . . à 1798*, p. 187ff: "L'emancipation politique et la Réforme."
78. *R.C.*, XII, p. 152 n. 1.
79. *Oeuvres de St. Francois de Sales*, XXIV, pp. 270–79, summarized by Ruth Kleinman, *St. François de Sales and the Protestants* (G., 1962), pp. 105 ff.
80. G. Bonnant, "Les relations politiques entre Genève et l'Angleterre sous Jacques Ier" (Prix Harvey, 1936), mss. at AEG. Jean Sarrasin, *Le citadin de Genève, ou responce au Cavalier de Savoye* (Paris: P. le Bret, 1606), summarizes and concludes eighty years of such legal arguments.

THREE

The Tumult of Independence, 1536–1555

For the first thirty years of her independence, the Republic of Geneva was firmly encased in a protective wrapping of Bernese *baillages*. Her importance, or even her existence, seldom came to the notice of outside powers. To the world at large, Geneva was merely a satellite in the orbit of Bern, as she had been a satellite in the orbit of the House of Savoy about 1500. Her 1536 treaty with Bern contained an important clause which forbade Geneva to contract any alliance or even to have diplomatic relations with other states without Bernese consent. For a full generation, Geneva's dealings with third parties, principally with other Swiss cantons or with the French crown, were on a rare and artificial basis. The fears expressed in August 1540 by the Emperor Charles V, who sent a letter to his Imperial city warning her against taking an oath of homage to Bern, were not entirely groundless.[1]

Geneva was not a tranquil satellite, however. Her first five years of independence, which culminated in a showdown between rival political factions in 1540, were unmitigated chaos, a tragicomedy acted out by exuberant amateurs. But behind this tumultuous facade, a great deal of constructive work was being done.[2] A mass of new institutions and new administrative measures needed to be introduced in order to answer the novel problems of civic independence. The Reformed church, the public school, and the public almshouse had to be staffed and paid for from various confiscated ecclesiastical properties. Religious orthodoxy and property titles within the walls of Geneva had to be clarified, standardized, and recorded; simultaneous investigations of these two points, house by house, took much of the

government's time in 1537. Official records were kept in the
new public archives. The change from Papist Latin to French
had to be made by Geneva's notaries and chancery.[3] Usurers
and printers were brought under strict surveillance. An important board of audit was created to control the numerous col-
lectors and spenders of public funds. In 1539, Geneva even
made an attempt to widen her streets. Her judicial system was
corrected and extended, and an appeals court was established
for civil cases. Rural lands which had belonged to the Prince-
Bishop or to the Cathedral chapter had to be taken in hand, and
the peasants made to obey their new masters. Parish priests in
the countryside around Geneva had to be forced to adopt the
Reformation. There were a thousand and one things for the new
state to do, from approving catechisms to reproving peasants.
Most of the time, no matter which political faction was in power,
the Genevan government did these things satisfactorily.

The simultaneous introduction of so many changes naturally
led to considerable confusion. An excellent illustration is the use
of French and Latin in Geneva's official records. All Genevan
public minutes are in Latin until February 1536, when under
the same secretary they suddenly change to French. That summer the Small Council ordered that all trials in town and country
be held in the vernacular; but in July the Council minutes suddenly revert to Latin and remain in Latin until the end of the
year. In 1537, the secretary began his entries in Latin, surged
bravely ahead for a line or two, then sometimes in mid-sentence
changed to French. "Joh. Balardi: expedevit quatour scut. solis
ultra sexdecim jam expedevit et se ypothequera sus ce qu'il
dira."[4] This macaronic style continues, with Latin steadily di-
minishing in proportion, until the autumn of 1537, when the
triumph of French becomes definitive. Nearly all other aspects of
Genevan life exhibit a comparable degree of confusion, from
religious creeds (as Calvin said long afterwards, when he came
there was preaching but little else) to financial records.

Compounding this confusion was the growth of factional
rivalry within the Genevan government. "The generation which
established the Reformation was torn apart by its own hands,"
as a nineteenth-century historian remarked, and it was a petty
quarrel between two magistrates, growing out of a single epi-

sode during the war for independence in 1535–1536, which began
this rivalry.[5] But it grew rapidly, and by 1537 Michel Sept led
the partisans of Farel, known as *Guillermins* or *Farets* (burned-
out candles) against militia commander Jean Philippe and his
friends, who were soon known to their enemies as *Articulants*
or *artichauds* (artichokes). Partly because of this rivalry, and
partly from the general instability of the times and the atmos-
phere of revolution, the turnover among Genevan officials, both
secular and religious, was remarkably high. Only four men
served continuously on the Small Council between 1536 and
1541, and only one pastor (Henri de la Mar) was continuously
employed during these years.

Geneva's political pace had quickened in 1537, when all four
syndics (including one who had been elected without being on
the preliminary list of eight candidates) were close friends of
Farel. Much of that year's activity was devoted to organizing
the Church of Geneva, drawing up a public confession of faith
and imposing it on the city's population. But this religious loyalty
oath met opposition in some quarters, especially from the German merchants in the rue des Allemands. Some of this opposition, like Jean Balard's, was both sincere and articulate, but
much of it came from little more than sheer inertia and dislike
for some of the more stringent regulations (such as regular attendance at Sunday sermons) which Farel and his friends wished
to impose. At the 1538 elections, the pendulum swung in the
opposite direction, and Farel's partisans were removed from all
the top public offices.

Immediately afer the elections, six *Guillermins* were suspended
from the Small Council and publicly charged with political intrigues with French agents.[6] Additional charges were made that
the *Guillermins* had mishandled the public mint (which was
probably true) and had falsified the secretarial records. Geneva's
pastors, led by Farel, began preaching against the new magistrates; they were sternly warned not to meddle in political questions and to follow the Bernese church ritual more closely. After
further misbehavior, Farel and Calvin were dismissed by the
Two Hundred and by the general citizen assembly in April.
"Well and good," said Calvin to the Small Council upon hearing
this decision, "if we had served men we would be ill rewarded,

but we serve a great Master who will reward us."[7] Bern, which had spent much time pressuring Geneva to adopt her form of church services (which included the use of baptismal fonts, wedding feasts, and the traditional services at Easter, Christmas, and Pentecost, all of which had been abolished by Farel in Geneva), now received the banished ministers gracefully and wrote an "admonition and request" to the Small Council to recall them. But the whole issue had become political and Genevan magistrates, their honor at stake, stiffly refused. Farel and Calvin, now thoroughly disgusted, left for Zurich and Strasbourg. Geneva merely hired some new ministers, relying mainly on local talent but also acquiring some men of reputation from Neuchâtel, and added a new schoolteacher later that year. Reforms continued without serious interruption. At Christmas, church buildings were repaired and peddlars were warned not to sell meat while the Sunday sermon was being preached.

The 1539 elections resulted in a choice of neutral syndics. Very few magistrates were replaced, and the *Guillermins* remained on the defensive, without any appointments to important jobs. The new government soon got embroiled with Bern over the precise extent of Genevan rights in the lands formerly held by the Cathedral chapter. These rights had been ill-defined in the 1536 treaty and there had been continual petty quarrels over which state had the right to arrest which peasant for which offense. Finally a deputation of three anti-*Guillermins* was sent to Bern to settle these disputes. They negotiated for a fortnight and returned with the guarded announcement that they had done the best they could. Two months later Bern sent a French translation of the clarifications to the 1536 treaty to which these ambassadors had agreed. It was immediately obvious that, contrary to their instructions, Geneva's ambassadors had conceded all the points in dispute.

Their fault was simple. Bern had insisted on conducting the negotiations in German, which only one of the three (Jean Lullin) claimed to understand. All three greatly admired the Bernese, and doubtless they relied on the good will and superior diplomatic finesse of their allies to produce an acceptable compromise. It is possible that Lullin had overrated his knowledge of Swiss German and that these three literally did not understand what was going on. The treaty clarifications were instantly repudiated by Geneva, and the same three men were ordered back to Bern. Lullin, humiliated, refused to go. Bern simply repeated her satisfaction with the clarifications, and the impasse remained. This gross diplomatic blunder was followed within a month by Francis I's seizure of the episcopal *mandement* of Thiez, an enclave within French soil, which was announced to the Genevans by a haughty royal herald who proclaimed that Geneva had "tried to seduce the people of Thiez to obey your faith, which greatly displeases us and which we cannot tolerate."[8] This double blow catastrophically undermined the public credit of Lullin's and Philippe's faction.

Yet all three *articulants* (as the 1539 ambassadors were now called, after the articles to which they had agreed) were re-elected to the Small Council in 1540 after an elaborate pre-election peace feast among all of Geneva's leading politicians. This equilibrium was soon to be destroyed by the power of the general citizen assembly, which reached its peak in the spring and summer of 1540. The storm broke in April, when Bern sent another embassy to prod Geneva into signing the clarifications to the 1536 treaty. Her ambassadors received a lukewarm reception from the upper councils, then appeared before the general assembly, which only two months before had voiced a need for better government and had simultaneously requested a French translation of the Bernese constitution.[9] This time, a riot ensued. Dozens of voices demanded the arrest of the *articulants,* and the meeting broke up in an uproar before the Bernese could be heard. All three *articulants,* warned in the nick of time by the Lieutenant of Justice, fled Geneva. The disgusted Bernese trudged home, followed soon by a Genevan embassy which tried unsuccessfully to mollify them.

A mammoth state trial now began at Geneva, as thirty-two witnesses exposed the conspiracy of the *articulants* to "deliver the state over to Bern." Efforts by Bern to intervene on behalf of the defendants simply confirmed Genevan suspicions of their guilt and speeded up the pace of the trial. On June 5, 1540, all three were condemned to death *in absentia.* The next day, Jean Philippe began blustering about the streets after a banquet.[10] He had been called an artichoke once too often, and either he or a close companion gave a severe wound to one "traitor" to prove it. There was a confused riot along the broad *rues-basses* and the waterfront, envenomed by an angry debate between Philippe and Michel Sept, who kept shouting at him from his upstairs window. Philippe had overestimated his popularity. He was soon outnumbered, two of his supporters were killed, and he was forced to hide. A manhunt discovered him the next morning under a bale of straw in a livery stable. He and twenty-five of his followers were arrested in the wake of this new conspiracy against the republic.

Once more, under incessant pressure from the general assembly, vigilante justice was pursued by the Small Council. Once again Bern attempted to intervene on behalf of the prisoners, but to no avail. Philippe and one of his bodyguards were executed, and his following disappeared like fog in the late morning. One syndic retired suddenly to his country estate, three members of the Small Council fled, another who was in Bern on business decided not to return. The Lieutenant of Justice remained at his post, but was soon purged by his victorious rivals. All vacancies were filled by staunch *Guillermins*.

Relations with Bern now reached the breaking point, for the ousted faction were strong admirers of both the Bernese state and church. Bern was also disturbed by the fact that their defeat was due principally to the machinations of a plebeian assembly; her embassy observed at one point that "these are strange doings and unworthy of magistrates." Geneva had in fact held twenty general plebiscites in five months, the highest figures in the Republic's entire history, and it seemed that mob rule and anarchy were imminent. The *Guillermins* soon made good use of a war scare to subdue the more unruly elements within the general assembly, but not until things had gotten so bad that some of the new preachers hired in 1538 had fled the city. As Bern increased her diplomatic pressures, Geneva responded with a blend of outright refusals and apologetic evasions — and repaired her fortifications.

The potential war was averted when Bern learned that Geneva had sent a special embassy to French authorities in Savoy. Fearing lest her *combourgeois* make a new alliance, Bern toned down her demands. By October, when Geneva had been pacified internally and externally, her new chiefs of state proceeded with their next order of business: the recall of Farel and Calvin. Farel had settled down in Neuchâtel and could neither be enticed away nor released by his Bernese employers. At Strasbourg, Calvin was even less eager than Farel to return to Geneva. "There is no place on earth of which I am more afraid," he had written only a few months before. But at last Calvin let himself be persuaded, just as he had been in 1536, and a young member of the governing clique named Ami Perrin was sent to bring him back. The remaining prisoners from the riot of June 6 were quietly released, and the outstanding disputes with Bern were handed over to an arbitration committee from Basel. Such disputes were really not worth fighting over. As Balard noted, the tumults of 1540 had been due "as much to M. Farel as to those articles."[11] Once the immediate goals of overthrowing Philippe and pacifying Bern had been attained, the real goal of the *Guillermins* could be undertaken. But they got a great deal more than they had bargained for. Instead of restoring the church of Farel, they had unintentionally inaugurated the church of Calvin.

✝

Fifteen years later, Geneva suffered another political crisis like that of 1540. The pattern of her first few years of independence was reproduced in slow motion: the growth of rival factions, charges of treachery with either France or Bern cast as enemies of the Republic, a defeated factional chief who doubled as militia commander, and mass removal of the defeated faction from the Small Council. Even the time when the decisive street fighting took place in 1555 was only three weeks earlier than in 1540.

Of course Geneva had learned a few lessons in 1540. Never again was a diplomatic mission to Bern composed entirely of members of one faction, and never again was the general citizen assembly used to upset the factional balance of power. Although factionalism continued to plague the Republic of Geneva, dividing the victors of 1540 just as it had divided those of 1526 and 1536, in many important ways the new state was becoming institutionally stabilized. The Small Council was beginning to grow into an oligarchy; fourteen of its twenty-five members served continuously from 1541 to 1555.

Far more important, the Church of Geneva stabilized both its doctrine and its personnel within a few years of Calvin's return. After his expulsion from Geneva in 1538, John Calvin had shed his youthful impetuousness. After guiding the French church in Strasbourg for three years, he had a fresh and important fund of practical experience upon which to draw. Now in his early thirties, returning to a city which he had good reason to fear, Calvin had once more been persuaded by Farel in February 1541 that it truly was God's will that his pastoral vocation be exercised in Geneva.

If he came reluctantly, Calvin also came with very definite ideas about what needed to be done in Geneva. On the very day of his arrival, September 13, 1541, he appeared before the Small Council to explain his long hesitation and to demand that the magistrates name a committee to prepare a written constitution for the Church of Geneva. Next Sunday, when Calvin preached at the cathedral for the first time since his return, he said not a word about the past but simply began where he had left off, explaining the same Scriptural verse he had reached when the sentence of banishment had come in 1538.[12] It was an impressive performance, and no doubt his firmness and maturity help explain the large degree of cooperation which he received from the Small Council in the next few months. The sketchy ecclesiastical ordinances of 1537 were revised and enlarged by Calvin and a superfluous six-man advisory committee in six weeks. This new code, slightly modified by the Small Council and the Two Hundred to increase the measure of lay supervision within the church (emphasizing that the pastors were appointed by *Messieurs* and that the elders were *commis* of *Messieurs*), was ratified within two months by the general citizen assembly. Geneva's famous Consistory began meeting within three months of Calvin's return.

On the day of his return from Strasbourg, Calvin had also told the Small Council that he wished to be of service to the city of Geneva. They took him at his word, and the day after the ecclesiastical ordinances were approved, they put him to

work on a committee charged with preparing a political constitution for the Republic. Calvin was entrusted with much of
the work, so much that he had to be given leave from some of
his other duties to finish it. However, his role was passive and
really little more than clerical. The finished product, Geneva's
1543 edicts on offices and officials, was essentially a codification
of current practices. The best political historians concur in the
judgment that Geneva's fundamental political dispositions were
in no way modified by them. Calvin himself probably found the
work very boring, for he never once mentioned it in his correspondence.[13] One of the few interesting features in this code
was its provision that the Two Hundred could only consider
matters already discussed by the Small Council, and the general
assembly, only matters already discussed by the Two Hundred.
This last provision had been voted down by a general assembly
as recently as November 1539, but was docilely accepted this
time.

The Republic of Geneva survived her first brush with the
plague not long after Calvin's return. It struck intermittently
in the autumn of 1542, then in the spring of 1543 (still not too
severely, since partial records indicate that two of every three
who caught it survived), and in the autumn of 1544. Besides
the usual consequences of a mild grain famine, and the reluctance
of various public officials (including the pastors) to fulfill their
duties, this Genevan plague ended in 1545 with a large-scale
witch hunt.[14] The hunt was apparently set off by a Bernese
official who had arrested a confessed plague spreader with Genevan accomplices. The irony was that the plague had pretty
well run its course when this panic struck Geneva, but the lessen-
ing danger only seemed to make public fear and hatred all the
more intense. There were forty victims in all. First it was the
plague spreaders, then the sorcerers who were uncovered. There
was the usual ghastly procedure of torture and confessions of
poisoning cattle, Witches' Sabbaths, and all the rest. Nearly all
the victims came from the *mandement* of Peney and were subjects rather than citizens of Geneva. Within Geneva, the usual
types of victims were unmasked and tortured; a few unfortunate
servants, the barber-surgeon, and a gravedigger employed at
the plague hospital were arrested for spreading the plague.

It was also during the early 1540's that Geneva finally succeeded in settling her dispute with Bern over the lands of Geneva's Cathedral chapter. The diplomatic settlement finally concluded between these states in 1544 admirably illustrates the flavor of Genevan politics.[15] In January 1542, the arbitrators at Basel reached their decision after eighteen months of deliberation. They had decided most of the disputed points in Geneva's favor, with two exceptions. The magistrates' first reaction was to disavow anything short of complete victory as unreasonable. But a special committee of eight councillors, plus Calvin and a neutral jurist from Chablais, concluded that Geneva's rights were not infringed upon in any vital respect and recommended acceptance. The Small Council, still unsatisfied, sent one last embassy to Basel in order to alter her decision on the two offending points, but to no avail. By April 1543, the Small Council created an entirely new committee to review their previous decision. While they were meeting, news arrived that Bern had rejected Basel's compromise. This reassured the Genevans, who agreed to reopen negotiations at Basel in September. Geneva now offered to abandon her claims to a part of the disputed lands if Bern would not demand the money still due for her military aid in 1536. Calvin exulted in a letter to Viret that his influence on the Small Council had triumphed over the demagogues, but his rejoicing was premature. By October 1543, the Council had once again decided to re-examine this question; the first to change his mind had been Ami Perrin. This new burst of chauvinism reached its peak in November, when the Small Council refused permission for an inn-keeper to do business under the sign of the Bernese bear. He soon reopened under the sign of the non-political ostrich.

Cooler heads in both Bern and Geneva reopened negotiations that winter. One conference was postponed after a disagreement about its location, with both sides desiring the cheaper role of host. Finally a seven-man Genevan committee spent a fortnight in Bern, where they were considerably harassed by the exiles of 1540. They made an agreement, which was quickly translated into French at Geneva and scrutinized by a large committee which included Calvin. The text proved to be identical with the first Basel compromise of January 1542, except for one additional clause providing for the full pardon of Geneva's three *articulants* of 1540. Geneva thereupon approved this treaty, with a few reservations. More negotiations in December 1543 reduced the points of contention to one, and this final block was removed two months later.

Genevan diplomacy, spurred by the sword's point of local patriotism and by the example of the *articulants,* could scarcely afford to yield a single point at the bargaining table. Their firmness often won them favorable promises and sometimes written concessions, but occasionally such fair promises proved worthless. A Genevan delegation headed by Ami Perrin was shamelessly hoodwinked by Francis I of France in 1544 and 1545 over its hopeless attempt to recover the *mandement* of Thiez.

The *articulants* received their pardon and re-entered Geneva in 1544. It so happened that the political schism of 1540 was the only one that did not result in a permanent corps of Genevan exiles, and its pacification within four years was a fine example of civic harmony. It may also have been due in part to the opportune disappearance of the most important *Guillermins,* whose chief (Michel Sept) and his two principal allies (Ami Porral and Claude Pertemps) had all died by 1544.[17] But this happy ending did not prevent the Genevan revolution from continuing to devour her own children. A new faction, based on little more than sheer chauvinism, was already beginning to form around the militia commander who had replaced Philippe, Ami Perrin.

Factional rivalry was already strong by the time of the first famous trial in Calvin's Geneva, that of Pierre Ameaux in 1546.[18] The outlines of this case are well known. Ameaux, who manufactured playing cards, wished to divorce his wife for adultery, but Calvin had been opposed to the idea for a time. Finally she was imprisoned and Ameaux divorced, but his anger remained and he now began turning it against Calvin and his teachings. The Small Council soon imprisoned Ameaux and told him to ask pardon of Calvin. But Calvin wanted a more severe penalty for Ameaux' blasphemy and finally won his point. Pierre Ameaux traversed Geneva in his shirt and bareheaded, pleading for mercy on his knees at three public squares, and promising to be obedient in the future. "Rough halters for rough donkeys," as Calvin said of the treatment which needed to be given to

Genevan malefactors; but there are a few details in this case that merit special emphasis. First, the issue was not Ameaux' guilt, but whether or not his punishment be public. Second, he was punished for blasphemy and *not* for offending Calvin. Third, despite three terms on the Small Council, Ameaux was not a political leader in Geneva nor was he connected with Perrin's blossoming faction.

Most of the other cases involving Calvin's authority in Geneva at this time involved more frivolous offenses by important people (such as the Favre clan who began a series of quarrels with the Consistory) or else involved serious offenses by frivolous people (such as the case of Jacques Gruet). Calvin's battles with the Favres lasted intermittently for three years, starting in the spring of 1546.[19] The patriarch of this clan was an old Eidguenot magistrate, now retired, who had no liking for religious authorities of any kind. His son and daughters, one of whom was married to Perrin, shared his opinions. Calvin fought them with ridicule. "Is the Favre family sacred and absolved from obedience to the laws?" he once asked, continuing that "perhaps they should build a city where they can live as they want, since they don't want to live here under the yoke of Christ." Calvin's colleagues were more blunt; one of them remarked that the old man was "as impudent as a dog." The Favres were at least equal to their opponents in giving abuse, especially Mme. Perrin whom the Consistory once had to silence by brute force. The misdemeanors of which they were accused were mostly minor — fornication, playing darts during Easter Communion, dancing, trying to obtain a divorce by mutual consent or "collusion," as the pastors' minutes called it — but their haughty and obstreperous attitude was a more serious problem. So was their social position. François Favre was merely told to re-appear before the Consistory in 1547, for example, after showing a degree of rebellion for which two lesser men were simultaneously put in prison. Perhaps the most important consequences of this guerrilla warfare was that Calvin became seriously and permanently embroiled with Ami Perrin, who had previously been among his most zealous supporters.

Gruet's crime was infinitely more serious to Calvin.[20] Not only had he written a vicious note against some of the pastors and

Stained-glass window made for the Bernese patrician family of Graffenreid, showing Genevan coat-of-arms upheld by sturdy Bernese bears. Note that the date (1540) corresponds to the moment of maximum Bernese power over Geneva. *Historisches Museum, Bern.*

stuck it to the pulpit in the cathedral, but his trial also proved him to be a candid and habitual blasphemer. Long after he had been executed, other writings, even more scandalous, were found among Gruet's effects. "Christ is treated as a swindler, a fantastic lout whose miracles were a lot of monkey business; the apostles are called rascals, brainless and blockheads; it is said that there is less good sense in all of Scripture than in Aesop's fables," reported the Council minutes, concluding that such hair-raising abominations were more than sufficient to damn an entire country. Gruet's manuscript, which was surely the most daring piece of anti-clericalism ever composed in sixteenth-century Geneva, was handed over to the hangman and publicly burned.

During this period, Geneva was stirred by a political trial of the first magnitude. In the autumn and winter of 1547, both Ami Perrin and *le magnifique* Meigret were imprisoned for treason.[21] Meigret was a close friend to Calvin, for whom he served as a kind of international news agency. (Meigret's business activities, which have never been clarified, apparently included opening such letters of the French royal post as passed through Geneva en route to their Swiss embassy.) Because of Meigret's connections in France and especially because of his activities in 1535,[22] Bern plunged wholeheartedly into his trial, attempting to secure his conviction and banishment from Geneva. Their Genevan ex-

The son of François Favre, one of Calvin's principal Genevan opponents, and his wife, together with the trademark of the Favre family. Both adorned the Favre home in the *Rues-basses* in 1551. *Musée d'art et d'histoire,* Geneva.

Renaissance stained-glass window (of disputed authorship) with earliest icono-
graphical representation of the Genevan motto, "Post Tenebras Lux" (1547),
and a text from Isaiah 40:8. Note that the Hapsburg double eagle and
Imperial crown still sit atop the Genevan coat-of-arms, as in the Graffenreid's
window. *Musée d'art et d'histoire, Geneva.*

pert, Nägueli (who had commanded the Bernese army in 1536)
communicated all the incriminating evidence he could find to
the Small Council. Ami Perrin, aided by Nägueli, was fighting
for his political life. Meigret, aided principally by Calvin, was
fighting for his honor and his Genevan pension.

The evidence on both sides was better suited for prosecution
than for defence. Perrin, very naive in diplomatic questions, had

eagerly listened to a French royal suggestion in 1545 that he take command of a troop of fifty French horsemen, use them as a garrison, and govern Geneva in the name of the King of France. Meigret had gotten wind of this suggestion and had communicated it to the Small Council. But he was too clever where Perrin was insufficiently so, for Meigret had recently caused the arrest of a prominent Genevan merchant in Lyon on suspicion of carrying a large sum of money to the Emperor. Perrin had secured the release of the presumably innocent merchant from the royal prisons. Nor was this the end of the charges against Meigret. The *monitoire* which was started after a suspect's arrest usually added a mountain of misdemeanors to the original indictment, and *le magnifique*'s dossier was soon filled with sixty-six charges, including (#40) "the ownership of a furnace suitable only for alchemy."

Both trials rapidly became questions of face for Geneva's rival factions. Ostentatious dinners were held in both men's cells by their respective backers. Perrin got the first break on October 20, when the President of the Parlement of Savoy informed the Small Council that the royal suggestion made to him had not been intended seriously. There was a brief flurry of sentiment to release both men. The public prosecutor, who disliked Perrin, then insulted the Syndics by calling them a pack of lawyers, and a new Bernese deputation arrived to fan the flames of anti-Meigret sentiment. On the advice of three non-Genevan lawyers, Perrin was liberated at the end of November, but was deprived of all his offices and banished for two years. The same lawyers then concluded that Meigret was a French spy. No sentence was passed on him for a month, during which Calvin made a dramatic appearance before a violently hostile Council of Two Hundred at some risk of his life. Finally on January 2, 1548, the Small Council decided to strip Meigret of his Genevan citizenship instead of banishing him; the vote was 9–8 against banishment, with five of Perrin's relatives ineligible to vote. Calvin immediately appealed to Farel and Viret to help him reverse this decision before the Two Hundred. Three days later, that body passed on omnibus resolution which both liberated Meigret without further punishment and reinstated Perrin on the Small Council. They behaved this way because Geneva's annual elections were only a fortnight away, and theatrical reconciliations of this sort were often staged by Geneva's political rivals at such a time. Neither Nägueli nor Calvin could claim a victory, and the delicate factional balance of power displayed here was prolonged for several years.

By 1548 Calvin was definitively estranged from Perrin's clique of friends and relatives. Their quarrels, begun in the Consistory in 1546, became even sharper. "Once upon a time," said Philibert Berthelier, spoiled son of an Eidguenot martyr and good friend of Perrin, "I fought with my sword in Lyon against men who spoke ill of Calvin, but now I wouldn't break my fingernail for him." Members of the Favre clan continued to appear before the Consistory, the women charged with having Gypsies tell their fortune and the men with arrogant and blasphemous talk. They continued to behave with "astounding insolence," even making obscene gestures before the assembled court on one occasion.[23] The issues were petty, but the war of nerves continued.

Among the few cases which involved serious offences, one in 1549 concerned the unpopular Roux Monet, whom both Calvin and Perrin disliked.[24] From fragmentary evidence, it seems likely that the accused was tortured and beheaded for his braggadocio about having the favors of four magistrates' wives and for carrying around a book filled with obscene pictures which he called his "Gospel." Undoubtedly the most serious case which arose in Geneva during these years was the attack on Calvin's doctrine of predestination launched by the ex-monk and doctor Jerome Bolsec; but this case properly belongs to the history of the Genevan church, for it was essentially a theological debate which was argued out before the civil authorities.[25] Bolsec was not a citizen of Geneva, Perrin never met him, and in brief this case had to be decided solely on its theological merits, which proved disastrous to Bolsec.

Similar to Bolsec in his criticisms was the ex-monk and notary Jean Troillet, who was a Genevan citizen and a crony of Perrin.[26] Troillet's suit against Calvin dragged on from June to November in 1552. It ended with a verdict in Calvin's favor, but only after Farel and Viret had been called in to help with his defense. Calvin guessed that Troillet had launched the dispute "in order to acquire glory among the ignorant by having disputed with John Calvin," and he objected strongly to Troillet's attempt to impose on him a "monkish jargon which I have never used." The Council's final decision upheld Calvin's *Institutes* and forbade anyone in future to contradict either the book or its doctrine. But Troillet was not punished, and even got a formal document from the Small Council a few days later which proclaimed him an honorable man and a good citizen.

Meanwhile, the political fortunes of Ami Perrin continued to rise after his narrow escape from exile in 1547. His partisans skillfully used the fears which circulated in Geneva after the Imperial *Interim* was pronounced and the Imperial Free City of Constance (like Geneva, allied to the Swiss cantons) was captured by Charles V in 1548. Pleading the urgent necessity of public defense, Perrin declared that he had been unjustly deprived of his office as militia commander, and successfully asked to be reinstated. As soon as this decision became official, Calvin took to naming Perrin "our comic Caesar" in letters to his friends.[27] This was a broad hint that Perrin intended in his clumsy way to become a *de facto* tyrant in Geneva, perhaps like the Medici in fifteenth-century Florence.

Another important consequence of the fall of Constance was that Geneva made strenuous but wholly futile efforts to enter the Swiss Confederation.[28] Under the immediate impact of Charles V's success, Bern had agreed in December 1548 to extend her *combourgeoisie* with Geneva for five years after its scheduled expiration in 1551. Geneva desired a firmer alliance because Bern and other Protestant cantons had failed to help Constance. News then reached Geneva that the French ambassador to Switzerland, who shared their worries, would do his utmost to get them admitted to the Confederation. The Small Council decided "not to make much noise about this right now," but to sound out their "secret friends" in Zurich. Geneva sent no fewer than five deputations to Bern in 1549, all trying to persuade their *combourgeois* to sponsor Geneva's entrance into the Swiss League. Privately, Genevan magistrates remarked that they ought to "abrogate the *clausule* of Article Two of the 1536 treaty" (which forbade them to deal with other states without Bern's consent) . . . "by the best way we can . . . and that it be done secretly." But Nägueli and his Bernese colleagues blandly replied that new alliances were not an issue, and ultimately agreed to reconsider the question sometime after the next *combourgeoisie*—in other words, at the Greek kalends. Geneva even attempted in 1550 to get Basel to sponsor her entry, but once again she was put off with vague promises. There the matter rested, and Geneva was in fact not admitted to the Confederation until 1815. The episode proved that Geneva still could not escape from the hegemony of Bern, or even circumvent her through third parties.

It was also during the period around 1550 that Calvin's Geneva saw her first great influx of religious refugees. The Small Council decreed in 1549 that a special register or *Livre des Habitants* should be opened for them. The effects of large numbers of French immigrants upon the older population of Geneva were soon felt. At the 1551 elections, the Small Council decided to ask the Two Hundred to bar all new *bourgeois* from sitting in the general assembly for twenty-five years, ostensibly in order to lessen the chances of evil machinations by these foreigners but really in order to preserve the current power structure. This edict did not pass. Consistory records from 1549 to 1552 are filled with reprimands for Genevans who accused the French of raising the cost of living, or who said that all devils were French. One magistrate, a Syndic in 1550, reportedly said "to the devil with whoever it was who brought so many Frenchmen here."[29] These currents of xenophobia were adroitly appropriated by Perrin and his followers, who prevented most of the newcomers from acquiring Genevan *bourgeoisie*.

†

Geneva's precarious factional balance was finally broken at the 1553 elections by skillful use of a demand for fresh blood on the Small Council. When the Two Hundred prepared to renew the magistracy, Perrin's friends proposed that sixteen new candidates stand for election alongside the sixteen incumbents, "so that there may be greater freedom of choice."[30] A compromise was arranged whereby only eight new candidates were proposed. Four of these new men were elected to the Small Council, three of them relatives and close supporters of Perrin. Thus the Perrinists, who now styled themselves *les Enfants de Genève*,[31] had brought about a new 1538, with Perrin himself as First Syndic. It was soon to prove as catastrophic for them as for the *articulants*.

Their regime was almost immediately faced with the nuisance of dealing with the celebrated heretic, Michael Servetus.[32] This man had recently published a shockingly heretical work named *Christianissimi Restitutio* in which he denied two cornerstones of Christian belief, the Trinity and infant baptism. Only four months before, Servetus had managed a sensational escape from the prison of the French Inquisition at Vienne, near Lyon. He was a thoroughly unsavory character, and it is not surprising that *any* Genevan government should prosecute him, briefly and unsuccessfully, as a dissolute personality and a disturber of the social order. But the bulk of the prosecution had to be entrusted to Calvin, his original accuser, since it was confined to theological issues which surpassed the knowledge of both prosecutor and judges at many points. The actual trial fluctuated wildly between abstruse issues and the abuse which Calvin and Servetus heaped on one another. Servetus insisted on calling his opponent Simon Magus, after the supposed father of predestination. Calvin observed that Servetus soiled every page of Scripture with his "futile triflings and impious ravings," and that he "habitually and brazenly cited authorities at which he had never looked." Servetus held his ground, clearly explaining his disbelief in the Trinity, and abhorring infant baptism as an invention of the devil. Finally, the Genevan government referred the case to other Swiss churches for their impartial opinions. Their replies were unanimous and rigorous, and Geneva's magistrates (including even Perrin as chief of state) had no choice but to condemn Servetus. Because he had "with malicious and perverse obstinacy sown and divulged even in printed books opinions . . . against the fundamentals of the Christian religion," they sentenced him to death by burning. Calvin tried to have the sentence lightened to simple execution, but without success. Servetus died on October 27, 1553. His was the only case, but at the same time an extremely significant case, of a man put to death for his religious opinions in Calvin's Geneva. Other victims followed him in nearby Protestant states; Bern, for example, beheaded the famous anti-Trinitarian Gentilis in 1566, and Zurich had been drowning Anabaptists since the 1520's. But the Servetus case earned immediate notoriety throughout Protestant Europe as a test case in religious persecution, thanks to the publication of Castellio's treatise on the punishment of heretics which appeared at Basel and drew swift replies from Calvin and Theodore Beza.

Soon after the Servetus trial the Perrinist government was faced with a new problem. The lingering debate between the magistrates and the Consistory over the question of excommunication was revived by Philibert Berthelier.[33] The issue was ultimately referred to the Two Hundred, who resolved that the Consistory could not excommunicate anyone without special permission from the Small Council in each case. Calvin and the rest of the pastors thereupon threatened to resign, and sent a circular letter to other Swiss reformed communities exposing their griefs. Geneva's Small Council, which was opposed in principle to granting Calvin's request for powers of excommunication, nevertheless prudently decreed that Christmas that Berthelier was not yet capable of taking communion. The whole issue was smoothed over rather than settled at a public reconciliation or *banquet des appointements* in January 1554, just a week before Geneva's annual elections. All parties appeared before the Small Council and swore with upraised hands to bury their differences. Next day, the council minutes report, "the entire Small Council, the officials of justice (including Philibert Berthelier), M. Calvin, and several others of the better sort in the city have dined together and confirmed the peaceful agreement made yesterday." All incumbents were thereupon returned to office.

Geneva spent most of 1554 wrestling with minor problems, and not until October did the great issue of excommunication present itself, again with Berthelier cast as the unrepentant sinner.[34] Another committee from the Small Council spent three months debating possible solutions and digesting evidence and advice from foreign cities and churches. Once again matters came to a head just before Geneva's annual elections. Once again an enigmatic decision was made to "respect the edicts passed by the general assembly in 1541," which implied but did not specifically state that the Consistory had the power to excommunicate. After the election of 1555, Calvin and the elders could claim victory on this vital issue.

For 1555 was a decisive year. This time all four syndics were Calvinists, and Calvin himself reported that an unexpected change occurred. When the Small Council came up for re-election, one vacancy due to death was filled by a zealous Calvinist, and one incumbent (Gaspard Favre, Perrin's brother-in-law) was also replaced by a Calvinist. Geneva's balance of power, always delicate, had been tipped in the opposite direction. And the issue which had caused this unexpected shift was *not* excommunication, but an attack against the overmighty strength of a single clan. Two eyewitnesses, Bonivard and Michel Roset, agree on this.[35] Bonivard reports that a quatrain (which he probably composed himself) was sung before the election:

> *Esliez comme ceux de Metz*
> *Tout vostre conseil d'un seul lignage*
> *Afin que, comme eux a jamais*
> *Vous puissiez tumber en servage.*[36]

Roset, in his laconic style, merely reports that his party won, "being aided by the votes of those angered by a government of relatives (*parentèle*) which was preventing them from getting their share of offices."

Such charges were apt, since the nucleus of Perrin's support on the Small Council had come from a wide circle of intermarried relations. Bonivard was mistaken in claiming that Perrin had fourteen of them on the council in 1553 and 1554, but a careful search does reveal half that number, related as follows (italicized names are those of 1553–54 councillors):[37]

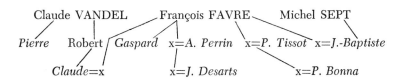

These intermarried clans obviously wielded a maximum of power in a state which forbade two brothers, or fathers and sons, from serving together on the Small Council. Relatives were usually, though not always, the most reliable of political allies. The exception to prove this rule is furnished by the Calvinist who replaced Gaspard Favre in 1555; Jean de la Maisonneuve was married to Gaspard's first cousin. Blood was certainly thicker than business connections, since Perrin's chief lieutenant, Pierre Vandel, had once worked as a foreign representative for draper Amblard Corne, leader of the pro-Calvin faction.

Perrin's opponents now had the momentum of electoral change behind them. They quickly followed up their advantage by purging the *Enfants de Genève* from the Two Hundred and replacing them with twenty-two young men who, as Bonivard noted, were the first generation raised in Geneva under the Reformation and thus "free from barbarian doctrine and habits." Next, civic rights were granted to a large number of French refugees who had been disarmed and systematically harassed by Perrin's adherents. Such a policy of mass enfranchisement was not unprecedented at Geneva, but it had always been regarded (in 1547, for example) as a fund-raising device. In 1555, Geneva's receipts from new *bourgeois* amounted to one-fourth of her budget and were used to pay off foreign debts.[38] Both these moves caught Perrin off guard, and no protests were raised for several months. When they finally did protest, using the aged Eidguenot Hudriod du Molard as their spokesman, nothing happened. So they reverted to their favorite device—threats.

Rumors had been spreading through Geneva for a fortnight before the famous brawl of May 16, 1555, took place.[39] That very evening, such rumors led the Small Council to replace the regular night watch by a special guard of four young men, all new members of the Two Hundred. Unlike its counterpart of 1540, this riot resulted in no deaths. Only a few people were even pushed around. The mayhem was verbal, and probably it was not premeditated. With the possible exception of Perrin himself, who had illegally seized a Syndic's black baton from him in order to wave it before the crowd and quiet them down (or so he claimed), few of the *Enfants de Genève* expected any serious repercussions from their activities that night.

Pierre Vandel, Perrin's best friend, attended the special session of the Small Council called at midnight on account of the riot, and helped disperse the crowd milling around the *Maison de Ville*. Perrin himself attended the next regular session, and his friends made their full share of counter-charges. They complained that most of the new *bourgeois* had lived fewer than eighteen months in Geneva and that they were unfamiliar with the byways of Genevan politics. Perrin himself was depicted as a peacemaker during the riot, not as an agitator. Twenty witnesses were heard on May 17, and twenty-five, mostly *Enfants de Genève,* were heard on May 18, although the secretary, a good Calvinist, recorded none of their testimony in the official minutes.[40] On May 19 twenty more witnesses, all Calvinists, were heard and their testimony was recorded. Perrin and Vandel continued to attend all council meetings until the next session of the Two Hundred a week later. In a test vote, this body decided to discuss the riot first, instead of considering Perrinist protests against the flood of citizenship grants to Frenchmen. Perrin and several others were promptly indicted for sedition. They left the city in haste, being warned (according to Bonivard) by a signal from one of their friends who had managed to leave the council room by feigning a call of nature.

This was the turning point.[41] The brawl of May 16, like the subject of most other Genevan inquests, tended to become more serious in retrospect, as more and more witnesses testified on their remembrance of things past. Perrin's flight seemed proof of his guilt to men who had apparently forgotten his flight in the wake of a highly dubious accusation in 1547. Then, Perrin had returned on the advice of his friends. Now he had no adequate counter-charges, nor did he receive sufficiently prompt help from Bern. Geneva instituted a brief reign of terror against his followers, twelve of whom were sentenced to death (eight of them *in absentia*). Perrin turned naturally to Bern, where Calvin's enemy Bolsec had found shelter for several years after his exile from Geneva, and whose rulers inclined to help men whose loudest boast was that they hated Frenchmen and loved the Swiss. Nägueli suggested that Perrin and his friends be given safe-conducts to stand trial in Geneva, but met with a peremptory refusal. Nägueli then arrived in Geneva himself, pointedly reminding the Small Council of the imminent expiration of the *combourgeoisie* and reproaching the Two Hundred because at Perrin's trial "witnesses were at the same time judges, which we find strange." The riposte was that Bern, by the terms of their alliance, should expel the fugitives from her territory, which she obviously had no intention of doing. All executions proceeded on schedule.

The official sentence passed against the Perrinists went beyond the riot of May 16 to describe an organized plot to "destroy the ecclesiastical discipline and the Reformation, principally the ordinances of 1541. . . . At a private meeting, they had decided to propose the abolition of the Consistory by the general assembly." These charges were almost certainly true. They also illustrate the intimate connection in Geneva between Franco-Swiss rivalry and the question of ecclesiastical discipline. Finally, in an afterthought prompted by the obvious parallel between militia commanders Philippe and Perrin, it was proposed by the Small Council and ultimately accepted by the general assembly that

for all time to come, no one speak of making any militia commanders under penalty of having his head cut off. As befits a good republic, everyone will be simply a citizen, without any desire to attribute to himself any authority or command over anyone else, except insofar as a judicial office confers such authority. In this way peace will be assured and seditions or tumults (*populaires*) avoided, and God will give us His blessing as a republic humiliated before Him, to His honor and glory.[42]

✝

Thus the last of Geneva's political factions was overthrown. An epoch had ended in Geneva by 1555, as the generation that had accomplished a political revolution and had introduced the Reformation completed the task of tearing itself apart. By 1558, none of the magistrates who had sat on the Small Council in 1536 was left in Geneva, and a third of them had children who were now exiled. They were being replaced, slowly but surely, by magistrates who believed in collective, orderly rule under Divine inspiration. A tenacious and devout type of Calvinist governor, whose increasingly oligarchic rule continued to mark the Republic of Geneva for the rest of its long existence, had taken control.

Geneva's first twenty years of independence was a time when the overwhelming problem for the republic was her attitude towards Bern. Both the Genevan state and the Genevan church had stubbornly preserved their independence from this powerful neighbor, despite some severe trials. Both Perrin and Philippe and their respective followers had been overly compliant towards Bern. Perhaps it was old memories from the days of the Eidguenots, perhaps simply their awe at Bern's military might; whatever the reasons may have been, these men sewed Swiss crosses on their clothes, wore Swiss pants, and admired the way in which Bern kept her preachers firmly under government control.[43] Calvin and his followers dressed and spoke differently. Under his direction, Geneva's church remained entirely independent of Bernese influence in both doctrine and ceremonies. Worse yet, from Bern's point of view, was that Calvin's wisdom and energy gave him great influence over their preachers in the French-speaking Pays de Vaud. This explains why a Bernese pastor told Bullinger in 1548 that his employers regarded Calvin as a rascal (*nebulone*) and added that he would be viewed with suspicion if anyone knew that he sometimes received letters from Geneva.[44] Little wonder that both the Bernese government and the city magistrates of Lausanne had long and complicated quarrels with Calvin's close friend, Pierre Viret.[45]

An epoch in Geneva's relations with Bern ended in 1555. The program shared by Calvin's friends, the Consistory and the French immigrants, was in strong opposition to that of Bern. Calvin's enemies, unlike the *artichauds* of 1540, were never reintegrated into Genevan public life. After 1555, Genevans tended to identify the furtherance of Calvin's type of reformation with a growing political independence from Bern. The paradox was now complete, since both Geneva's independence and her reformation would have been impossible without the imperialistic intervention of Bern in her affairs thirty years before.

NOTES

1. Roget, *HPG*, I, pp. 270–71.
2. Only by consecutively reading #700–775 in the *Sources du droit* can the size and scope of Genevan reforms from 1536 through 1540 be understood properly.
3. Bern had done the same thing in the Pays de Vaud in 1536 (Gilliard, *La Conquête du Pays de Vaud par les Bernois,* p. 247), and Francis I would order all his notaries and parish priests to keep their records in French in 1539.
4. Chapponière, *Journal du Syndic Balard,* p. lxviii n. [2–1–1537]. Other examples in *C.O.,* XXI, cols. 206 [15–1–1537], 210 [19–3–1537].
5. Roget, *HPG,* I, p. iii. Best account of the origins of this rivalry in C. A. Cornelius, *Historische Arbeiten, vornehmlich zur Reformationszeit* (Leipzig, 1899), pp. 124ff ("Die Dritte Spaltung der Genfer Burgerschaft").
6. Next four paragraphs based on Roget, *HPG,* I, pp. 113–229, and Cornelius, *Historische Arbeiten,* pp. 137–282.
7. *C.O.,* XXI, cols. 226–27.
8. Roget, *HPG,* I, pp. 199–200. See Paul-E. Martin, *Trois cas de pluralisme confessionel* (G., 1961), pp. 25–39, on the Genevan occupation of Thiez.
9. Roget, *HPG,* I, p. 209 and n. 1.
10. Best account in *ibid.,* pp. 231–54.
11. Copied by Savion, in P.-F. Geisendorf, ed., *Les Annalistes genevois du début du XVIIe siècle* (G., 1942), p. 488. Geneva's Protestant chroniclers, Bonivard and Roset, do not share this opinion. The latter (*Chroniques,* Bk. IV, ch. 37) says only that the loss of Thiez and the articles of the treaty together roused public opinion.
12. Williston Walker, *Jean Calvin, l'homme et l'oeuvre,* trad. N. Weiss (G., 1909), pp. 284–85. The French edition has better notes than the English original.
13. Roget, *HPG,* II, pp. 62–68. The code is in *Sources du droit,* #807; Calvin's notes while working on this project are in *C.O.,* X, cols. 125–46, with some additional notes found in Gotha and printed by M.-E. Chenevière, *La pensée politique de Calvin* (G., 1937), pp. 211–17.
14. Roget, *HPG,* II, pp. 60f, 70–78, 154–67. Some additional texts may be found in Oskar Pfister, *Calvins Eingriefen in die Hexer- und Hexenprozess von Peney, 1545* (Zurich, 1947), pp. 15–57, but this work should be used with extreme caution, since it is rabidly polemical and sometimes inaccurate.
15. Roget, *HPG,* II, pp. 85–109.
16. *Ibid.,* pp. 122–35.
17. Walker, *Jean Calvin,* p. 304.
18. Roget, *HPG,* II, pp. 209–23. Trial records published by J.-B.-G. Galiffe, "Nouvelles pages d'histoire exacte," in *MIG,* 9 (1863).

19. Roget, *HPG*, II, pp. 226–32, 265–69, 272, 284–85; *R.C.P.*, I, p. 41. Texts published by Henri Fazy, "Procédures et documents du XVI° siècle: Favre et le Consistoire," in *MIG*, 16 (1886).

20. Roget, *HPG*, II, pp. 289–309, 324–29. Trial records published by Henri Fazy in *MIG*, 16 (1886).

21. Roget, *HPG*, III, pp. 1–39. Documents on these twin trials in Cornelius, *Historische Arbeiten*, pp. 523–57; additional information and pro-Meigret arguments in A. François, *Le Magnifique Meigret* (G., 1947), pp. 99–154.

22. *Supra*, pp. 54–55.

23. Roget, *HPG*, III, pp. 44, 46–48 and notes, 62, 255.

24. *Ibid.*, pp. 112–16, esp. 115 n. 1.

25. *Infra*, pp. 128–31.

26. Roget, *HPG*, III, pp. 57, 235–43, 246–48.

27. *Ibid.*, pp. 73–79.

28. Léon Gautier, "Les efforts des Genevois pour être admis dans les Ligues suisses de 1548 à 1550," in *MDG* in 4°, IV (1915), pp. 99–128.

29. Roget, *HPG*, III, pp. 132–37, 149, 208, 219–21; IV, p. 156 n. 1.

30. Roget, *HPG*, III, pp. 275–77.

31. The term "Libertines," so often applied to Perrin's faction, is an anachronism which dates from the 1580's: see F. Kampschulte, *Johann Calvin, sein Kirche und sein Staat in Genf* (Leipzig, 1869–95), II, p. 19 n. 1. Bonivard (*Ancienne et nouvelle police*, p. 54) uses "esgrenez" or chaff, which could only be posterior to their flight in 1555. The other faction, less tightly knit, appears in the records only as "Calvinistes," which of course was a term of opprobrium before 1555.

32. Best account by R. H. Bainton, *Hunted Heretic: The Life and Death of Michael Servetus, 1511–1553* (Boston paper ed., 1960), pp. 183–215.

33. Roget, *HPG*, IV, pp. 142–56.

34. *Ibid.*, pp. 174–76, 186–92.

35. *Ibid.*, pp. 197–202. Cf. Bonivard, *Ancienne et nouvelle police*, pp. 116, 125; Roset, *Chroniques*, Bk. 5, ch. 62 (p. 366).

36. *Elect the way they do in Metz*
    All your council from a single clan
    So that, like them, you can
    Fall into serfdom forever.

37. *Ancienne et nouvelle police*, pp. 116, 64. Genealogical information from A. Choisy, *Généalogies genevoises* (G., 1946), pp. 118–38, on the Favres, and from the less accurate *Notices généalogiques* of the Galiffes.

38. *Studies*, p. 25 n. 34; compare Roget, *HPG*, III, p. 133 n. 1.

39. Account based on Roget, *HPG*, IV, pp. 245–67.

40. Their side of the story may be reconstructed from a justificatory memoir which they presented to the Swiss Diet in 1556, which is fully summarized in J.-A. Gautier's *Histoire de Genève*, IV, pp. 34–41, and partly printed in the original German by Emile Dunant, *Les relations politiques de Genève avec Berne et les Suisses de 1536 à 1564* (G.,

1894), pp. 211–14. Their case was sufficiently damaging for Geneva to issue two refutations. One, composed by Calvin, went to Basel and Zurich in Nov. 1555; a second and lengthier refutation was sent to all Swiss cantons after the 1556 Diet.

41. Roget, *HPG*, IV, pp. 274–329.
42. *Sources du droit,* #924.
43. Roget, *HPG*, III, pp. 56–59; Walker, *Jean Calvin,* p. 334.
44. *C.O.,* XIII, #1055 (p. 19).
45. See Henri Meylan, "Viret et MM. de Lausanne," in *Revue hist. vaudoise,* 69 (1961), pp. 113–73, and Robert Linder, *The Political Thought of Pierre Viret* (G., 1965).

FOUR

Calvin's Zenith, 1555–1564

In the spring of 1564, Calvin lay dying in his modest home on the rue des Chanoines. He had been seriously ill at frequent intervals for the last few years, but this time matters were perceptibly worse. He had stopped giving sermons and lessons in theology at the Academy since early February, and he seldom left home. The Small Council was informed early in March that he was in danger of dying, and they ordered prayers said for his health. Calvin summoned up his remaining strength in order to take Easter Communion at the cathedral, but his condition worsened soon afterwards and he became a virtual invalid. On April 25 he made his will, dividing his modest estate of 225 écus among four nieces and three nephews, after first giving a tenth of his property to various Genevan charities. Two days later, he sent a messenger to the Small Council to request a final interview with them. They agreed to take the unprecedented step of visiting him in his home.[1]

As they arrived, Calvin thanked them for the unwarranted honor which they had bestowed upon him. Then, said the secretary, Calvin remarked that "while he has been here, he has had several quarrels and arguments which weren't the fault of *Messeigneurs*." He asked them that, if he hadn't always done what he ought to have done, they consider that at least he had always meant well.

He has desired and procured the good of this city, but sometimes his efforts were far wide of the mark. It is also true that he doesn't deny that God has used him in the little he has done, and that if he said otherwise he would be a hypocrite.

93

Calvin especially asked the magistrates to forgive him his "overly vehement affections . . . and other vices which God has put in him." Otherwise, he protested before God and *Messieurs* that he had always tried to preach the Word of God purely and without error, as his calling demanded, and that he had tried to avoid the snares of the devil who perverts Scripture through men's fickle minds.

Next, Calvin gave a "small word of encouragement" to the magistrates. Whenever you feel menaced, he said, always think that God wishes to be honored and that only He can preserve and maintain states. Citing the example of David, who had sinned in the midst of prosperity, he observed that "we have good reason to humble ourselves and to hide under God's wing." Even though our fate may seem to hang by a thread, said Calvin, nonetheless God will continue to preserve Geneva in the same way as before.

If the Lord gives us prosperity, we rejoice; but when we are besieged by a hundred different evils on all sides, we must not fail to put our trust in Him. . . . Whenever something important happens, know that God is testing us in order to humble us. If we want to preserve our present condition, we must not dishonor the seat into which He has put us, for He has said that He will honor those who honor Him, and will cast down those who scorn Him. I say this in order that we follow His Word more carefully than ever, for we are still a long way from keeping it as fully as we should.

"Moreover," continue the official minutes,

he said that he had some knowledge of our habits and ways of action, so that each of us could be exhorted to better his imperfections. It is up to us to consider them and to battle them. Some magistrates are cold, given over to their private business and seldom serving the public. Others are abandoned to their passions. Others, to whom God has given a prudent spirit, do not use it. Others are opinionated and wish to acquire undue credit and reputation. May the old not envy the young any graces they may have received; and may the young modestly content themselves without wishing to advance too rapidly. We should not become discouraged, nor get in one another's way. When annoyed, we should not give rein to our passions. Everyone should work according to his station and faithfully employ whatever God has given him in order to maintain this republic.

Finally, after requesting to be excused from all further responsibilities on account of his illness, Calvin closed this meeting with a brief prayer. He then shook hands with each of the twenty-five members of the Small Council, and thus he took leave of the civil power. It had been a polite but sorrowful meeting, at which Calvin was addressing them like a schoolmaster at an annual commencement exercise. Admonitions and still more admonitions, mixed with a vague glimmering of hope for the future, were his last words to them.

The day after this ceremonial farewell, Calvin received the Company of Pastors in his home for the last time. This meeting, where Calvin was advising his own colleagues, has a startlingly different tone and message from his pious remarks to the magistrates of Geneva. It is a remarkably candid speech and a surprisingly subjective one, whose tone is rarely matched elsewhere in his works. The only similarity with his remarks to the magistrates was at the beginning, when Calvin stressed the seriousness of his current illness and announced that this would doubtless be the last time that he would see them. Then he proceeded to give an account of his career in Geneva, which we have translated in full according to the lengthy and polished account of pastor Jean Pinault.[2]

When I first arrived in this church there was almost nothing. They were preaching and that's all. They were good at seeking out idols and burning them, but there was no Reformation. Everything was in turmoil. To be sure, there was good master William [Farel] and also blind Courault. Moreover, there was Master Antoine Saulnier and that fine preacher Froment, who, having put aside his apron, mounted the pulpit and then climbed back down to his store where he would gab, thus preaching a double sermon.

Here I have lived through wondrous battles. I have been saluted in derision outside my door in the evening by fifty or sixty arquebus shots. You may well imagine how this could astonish a poor, timid scholar such as I am and always have been, I confess.

Then later I was expelled from this city and went to Strasbourg, where I lived for a time before I was called back; but I had no less

trouble than before in trying to do my duty. Crying 'wretch! wretch!,'
they set dogs at my heels and they caught at my robe and my legs.
Once I was going to the Council of Two Hundred during a fight,[3]
and I held back the other ministers, those who wished to enter and
those who did not; and although others brag of having done it all, like
M. de Saulx [Nicholas Desgallars], I was there, and as I entered they
said, 'Withdraw, *Monsieur;* they bear *you* no grudge.' I told them,
'I will not; go on, villains, kill me and my blood will be on you and
these very benches will shout it.'

Thus I have been in the midst of battle, and you will experience
ones not less, but greater. For you are in a perverse and unhappy
nation, and although she has some honorable men, the nation is perverse and wicked. You will have your hands full after God has taken
me away. For even though I am as nothing, I know that I have prevented three thousand tumults that might have taken place in Geneva.
But take courage and fortify yourselves, for God will use this Church
and will uphold it; I assure you that He will preserve it.

I have had many infirmities which had to be borne and yet, all that
I have done is worth nothing. Evil men will seize upon that word;
but still I say that all I have done is worth nothing and that I am a
miserable creature. But I can say that I meant well, that my vices have
always displeased me, and that the root of the fear of God has been
in my heart. And you can say that my intention has been good. I beg
you to pardon me the bad; but if there be some good, may you confirm it and follow it.

As for my doctrine, I have taught faithfully and God has given me
the grace to write, which I have done as faithfully as I could. I have
not corrupted a single passage of Scripture nor knowingly twisted it.
And when I would have brought in subtle meanings, if I had previously studied subtlety, I cast all this underfoot and have always striven
for simplicity.

I have written nothing from hatred of anyone, but have always faithfully propounded what I considered to be for the glory of God.

As for our internal affairs, you have elected M. de Bèze to take my
place. Take care to help him, for his burden is heavy and so difficult
that he must necessarily be overcome by it. Take care to support him.
As for him, I know he has a good will and will do what he can. May
everyone keep his obligations, not only to this Church, but also to the
city which we have promised to serve in adversity as well as prosperity,
so that each man may continue his calling and try neither to withdraw nor to intrigue. For when one goes underground to escape, one
generally says that it was not premeditated, and that he has not sought

this or that. May you heed the obligation before God that you have here.

Take care also that there be no teasing nor harsh words among you, since gibes will sometimes be tossed about. For even though this be in jest, the heart will hold bitterness. Those things are trifles and, besides, they are not Christian. So refrain from them and live in good harmony and sincere friendship.

I also ask you to change nothing, to make no innovations, for novelty is often requested. It is not that I desire from personal ambition that what is mine remain and that it be kept without seeking anything better, but because all changes are dangerous.

Upon my return from Strasbourg, I wrote the catechism hastily, for I would never have accepted this ministry if they had not pledged me these two things; namely, to keep the catechism and the discipline. While I was writing it, they came to fetch away pieces of paper as big as your hand and carried them to the printers. Even though Master Viret was in this city, imagine that I never showed him anything. I never had the leisure, though I did sometimes think to put my hand to revision if I ever did have the leisure. As for the Sunday prayers, I used the Strasbourg form and borrowed the greatest part from it. I couldn't take the other prayers from them because they didn't have any, but I took the whole thing from Scripture. I also had to compose the baptismal formula at Strasbourg, when they brought me Anabaptist children from five and six leagues around to be baptized. I made this crude formula then, but such as it is I advise you not to change it.

The Church of Bern has betrayed this Church and they have always feared me more than loved me. I would like them to know that I die with this opinion of them: that they have feared me more than loved me, and still fear me more than love me, and have always been afraid that I will meddle with their Eucharist.

On this note Calvin abruptly ended his speech. He shook hands with each member of the Company of Pastors, most of whom burst into tears. Less than a month later he died.

†

Calvin's farewell address to the pastors is a curious document. It is silent about many of the greatest sides of his career, passing over his scores of publications in one phrase, completely ignoring his dealings with the kings and princes of half a dozen countries, and making no reference at all to the international activities of the Venerable Company of Pastors. It concentrates on his life in Geneva as a member of the Company, and even here it is not so full as it might be. There are no final comments about the most famous episodes in the history of sixteenth-century Geneva—not a word about Servetus, or Bolsec, or Perrin. Nevertheless, the burden of his remarks is of major importance, for they show what he thought on his deathbed about revolutionary Geneva ("they were . . . seeking out idols and burning them, but there was no Reformation") and about Genevans in general ("you are in a perverse and unhappy nation"). Calvin also outlined some of the main points of his theology and many of the main traits of his character: his total lack of egotism and his cynicism about human capabilities ("all I have done is worth nothing and I am a miserable creature"); his purity of verbal expression ("I have always striven for simplicity"); and his deep conservatism ("I ask you to change nothing . . . because all changes are dangerous"). The self-portrait which Calvin attempted here is an honest one, fully in keeping with the awesome integrity and seriousness of the man.

Calvin does not say much about his personal idiosyncracies, remarking only that he was and always had been a "poor, timid scholar." In reality, he had few unusual or remarkably significant personality traits; if studied merely as a man, Calvin is not particularly interesting. Of course, he was an habitual insomniac who "had lain awake more than five hundred times while others slept."[4] He had a sharp temper, sometimes with an overly short fuse, for which he had particularly apologized to the magistrates. He had some slight tendencies toward misogyny; when the Anabaptist widow whom he had married eight years before died in 1549, he could muster no warmer tribute to her than to say that she had never interfered with his work.[5] Such details add up to very little; Calvin's personality remains unremarkable. He himself would be the first to tell us that he was no different from other men, hopelessly poor and corrupt sinners.

Calvin was not so much a personality as a mind. Basically, he lived for his work: teaching, preaching, and writing. His work was essentially moral and intellectual, and his authority within Geneva was essentially moral and intellectual. In most cases

Calvin's influence was based upon the fact that he knew more about something than anybody else, expressed himself about it more readily, and seldom changed his mind. His mental equipment was peculiarly excellent for a sixteenth-century man. This does not mean that Calvin had an original or inventive mind. His excellent humanistic teachers helped instill in him an aversion to modern innovations; and as a reformer, Calvin was out to rebuild the ancient church, not to establish a new one. Like the other men of his century, he did not have a rigorously logical or deductive mind — certainly not if we compare him with Descartes or with the best of the Schoolmen.[6] If Calvin excelled neither in originality nor in logical rigor, his mind still had two superlative assets: a superbly stocked memory, which was almost perfect where Scripture was concerned; and a fluency of expression which made him one of the earliest masters of French prose. Calvin could illustrate his arguments marvellously well, and he could explain them clearly. More than this his age did not ask. Perhaps his greatest mental asset was his total mastery of Holy Writ, which was outstanding even in an age when all Reformed theologians knew it extremely well. Calvin had committed all of Scripture to memory, much as Erasmus in *De Copia* had advised young men to do with the corpus of ancient literature.

Armed with such advantages, Calvin secured his place in Geneva after the rout of the Perrinists in May 1555. His triumph was definitive; thenceforth Geneva truly became Calvin's Geneva. As a local chronicler observed, "everybody went to sermons regularly now, even the hypocrites."[7] There were several reasons behind Calvin's permanent triumph, which ushered in the brightest decade of Geneva's history; let us examine a few of the most important among them.

First, Calvin faced no local opposition of any stature whatsoever. There were very few educated men who might have opposed him in Geneva, and none who had any real eloquence or independence of mind. No doubt many of his projects had irritated many Genevans, but none of them could oppose him articulately or coherently. In fact, this absence of important opposition extended beyond Geneva to her two most important neighbors, Bern and France. During Calvin's lifetime, there were no internationally respected theologians working in Bern; there was not even a Bernese pastor who ranked as a political adviser to his rulers, comparable to Bullinger in Zurich. And if we scan the whole panorama of the French Reformation in the 1530's and 1540's, it seems to have contained few first-rate minds and none which could challenge Calvin's claim to leadership after the appearance of the *Institutes of the Christian Religion.* Calvin was well aware of both these facts. He had some of the contempt of an aristocrat of the mind for lesser minds, and recognized few peers among the Reformed theologians of his age, except for Melanchthon in Wittenberg.

Second, Calvin and his colleagues monopolized Geneva's only mass medium. Sermons were one principal form of public communication in the sixteenth century, and in Geneva sermons were remarkably frequent. In the 1550's, sermons were being preached in her four churches on an average of a dozen times each week. The effects of Calvin's sermons and those of his colleagues is of course impossible to measure precisely, but it must have been immense. It has been claimed by Lucien Febvre that sixteenth-century men perceived things better by hearing than by seeing; though this argument may be exaggerated,[8] it is undeniable that men in this age listened attentively and that they heard many more things than they read. The Word of God was the single most important part of a Christian's life, at least in Protestant communities. Preaching this Word, as Calvin reminded his colleagues, was a critically important duty. It must be done purely and simply, without frills, or subtlety, or such scholastic devices as allegories. Yet we still know very little of Calvin himself as a preacher; many of his sermons have survived through shorthand notes taken by his secretary, but are only now in process of publication.[9] It seems certain that Calvin's effectiveness as a preacher must have been great. On rare occasions we can perceive the effect of a sermon; for example, a Genevan magistrate recorded one of Calvin's remarks about the downfall of kingdoms and the deliverance of God's church which was remarkably demonstrated a few weeks later by the timely and unexpected death of Henri II of France.[10]

Third, Calvin's program was enforced in Geneva by very thorough indoctrination. Genevan children were drilled on their catechism every Sunday noon until they could repeat from memory the essentials of their faith. Adults too were expected to undergo the same course of religious instruction. As late as 1557, the Consistory discovered five old men who still "could not give an account of their faith," and ordered them to hire a tutor and learn their catechism before the next public Communion.[11] Both children and adults found it easier to submit to Calvin's system of discipline than to resist. No doubt this was partly because they did not wish to argue against their teachers, and because if they did so argue they were likely to be punished for rebellion. But it would be a gross error to assume that Calvin's Geneva enforced this program of religious education through simple coercion. In January 1549, for example, Geneva's pastors and government agreed that great troubles were descending on their city. To forestall these calamities, they decided to announce to all heads of families that everyone should attend church more regularly, and that children and servants should attend catechism.[12] Much is said in this document about the intentions of Geneva's rulers and her clergy, and much is said about the examples they were setting, but nothing at all is said about punishment. It is pure exhortation, unmixed with threats. And there really were no material penalties inflicted on Genevans who did not attend church, though rural subjects might be fined for such offenses.

The enforcement of God's and man's law in Calvin's Geneva is something of a mystery. The city had no true police. As in a totalitarian state, every man was encouraged to report his neighbor's unorthodox behavior, but the neighbor was not put to the torture or even fined, except in the most serious cases. Genevan authorities could rely on the public fear of "scandals" to ensure that most of the laws were kept most of the time. The unanimity with which official Geneva (and the general public) shuddered at the gross blasphemies of Jacques Gruet or Michael Servetus illustrates the local consensus about what constituted a really serious moral crime.[13] No doubt it was primarily the fear of bringing down the wrath of God upon their city which prompted many lesser Genevans to report their neighbor's faults to the ecclesiastical authorities; these authorities, in turn, had been instituted to admonish rather than to punish the guilty.

✝

Unarmed, relying on the power of words and of the Word, and unopposed by men of real ability, Calvin became the dominant figure in his adopted city. How did the citizens of Geneva adjust to his authority and his teachings?

In general they absorbed Calvin's doctrine quietly and without objection. Of course, a few people did object, and we know a good deal about them. The remnants of the old Eidguenots and their families, men like François Favre or the son of the patriot and martyr Berthelier, were Calvin's typical opponents. Behind them, quieter but perhaps more obstinate, were the children of a few Genevan families which continued to indulge in crypto-Catholic practices. Jean Balard's daughter was frequently accused of such practices by the Consistory. The daughter of another conservative magistrate, Girardin de la Rive, was censured by the Consistory as late as 1557 for keeping an altar with Papist images in her room.[14] However, Geneva contained only a few families like them, and these families were losing their political influence by 1550. More typical was the case of magistrate Amblard Corne, who was sharply censured by the Consistory in 1546 and who cheerfully conformed to Calvin's discipline thereafter.[15] Nobody in Calvin's Geneva kept a diary, and the vast silent majority of her citizens left no traces of misbehavior in the public records. Law-abiding people usually have little history. Most Genevans, especially those boys who had attended Calvin's Sunday schools in the 1540's and 1550's, were sober and upright types. Bonivard, in sketching the fall of the *Enfants de Genève* in 1555, noted that this younger generation "were not raised in a time of barbarian doctrine and habits like most of their elders;"[16] such youths were wholly repelled by the peccadilloes of Perrin and his allies. The typical figure of the generation raised under Calvin was the pious, public-spirited magistrate and chronicler Michel Roset.

The new generation had learned Calvin's lessons well, since the fundamentals of his doctrine had been drilled into them for many years. If we wish to know exactly what they had learned, we have no better source than the Genevan catechism which Calvin composed immediately after his return in 1541. On his deathbed, Calvin placed this document on a par with Geneva's ecclesiastical discipline and regretted the fact that he had never been able to revise it. If we wish to know what Calvinism meant to the ordinary Genevan, particularly to one born after 1530, we should begin with the catechism. This will give us a glimpse of Genevan Christianity from underneath, in its simplest and nevertheless very complete form of indoctrination for children.

Calvin's catechism was a lengthy document which filled sixty-seven folios in its first printed edition of 1545.[17] Commentators have sometimes found its length excessive when compared to other catechisms such as Luther's. However, Calvin minimized the dangers of excessive length in two ways: first, by dividing the body of the catechism into fifty-five separate lessons, one of which should be studied each Sunday; second, by summarizing the whole teachings of his catechism in the examination[18] which the pastor gave to each Genevan child before admitting him to his first Communion. In other words, this document provides a reasonably complete summary of what Calvin considered to be the essentials of a Christian education. No doubt this is what the five old men who were told to "give an account of their faith" in 1557 were expected to learn.

What are the basic themes in Calvin's religious primer? Surely a child best remembers the beginnings of something he has had to memorize, so Calvin made sure to begin his catechism with some basic material:

TEACHER: What is the principal end of human life?
STUDENT: It is to know God.
T.: Why do you say that?
S.: Because He has created us and put us on earth to be glorified in us. And it is surely right that we dedicate our lives to His glory, since He is the beginning of it.
T.: And what is the sovereign good of men?
S.: The same.
T.: Why do you call it the sovereign good?
S.: Because without it our condition is more unhappy than that of brute animals.
T.: Thus we see that there is no unhappiness so great as that of not living under God.
S.: Certainly.

T.: But what is the true and correct knowledge of God?

S.: When we know Him in order to honor Him.

T.: What is the proper way to honor Him?

S.: By putting all our trust in Him; that we serve Him by obeying His will; that we go to Him in all our needs, seeking health and all good things from Him; and that we acknowledge, in our hearts as well as with our mouths, that all good comes from Him alone.

Calvin began his catechism like his *Institutes,* by insisting that man's fundamental activity is to know God. His second lesson dealt with the foundation of man's trust in God, best expressed by the "common confession of faith of all Christians;" this was the ordinary Apostles' Creed which is still used in many Christian churches.

Calvin's catechist explains the *credo* by subdividing it into four parts, one dealing with each person of the Trinity and the fourth with the Church (Calvin had already adopted this four-fold division in his *Institutes*). The next twenty Sundays are spent on these four topics. The same amount of time is not spent on each topic, and the proportions are very different from those of the *Institutes.* Only a small part of it (three lessons) are devoted to the omnipotence of God the Father. Almost nothing is said about the mysterious workings of the Holy Ghost; only one lesson, the fourteenth, is devoted to this topic.[19] There is not a word about the doctrine of election, that system of pre-destination in which nineteenth-century theologians saw the center and focus of Calvin's system. Perhaps it was omitted from the catechism because it was difficult to explain to children — although other doctrines which are equally difficult, such as the nature of the Eucharist or the uselessness of good works, are explained at great length. Or perhaps it was omitted because it might frighten the children needlessly.

The bulk of Calvin's exposition is devoted to two subjects: the activities of Jesus Christ as savior (eight lessons) and the nature of the true church (seven lessons). The sections on the church are particularly interesting, especially when they dwell upon the imperfections of the visible church or when they emphasize salvation by faith. Calvin carefully stresses the uselessness of works without faith, and even explains that good works by the elect are not in themselves pleasing to God, though such works are both useful and necessary.[20] Faith, says the catechism, is the root of works, and faith is a gift of the Holy Ghost; man cannot obtain it by himself, "because our understanding is too weak to comprehend the spiritual wisdom of God, which is revealed to us by faith. Our hearts are inclined to mistrust, or rather to perverse trust in ourselves or in other creatures."[21] Salvation by faith is of course the great touchstone of all Reformation doctrine, but the particular emphases on human weaknesses add a special Calvinist note to this presentation.

The sections on the Trinity and the Church fill about two-fifths of the catechism. The remainder is split into three nearly equal sections: one on God's commandments, one on prayer, and one on the sacraments. In the first of these sections, on the Commandments, Calvin's principal problem was to get beyond the letter of the law to the broader and more symbolic ways in which they should be observed. He is careful to explain that the commandment about keeping the Sabbath applies more to Jews than to Christians, that the number seven is symbolic and ceremonial; he is also careful to point out to children that the commandment to honor one's father and mother really applies to *all* superiors. Generally, Calvin tried to spiritualize the commandments by pointing out that they applied to intentions as well as to deeds.

The section on prayer began with the Lord's prayer, which Calvin subdivided into three parts dealing with the glory of God and three parts dealing with the individual suppliant. He explained each point by point, stressing the symbolic nature of such phrases as "our Father in Heaven" and "Thy Kingdom come," which he said were true only in part. Calvin was equally careful to point out that prayers must be sincere, spoken in a tongue which the speaker understands, and not directed to saints or angels. Prayers are useless unless grounded in faith. Even when they are so grounded, God will only grant the suppliant's wish "if it be expedient."[22] Calvin placed the efficacy of children's prayers within very narrow limits.

The final section begins with a brief discussion of Scripture, "which is like an entry into His celestial kingdom,"[23] and which should be studied both at home and in Christian assemblies where it was explained. God communicates with us, said Calvin, through His Word in Scripture and through the sacraments. These are "external proofs of the grace of God, who represents spiritual things to us through a visible sign in order to imprint His promises more strongly in our hearts." The catechist thereupon objects that this is properly the work of the Holy Ghost, not of the sacraments. True, says the student, but

> there is a great difference between the one and the other. For truly the Holy Ghost is the only one who can touch and move our hearts, and illuminate our understanding; . . . However, the Lord makes use of the sacraments as inferior instruments, as it seems good to Him, without diminishing the virtue of His Spirit thereby.[24]

There are only two sacraments, baptism and communion, both of them symbolic promises. Calvin's catechist spent the next four Sundays explaining the presence of Christ in the Lord's Supper, pointing out the inadequacies of both the Lutheran and Catholic opinions on this point.

Near the end of this section, Calvin made the same point that he had previously done with good works, with prayer, and with the commandments; namely, that without the gift of faith sacraments too were worse than useless. His very last lesson explained why certain hypocrites were not allowed to pollute the sacrament, explaining however that not all the ungodly could be excluded without "sufficient approval and judgment of the Church."[25] In a well-governed church, said Calvin, men are specially deputized in order to prevent such scandals. After concluding his discussion of excommunication and ecclesiastical discipline, the pastor assumed that the student was ready for his first communion, to which he would be admitted after passing an examination on the whole program of instruction (confession of faith, commandments, prayer, and sacraments).

Religious education in Calvin's Geneva made only a few concessions to the youthful and imperfect minds of her students. One has the impression that the program of Sunday schools and catechisms was made as difficult and rigorous as possible, but that it was somehow kept within the bounds of intelligibility. Such intricate doctrines as redemption and the Eucharist were only slightly simplified. The doctrine of predestination was omitted, but in 1542 it did not as yet occupy an especially important place even in Calvin's more advanced handbook, the *Institutes*. Many of Calvin's principal theological teachings lie scattered throughout his catechism. His primer begins with the basic proposition that man's purpose on earth is to know God in order to honor Him. Several passages stress human weakness and repeat that man is incapable of attaining faith or salvation by his own efforts. Of course, in its distribution of emphasis, the catechism is very different from the *Institutes* or from other of Calvin's works. The importance of this extended description of his catechism is that these are the fundamentals that Calvin drilled into his immediate audience. Here we have not his finished theology but its essential ingredients, adjusted for local youth.

In attempting to judge Calvin's influence at its peak after 1555, it is necessary to dwell upon his program of religious education and discipline, upon his influence as a preacher. Calvin was a pastor — as well as the permanent Moderator of the Genevan Company of Pastors — and he had no other kind of authority in Geneva. Calvin's influence within Geneva was remarkable, particularly after 1555, but this influence was not primarily political. The obscure French church which addressed him in 1561 as "Bishop and Syndic" of Geneva was miles wide of the mark.[26]

To be sure, Calvin's advice was sought on a variety of problems, including whether or not an improved Swiss furnace should be adopted in 1557. He also made several suggestions, including one that balconies be added to all Genevan buildings for the greater safety of children. Calvin served the Republic of Geneva as a legal consultant and sometimes as a diplomat; on rare occasions he even made entries in the official records. But he did not habitually attend all sessions of the Small Council and give advice on each and every question, as the Swiss Reformer Zwingli had done. Furthermore, there were times even after 1555 when Calvin's advice was rejected by Geneva's rulers. In 1560, for example, they opposed his suggestion that copper slugs be distributed to all qualified laymen in order to admit them to the next Communion, and they later rejected another suggestion that a Savoyard ambassador be put in jail as a seducer.[27] In most cases, of course, Genevan authorities accepted Calvin's suggestions. Cooperating with the civil authorities, Calvin helped his adopted city through some difficult moments during the final decade of his life. But Calvin's basic achievement was elsewhere. It had been to instruct an entire generation of Genevans, thoroughly and systematically, through his catechism and his sermons and his system of ecclesiastical discipline (about which we shall talk later). By the time Calvin died, there were few if any European cities so well indoctrinated and accustomed to rigorous discipline as was Geneva. Calvin had tried to enforce respect for the laws of God and man on a turbulent and newly independent city, and after considerable struggle he had succeeded.

✝

Calvin's Geneva had become an important city. "Before 1555," a Genevan historian recently remarked, "the history of Geneva is that of a city allied to the Swiss League; afterwards, it splits off and follows a distinct path as a figure unto itself in European history, the city of Calvin."[28] Internal questions fell into the background, while international questions now occupied most of Geneva's attention. Several different problems required the attention of her rulers and the advice of Calvin. Four among them were especially important for the political history of Geneva.

First, there was the continuing problem of Geneva's alliance with Bern. Relations between them had worsened steadily after Perrin's flight, reaching a nadir in 1556 when diplomatic contacts were ruptured and the *combourgeoisie* between them was allowed to expire. A Bernese court of appeals confirmed a judgment which awarded Perrin and his fellow fugitives an enormous sum in damages, and permitted them to seize Genevan property anywhere in Bernese territory as compensation. Geneva tried to break through her diplomatic isolation in the summer of 1557 by sending embassies to other Swiss Protestant cantons, and Calvin wrote to Bullinger at Zurich in support of Geneva's demands. But once again, as with earlier attempts to circumvent Bern, Geneva got only vague promises from the Swiss.

The international scene changed suddenly in the late summer of 1557. A Hapsburg army, commanded by Emmanuel-Philibert of Savoy, crushed the French in the battle of St. Quentin. The House of Savoy was suddenly in an excellent position to reclaim the lands seized from her by France and Bern in 1536.[29] Both Bern and Geneva were alarmed by the news of this battle and immediately proceeded to renegotiate their *combourgeoisie*. Bern made several concessions, two of which were crucial: first, the case of the Perrinists was omitted from these negotiations and left to the later decision of a Swiss arbitrator; second, this time the alliance was not to be for twenty-five years, as Bern had wished, but permanent. Michel Roset, the twenty-three-year-old Secretary of the Republic of Geneva who had played a vital role in these negotiations, wrote a lyric poem in honor of this new and perpetual *combourgeoisie*. Calvin approved it, as Roset proudly noted in the public minutes, and it was recited when Nägueli and five other Bernese deputies arrived to confirm the treaty in January 1558. A play was performed (also with Calvin's approval) and trees were planted around the city to celebrate this event.

But Nägueli had not persuaded Geneva's councils to grant pardons to Perrin or to the other exiles, "those thistles of hell who would be the occasion of the common ruin of both cities," and tensions between the newly reunited allies continued. Geneva's judges finally argued their case (in German) before the Basel arbitrator early in 1550. Six months later he ruled in Geneva's favor. The city held public prayers of rejoicing, and gave him a handsome reward of 200 écus for his labors.[30] The highly chagrined Bernese protested ineffectively against this decision, which left Geneva free to dispose of the exiles' property as she wished. The *combourgeoisie* with Geneva remained legally in force, although with muted enthusiasm on Bern's part.

Geneva's legal victory over Perrin was only one among several memorable events of the year 1559. In that year, Calvin published the definitive edition of his great handbook, the *Institutes of the Christian Religion*. That year the flood of refugees to Geneva reached its peak. That year peace was made between the Hapsburgs and the Valois, to the great consternation of Geneva, who feared that Henri II of France was about to turn

Another Genevan coat-of-arms that adorned the new Academy in 1558. Note the extreme simplicity of the design by comparison with the window bearing the earliest representation of Geneva's motto a decade earlier (page 78). *Musée d'art et d'histoire, Geneva.*

his sword against them. In several different ways, 1559 marked the high-water mark of Calvin's Reformation in Geneva, and it seems especially appropriate that the Small Council offered him citizenship that Christmas — and that he accepted it, long after the rest of his pastoral colleagues and thirteen years after his brother Antoine.

Probably the most important event of the year 1559 in Geneva was the public dedication of her Academy on June 5.[31] This had long been an important item on Calvin's agenda. Ever since his return from a visit to Strasbourg in 1557 he had put pressure

This somewhat idealized portrait of Calvin was the property of his successor as Moderator of the Geneva Company of Pastors, Theodore Beza. *Musée historique de la Réformation, Geneva—Jean Arlaud, photographer.*

on the Small Council to construct a free public school in Geneva, and early in 1558 he had helped pick the site where this new building should be erected. Construction was begun that fall by an impecunious government, while Calvin began combing Europe for men who might be induced to teach there. As Michel Roset lucidly noted, this was an enterprise in which the enthusiasm of the magistrates and the people rose above their poverty. The school existed before its building. After some eminent teachers had refused Calvin's invitation, he was able in January 1559 to invite several members of the nearby Bernese Academy in Lausanne who had just been expelled by their rulers for demanding the right to excommunicate. It was an odd coincidence, and in Bern Calvin was accused of fomenting the crisis so that he might have his pick of their French-speaking pastors and professors; but the accusation was unfounded, since Calvin was bedridden at the height of this crisis. Otherwise, he would surely have gone to Bern, as he had several times before, in order to appease the quarrel. The most important among the new men thus acquired for Calvin's Academy was Theodore Beza, who was chosen by the pastors to serve as Rector of their new institution.

The official inauguration, attended by a crowd of 600, was held in the cathedral. The statutes of the school were read by secretary Roset, and the new Rector and professors were formally installed. Beza delivered a long harangue in Latin, summarizing the history of education and congratulating Geneva on her provision for liberal studies which were free from superstition. Calvin spoke briefly in French, and closed the meeting with a public prayer. Thus the new school was launched. It consisted of two parts: a primary school, the *collège* or *schola privata,* divided into seven grades and designed to serve all the youth of Geneva (the topmost class had 280 pupils that first year, and an extra teacher had to be hired at once); and a more advanced Academy or *schola publica,* which was intended primarily to provide advanced training in theology. At first it was composed of two chairs of theology (for Calvin and Beza) and one chair each of Hebrew, Greek, and philosophy. Unlike the *collège,* the Academy aimed to draw students from all parts of Christendom, and it succeeded admirably in this goal. By 1562, no fewer than 162 students had enrolled in it; four-fifths of them were French and only four were native Genevans.[32] During the first three years of its existence, the Academy counted such students as Gaspard Olevanius, who later became coauthor of the Heidelberg Catechism; Philippe Marnix van Sint-Aldegonde, later the intimate councillor of William the Silent; Florent Chrestien, later tutor of Henri IV; Thomas Bodley, later founder of the Bodleian Library at Oxford; and François du Jon, later professor at the new University of Leiden. By the time of Calvin's death, his fledgling Academy had enrolled over 300 students. It continued to be the single most important of his institutional legacies to his adopted city throughout the following centuries. His Academy conferred no academic degree, but only a certificate of attendance and good conduct. The Academy statutes provided for the eventual establishment of chairs in the liberal professions of law and medicine, but during Calvin's lifetime these subjects were never taught. Basically, Calvin's new upper school served as a theological seminary for the Reformed church in France.

The Academy was an invaluable addition to Geneva and a far greater success than many had dared to hope. But it was also terribly costly to build and to maintain. When construction began in 1558, Geneva made ingenious efforts to meet the strain on her public finances.[33] Soon the city's notaries were requested to ask all dying citizens to leave a bequest to the new school in their wills. In 1559, twelve such bequests totaled 1074 florins, and more than forty such legacies were made in the next three years. But, by one of the great ironies of Genevan history, most of the construction costs of Calvin's Academy were unwittingly borne by his political enemies. As soon as Geneva had won her case against Perrin at Basel, the Republic proceeded to a mass auction of their estates. In the next two years, Genevan treasuries pocketed about 60,000 florins from the *biens des sept condamnés*, and spent about 50,000 florins constructing the school building. However, the roof was not on in the autumn of 1561, and the building was not completed until 1562.

Bern had supposed that this venture would fail because Geneva was a dangerous and expensive place for students to live. Roset, in reporting the official dedication of June 5, candidly recognized such fears, but concluded that "it was an admirable example of resolution and constancy not to abandon these projects, when a city so devoid of resources should be thinking about everything else except studies, which imperiously demand peace and quiet."[34] Indeed, Calvin's Geneva had taken a calculated risk in dedicating her school in the summer of 1559, for her ceremony coincided with the signing of the Treaty of Cateau-Cambrésis between France and Spain.

✝

If construction of the new Academy was the second major area of activity for Calvin and for Geneva's rulers, their tense and ill-defined relationship to the French crown after 1559 was the third. As both Calvin and the Council had feared, Cateau-Cambrésis was the prelude to an intensified campaign against Protestants in France. Even the sudden death of Henri II in a tournament later that year provided Geneva with only a temporary respite. By March 1560, the French Royal Council was strongly censuring Geneva's role in sending preachers, "mostly artisans with no learning," and a "malicious dispersion of damnable books" to disturb the kingdom.[35] This was only the prelude to a more serious act by Charles IX in January 1561. He sent a special courier to the republic's syndics, complaining that the troubles of France came from a group of preachers sent by Geneva, who had "dared publicly to stir up our people to overt sedition." He commanded them to stop such activities at once, and threatened reprisals if they did not obey. In their reply, the Small Council denied that they had ever sent a single man to France; although they admitted that Geneva's pastors may have sent some men to France, they insisted that such men had done their best to prevent conspiracies and sedition.[36] (Calvin had in fact *not* kept Geneva's rulers informed about the men whom the Company of Pastors were sending to France, but he had done so at the Council's own insistence; on the one occasion when this silence had been broken, in 1557, Calvin told them that "these things, if very secret, would be less dangerous," and the Council minutes added in the margin that "it would not be good if it was said that the *Seigneurie* did this."[37]) For a moment, a serious threat of a French attack on Geneva hung in the air. But again, a sudden reversal of royal policy removed this threat within a few months, and French Protestant chiefs soon invited Beza to the Colloquy of Poissy to argue their case before the French court.

It is true that between 1559 and 1561 Calvin and his colleagues had intervened often in French affairs, especially by sending more than fifty pastors in answer to requests from French Reformed churches, and even by sending men to the court of the King of Navarre. It is also true that some of the French refugees at Geneva were deeply implicated in the unsuccessful Conspiracy of Amboise in May 1560.[38] Geneva's government, worried about repercussions at the French court, started lawsuits against one of these refugees, whom they accused of falsely telling French Reformed churches that Genevan officials had favored this plot. Calvin and Beza also brought suit against two other refugees on substantially the same charges. Most of the evidence introduced during these trials was equivocal, except for Calvin's position. He clearly opposed any such plot unless a prince of the blood royal were privy to it. During a period when dogmatic lines were not yet finely drawn in France, and when French noblemen were converting en masse to the banners of the Reformation, Calvin's Geneva had fished successfully in some very troubled waters.

In the spring of 1562, the long-awaited civil war between Huguenots and Catholics broke out in France. Geneva was informed of the outbreak of hostilities by a letter from the head of the rebellion, the Prince of Condé (whose secretary and press agent at that moment was none other than Beza), which justified his seizure of Orléans and requested Geneva's support.[39] Geneva's response depended upon Bern, and her ally decided to remain neutral. But as soon as Swiss Catholic cantons began to raise troops to help the royalists and the Guisards, both Bern and Geneva found it impossible to prevent volunteers as well as war materials from reaching the French Protestants. News of the Huguenot seizure of Lyon led Bern to send a large army to that city to fight alongside the Huguenot troops. While this force was en route to Geneva, her magistrates decided to break their policy of neutrality and send a cavalry escort of fifty men under the command of a syndic to accompany the Bernese as far as

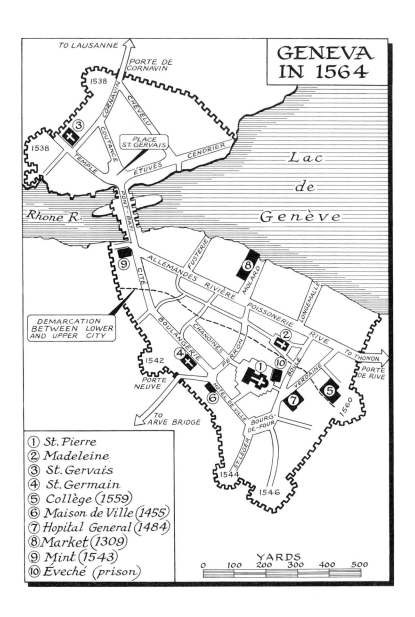

GENEVA IN 1564

TO LAUSANNE

PORTE DE CORNAVIN

1538

CORNAVIN

CHEVELU

COUTANCE

TEMPLE

1538

③

PLACE ST. GERVAIS

ÉTUVES

CENDRIER

Lac de Genève

Rhone R.

PONT BAT

CITÉ

⑨

FUSTERIE

RIVIÈRE

ALLEMANDES

MOLARD

POISSONERIE

LONGEMALLE

RIVE

DEMARCATION BETWEEN LOWER AND UPPER CITY

BOULANGERIE

CHANOINES

PERRON

②

TO THONON

PORTE DE RIVE

1542

④

⑩

①

BOULE

VERDAINE

⑤

1560

PORTE NEUVE

⑥

HOTEL DE VILLE

⑦

TO ARVE BRIDGE

BOURG-DE-FOUR

ST-LEGER

1544

1546

① St. Pierre
② Madeleine
③ St. Gervais
④ St. Germain
⑤ Collège (1559)
⑥ Maison de Ville (1455)
⑦ Hopital General (1484)
⑧ Market (1309)
⑨ Mint (1543)
⑩ Éveché (prison)

YARDS
0   100   200   300   400   500

116

Lyon. Geneva financed this force by voluntary contributions, to which Calvin donated two écus.[40] Upon reaching Lyon, their commander sent back a series of letters begging for permission to join in the fighting north of Lyon. On Calvin's advice, permission was granted. After some desultory fighting, the fifty cavalrymen returned to Geneva in September, when Bern also recalled her forces. The Genevan syndic in command complained that Huguenot commanders in Lyon had treated him with insufficient respect.

Throughout this rebellion, both Condé and the Church of Lyon addressed requests for cash loans to Genevan authorities. With one exception, these loans involved sums larger than the city could possibly raise, and larger than the Swiss Protestants were willing to raise. The exception was a request from the Lyon Church in February 1563 to borrow 3000 écus to help pay the German mercenaries guarding the city. Geneva wrote to Basel, who advanced the money, while insisting that the city of Lyon not be mentioned in the official documents. Thus it appeared on the books as a loan from Basel to Geneva, and this was actually what happened. The money was forwarded from Geneva to Lyon, and almost immediately repaid; Geneva, however, did not send the money back to Basel after the war ended, but simply kept it and paid the 5% interest on it. "It is obvious," wrote R. M. Kingdon, "that Geneva's direct financial contribution to the Huguenot cause was not very substantial"; but he concluded that Geneva had systematically violated her neutrality by sending men, money, and large quantities of gunpowder to the Huguenot armies in France.[41]

✝

The fourth major field of Calvin's and Geneva's interest during the last decade of his life was also an outgrowth of the Treaty of Cateau-Cambrésis. The re-establishment of the House of Savoy posed a far more immediate and far more serious threat to the religious and political fate of Geneva than did the troubled affairs of France. The real dimensions of the Savoyard threat became apparent when the new Duke, Emmanuel-Philibert, renewed an ancient alliance with the Swiss Catholic cantons and then demanded back *all* his father's lands of 1535, including the conquests of Bern. He put pressure on Bern through the Swiss Diet, saw his claims submitted to arbitration by 1561, and won an award which gave him the lands around Geneva but not the pays de Vaud; he rejected this as insufficient. Meanwhile, he had begun to sound out public opinion in Geneva as early as the autumn of 1559. The first magistrates whom his emissaries encountered answered his overtures with the abrupt remark that "we will venture our lives for our sovereignty and for the Word of God." Geneva's rulers decided, as in all moments of crisis, "to put our trust in God and to keep a sharp watch," which was their version of Oliver Cromwell's famous "trust in God and keep your powder dry." Later that winter, the new Duke sent one of his subjects, a Bishop who had been born in Geneva, on an official mission to the city. The Bishop was spied on by an Italian in his inn, shunned by all the magistrates as if he had the plague, and was kept waiting six days for an audience. After he had made his speech and revealed Emmanuel-Philibert's peaceful intentions and his ancient rights, the magistrates summoned Calvin to give them advice. "He kept repeating," said the Bishop's report, "that I was there to put bells on their ears, and he demanded that I be put in prison as a seducer."[42] Calvin's advice was not followed on this occasion, but, needless to add, neither was the Bishop's. This same cleric soon afterwards tried to take his revenge on Calvin by organizing a plot to assassinate him.[43]

For the moment, Emmanuel-Philibert was busy organizing his restored lands and modernizing their institutions. He established his capital in Turin, reformed the coinage, cleverly succeeded in permanently abolishing his Estates-General in 1560, and revolutionized his finances by instituting a *taille,* which he collected directly through the peasant communes instead of from feudal notables. Within a very short time he had established a new state, which was far more powerful than the Duchy of Savoy had been under his predecessors. But for the moment, promises had gotten him nothing at Geneva, and threats had gotten him an insufficient reward from Bern. In 1561, Geneva merely rooted out a few spies and privately told another ducal emissary that they could not negotiate with him until he had reached an agreement with Bern. The principal result of two years of Savoyard pressure had been to drive Bern and Geneva to forget many of their differences.

In 1563, Geneva received a nasty surprise. After the House of Savoy had made one more unsuccessful attempt to establish diplomatic contact with Geneva, this time through the new Duchess Margaret (a French princess) who had written directly to Calvin, some lesser minions of Savoy decided to take more direct action.[44] They hired some of the old Perrinist exiles, who were long since discredited at Bern, and told them to collect a force of 600 men. This army was to slip into Geneva at night along the lakefront, surprise the city and claim her for Savoy. They were to promise freedom of worship to the inhabitants of Geneva, but (according to the man who revealed the plot to Genevan authorities) they also had instructions to capture Calvin and put him in an iron cage, then to proceed north and invade the pays de Vaud. Geneva quickly put a counterspy into the midst of this plot and squelched it. Fifteen residents of Geneva were arrested for complicity in it and two of them were executed, although the ringleaders escaped. The valiant counterspy was rewarded with an annual pension and a gift to liquidate the mortgage on his home. Thus Geneva successfully survived the first and by no means the most serious in a long line of Savoyard plots against her independence.

✝

An exciting decade closed in 1564. It had been filled to overflowing by the successful installation of the Academy, by the fragile restoration of the *combourgeoisie* with Bern, by ecclesiastical and occasionally political intervention in French affairs, and by the successful repulse of the threat posed by a restored and vigorous Duchy of Savoy. Calvin had been particularly involved in the Academy and in French affairs, but his prominence within Geneva was such that he could not help becoming involved at important points in all four matters. This preacher, educator, and adviser had become an overpowering moral force within Geneva, and his influence was spilling over into many fields outside the ministry. When he died in 1564, Geneva lost the man who had given her the supplies of men, institutions, and ideas which would enable her to survive as a Protestant enclave in Catholic lands, as a tiny city state surrounded by princely absolutism, and as a model for all the Reformed communities and Churches of his century. The fate of Geneva — as model community, religious enclave, and political anachronism — was unique in sixteenth-century Europe. It had been made possible by the work of a single immigrant who had been a citizen for less than five years when he died — and who on his deathbed could refer to Geneva as a "perverse and unhappy nation."

The importance and peculiarities of Genevan history are basically due to Calvin, and the city's international reputation to the refugees whom he attracted there. Geneva's reputation was greatly expanded during the decade that ended in 1564. Calvin's death coincided almost exactly with the long-delayed signing of the Treaty of Lausanne, by which all Bernese conquests around Geneva were to be returned to the Duke of Savoy; as a Genevan chronicler noted, 1564 had been an especially bad year, "not only because of the new neighbor who prepared his arrival, but also because of the death of John Calvin."[45] After this protective covering of Bernese *baillages* had been removed, Geneva stood as a city with stout walls and a sense of mission. Calvin's Geneva had used her last ten years of poltical security to tremendous advantage.

NOTES

1. *C.O.*, IX, cols. 887–91; Roget, *HPG,* VII, pp. 58–63.
2. *C.O.*, IX, cols. 891–94; Roget, *HPG,* VII, pp. 63–68. Compare the slightly different version by another pastor, Bonaventure Bertram, which we have reproduced as an appendix. The variations between them, as Roget long ago noted (VII, p. 68 n. 1), are minimal.
3. Dec. 17, 1547, during the trial of *Le magnifique* Meigret; cf. *supra,* pp. [ch. 3, pp. 12 ff].
4. *Infra,* p. 240.
5. Walker, *Jean Calvin,* p. 258; *C.O.,* XIII, col. 230. See Richard Stauffer, *L'humanité de Calvin* (Neuchatel, 1964) on his personality.
6. The two principal contemporary French Protestant students of Calvin agree on this. See Henri Strohl, *La pensée de la Réforme* (Strasbourg,

1951), p. 123, and François Wendel, *Calvin: sources et evolution de sa pensée religieuse* (Paris, 1950), pp. 247 ff.

7. Roset, *Chroniques*, Bk. VI, ch. 1 (p. 377).

8. L. Febvre, *Le problème de l'incroyance au XVIe siècle: la religion de Rabelais* (Paris, 1942), pp. 462ff, largely reproduced by R. Mandrou, *Introduction à la France moderne: essai de psychologie historique* Paris, 1961), pp. 70ff; but see also the criticism by Alain Dufour, "Historie politique et psychologie historique," in *BHR*, 25 (1963), p. 18 f.

9. See *R.C.P.*, II, pp. 115ff for a catalog of extant sermons by Calvin; also B. Gagnebin, "L'incroyable histoire des sermons de Calvin," in *BHG*, 10 (1956), pp. 311–34.

10. Roset, *Chroniques*, Bk. VI, ch. 49 (p. 430).

11. Roget, *HPG*, V, p. 101 f.

12. *R.C.P.*, I, p. 45 f.

13. *Supra*, pp. 75–77, 83.

14. Roget, *HPG*, V, p. 101. Her father was one of the last magistrates to accept the Reformation: see A. Roget in *Etrennes genevoises*, I (1877).

15. *Infra*, p. 138.

16. Bonivard, *Ancienne et nouvelle police*, p. 127.

17. Printed in *C.O.*, VI, cols. 7–134.

18. In *ibid.*, cols. 148–60.

19. *Ibid.*, col. 37.

20. *Ibid.*, cols. 47, 49.

21. *Ibid.*, col. 45.

22. *Ibid.*, col. 87.

23. *Ibid.*, col. 107.

24. *Ibid.*, col. 111.

25. *Ibid.*, col. 133.

26. *C.O.*, XIX, col. 34. These judgments closely concur with those of John T. McNeill, *The History and Character of Calvinism* (Oxford, 1954), pp. 185, 190, and those of Ernest Pfisterer, *Calvins Wirken in Genf*, 2 Aufl. (Neukirchen, 1957), pp. 137 ff.

27. *Infra*, pp. 118, 139.

28. Alain Dufour, "Le mythe de Genève au temps de Calvin," in *Schweizerische Zeitschrift für Geschichte*, n.s. 9 (1959), p. 517.

29. Roget, *HPG*, V, pp. 81–94.

30. *Ibid.*, pp. 202f, 268–71.

31. All subsequent accounts have drawn on Chas. Borgeaud's monumental *Histoire de l'Université de Genève: I, L'Académie de Calvin, 1559–1798* (G., 1900); see the good recent summary by Paul-F. Geisendorf, *L'Université de Genève, 1559–1959* (G., 1959), pp. 20–36.

32. Borgeaud, I, pp. 55–63. See S. Stelling-Michaud's edition of the *Livre du Recteur de l'Université de Genève, tome I: le texte* (G., 1959), pp. 81–84. A second volume giving the biographies of Genevan students is promised soon.

33. Borgeaud, I, pp. 34–36; *Studies*, p. 25f.

34. Roget, *HPG*, V, pp. 240, 195.
35. Roget, *HPG*, VI, pp. 21–22.
36. *Ibid.*, pp. 67–70.
37. R. M. Kingdon, *Geneva and the Coming of the Wars of Religion in France, 1555–1563* (G., 1956), p. 33 f.
38. *Infra*, p. 183 f.
39. Excellent account in Kingdon, pp. 106–26.
40. *Studies*, p. 26 n. 39.
41. Kingdon, p. 119.
42. Roget, *HPG*, VI, pp. 1–17, 173–88, 309–312.
43. Henri Naef, *La Conjuration d'Amboise et Genève* (G., 1922), pp. 98, 122 n. 2.
44. F. de Crue, "Le complot des fugitifs en 1563," in *MDG*, 20 (1879–88), pp. 385–428; Roget, *HPG*, VII, pp. 27–35.
45. BPU, Ms. Suppl. 433 (copy of Ami Favre's *Chronique*, 1563–1571), fol. 15.

PART B

Pillars of Calvin's Geneva

FIVE

The Church of Geneva to 1564

The history of the Church of Geneva from the establishment of the Reformation to the death of Calvin has almost never been treated as an intelligible and distinct historical unit. Usually it is sacrificed to the needs of biographers of Calvin, who divide it into periods covering Calvin's first stay in Geneva, his exile, and the period after his return. The years after 1541 are subdivided by the phases of Calvin's struggles against the civil authorities and against various heresies. Finally, after 1555, the history of Calvin's Church enters a triumphant phase, culminating in the foundation of the Academy in 1559.

There are a few flaws in this standardized picture, which presupposes Calvin's complete dominance over the church established in Geneva by Farel. Some details need to be modified, because the Church of Geneva was something slightly different from the personality of Calvin. The relationships between the man and his professional institution have been clarified in the last few years, primarily through the publication of the official records of Geneva's Company of Pastors from 1546 to 1564.[1] It is now easier to trace and to explain the history of this institution. Of course, the history of the Church of Geneva in the first decade after the Reformation must still be interpreted from the older sources, but here too some standardized misconceptions and arbitrary divisions need to be modified.

In the first place, the personnel of Geneva's new church underwent some rapid turnovers during the tumultuous years after independence, and not only when Farel and his young protégé were expelled in 1538. The rural districts, where parish priests were ordered to submit to the new order, show scenes of turmoil even greater than those within the city of Geneva. These priests (who cautiously prayed every Sunday for the health of both *Messieurs de Genève* and the Pope, or who gave their pulpits to visiting friars who proclaimed that anyone who accepted the Reformation would die of the plague) were a major headache for the city's authorities.[2] They were probably no worse than the "meddling" of Farel's blind friend who had called the magistrates a bunch of drunks and precipitated the expulsion of Farel and Calvin in 1538. Furthermore, while the rural priests remained a problem, Genevan authorities made serious efforts to replace Farel and Calvin with the best men they could find. The governors of Neuchâtel gave Antoine Marcourt, who was already known among French Reformers as the author of the famous Paris placards of 1534. He and Jean Morand, another important replacement, were capable men who instituted some minor reforms, such as keeping parish registers of baptisms.[3] If Marcourt and Morand had not fled the city during the war scare of 1540, the recall of Calvin would have been less necessary. Finally, in surveying the evolution of Geneva's corps of pastors from 1536 to 1545, one is struck by the fact that there is always a certain minimum continuity as well as a rapid turnover among their personnel. This turnover was proportionately no greater than that among the membership of the Small Council. We should also consider that Geneva's pastors were nearly all Frenchmen who were accustomed to frequent migrations in these early and hectic years of the French Reformation under Francis I.

Turnover among Genevan pastors continued to be rapid after Calvin's return in 1541. Four new men were brought in by 1543, two more in 1544, and two more in 1545; all eight were Frenchmen. All the men Calvin found in office when he returned were gradually transferred to rural parishes to replace the old priests. In addition, Calvin replaced Sebastien Castellio, the principal of Geneva's public school and future apostle of religious toleration. Only after all these changes had been made did the corps of Genevan pastors become virtually homogeneous, with Calvin as its guiding spirit. Not only had Calvin purified the corps of urban pastors, but he had also greatly extended the network of the Church of Geneva in 1544. The final settlement with Bern permitted Geneva to take full control of a dozen rural parishes where her rights had previously been in dispute. On this occasion all the old priests were finally removed, and eight new Reformed preachers (many of them transferred from city posts) were sent to replace them.[5] After this change had been completed, and both the pastors' custom of mutual censorship (*grabeau*) and the tribunal of elders were working to Calvin's satisfaction, one may safely assume that the second Reformation of the Church of Geneva was complete. It is only then, in 1546, that the official minutes of the Company of Pastors (as we possess them) begin.

Inside the cover of their register is the only extant copy of the famous Ecclesiastical Ordinances of 1541, drafted by Calvin and twice amended by the various Genevan councils. This document remained as the great charter of the Church of Geneva, at least until the major revision of 1561. On the very day when he returned to Geneva, Calvin had insisted on the necessity of preparing such a document, and thanks to his insistence Geneva's Church possessed her organizational charter two years before Geneva's state. The 1541 Ordinances explained the working order of the four parts of Calvin's church — pastors, teachers, elders, and deacons — but only in preliminary and incomplete fashion did they define the exact boundaries and connections between civil and ecclesiastical power. The Ordinances were not a closed system. On the touchy question of excommunication, for example, they decreed that the elders in Consistory had the right to separate an unrepentant offender from the body of the church, but they also stated that the elders possessed no legal powers. They said nothing about the right to appeal a sentence of excommunication to the Small Council, nor did they say who had the power to remove excommunication. The margin for interpretation was large; some of these latent problems were only resolved after the famous Berthelier case in the summer of 1553. They have also bedeviled innumerable modern interpreters of Calvin.[6] Although some other articles were also drawn up hastily and incompletely, the Ordinances proved good enough to guide the Church of Geneva through a difficult period. As Calvin said, it was not perfect but it was the best available under the circumstances.

The history of Calvin's church, as revealed by its registers, is marked between 1547 and 1558 by a few major struggles and several minor ones. Major issues confronting them appear to have been the union of the Swiss Protestant churches, predestination, anti-Trinitarianism, and the affirmation of the Consistory's powers, especially the power of excommunication. Running as a constant motif through these major themes is the opposition to the Calvinist or majority opinion by a few Genevan laymen and, more surprisingly, by an obstinate minority of the corps of pastors.

Calvin's concern with the doctrinal solidarity of Swiss Protestantism preceded by a decade a similar concern for the common confession of the Reformed Church in France. It explains why the Zurich Consensus of 1549, hammered out in discussions between Calvin and Bullinger, was copied *verbatim* into the Company's minutes, where it filled twelve folio pages. Calvin and Bullinger both hoped that this document would prove acceptable to Melanchthon and thereby serve to unite the Lutheran and Reformed churches; unfortunately this never happened.

The critical importance of predestination, raised in the trial of Jerome Bolsec, ex-Carmelite monk and personal physician to M. de Falais (former courtier of Charles V and personal friend of Calvin) appears clearly in the records. Seventy-eight folios of their first volume of minutes are filled with the memoranda of this case, which had serious reverberations not only in the community of Geneva but even among the pastors themselves. Perhaps on no other issue was Calvin's control of his Company at stake, and nowhere else did he encounter such opposition from pastors in the Bernese Pays de Vaud. Bolsec saw his encounter with Calvin in terms of a great disputation, inaugurated by an outsider (he was careful to describe himself at the outset as a subject of Bern) but designed to be definitive:

if it be proved by the Word of God that the petitioner be in error (which he doesn't believe), then authors holding his doctrine should be condemned and their books forbidden to be printed, sold, or owned in your city [Geneva], so that no one will be deceived by their false doctrine. Similarly, if the contrary be true, if your ministers hold and teach an opinion not in accord with the Word of God, may their doctrine be prohibited and condemned along with the books which teach it.[7]

Relying on the authority of his protector M. de Falais, whose public apology for his conversion to Protestantism had been drafted and printed by Calvin three years before, Bolsec launched his attack. He attempted to paint Calvin and his adherents as the heirs of an heretical tradition which began with Lorenzo Valla and was repeated by Zwingli in *De Providentia* in its most absurd form. (Calvin, incidentally, said he had only glanced lightly at Zwingli's work.) Bolsec depicted himself as representing a doctrine of election "about which the ancient doctors agreed, and at the present time three learned and respected persons, namely Melanchthon, Bullinger, and Brenz."[8] Bolsec preferred to narrow the debate to a single question, affirming that "he had never heard M. Calvin preach anything that wasn't holy or good, except for what he told his congregation about the reason for the perdition of the damned." On this issue Bolsec proposed that the simplest Scriptural answer was the best; he "had always claimed that God's election was eternal and that we are saved by grace, but he has also said and said again, note well that Scripture doesn't say that we are saved because God has elected us, but because we have believed in Jesus Christ."[9]

With the issue so clearly joined, Calvin's defense (in the name of the whole Company) was simple. He bore down upon the basic corruption of man, and attacked Bolsec's claim that his theory was in accord with the Fathers of the Church. "That was too great an imprudence, since St. Augustine says the contrary [about divine election] in over two hundred passages"; as for his claim to modern support, "he has understood Melanchthon badly." They accused Bolsec of making false glosses on biblical passages, and on at least one point they were able to make the telling accusation that Bolsec "spoke like a true Papist" by making human free will the companion to the Holy Ghost in the process of salvation. The pastors' critical point must have been the refutation from St. Augustine, for they carried his *De Predestinatione* along with the Bible right into Geneva's city hall

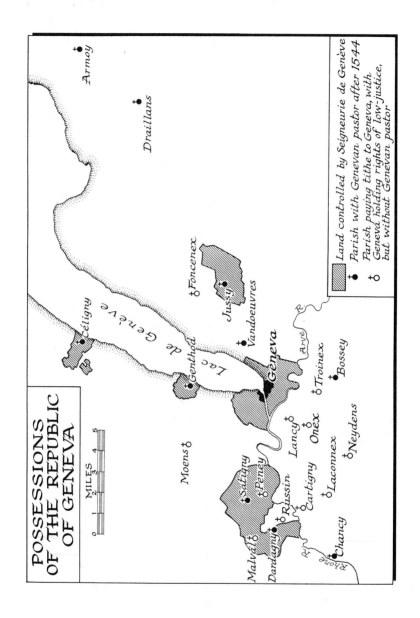

POSSESSIONS
OF THE REPUBLIC
OF GENEVA

MILES
0 1 2 3 4 5

Land controlled by Seigneurie de Genève
Parish with Genevan pastor after 1544
Parish paying tithe to Geneva, with
Geneva holding rights of low-justice,
but without Genevan pastor

Armoy

Draillans

Foncenex

Céligny

Lac de Genève

Genthod

Jussy

Vandoeuvres

Geneva

Arve

Troinex

Bossey

Moens

Malval

Saltigny

Peney

Lancy

Onex

Neydens

Laconnex

Dardagny

Russin

Cartigny

Chancy

Rhône

in order to confront Bolsec with the relevant passages on two successive days. This backed their opponent into a corner. "M. Jerome didn't know what to say," note their minutes, "and couldn't get out of the soup, until finally he said that the advice of neighboring churches was necessary and that he would submit to their judgment, to which the ministers agreed."[10] Actually, Bolsec had already lost his case and was condemned to perpetual banishment from Geneva just before Christmas 1551, "so that if anyone was infected with his error, this might be remedied and the sacrament [of communion] not be polluted by him."[11] This decision was taken *before* most of the neighboring churches (with the significant exception of Zurich) had replied to the questionnaire sent out by Geneva's magistrates.

The other great doctrinal issue encountered by Geneva's pastors less than two years later was the issue of the Trinity raised by Servetus. This famous case filled thirty-two large folios of the Company's minutes, but except for the care with which the records were preserved, it had few similarities with Bolsec's. In the first place, their opponent was put in prison "so that he may no longer infect the world with his blasphemies and heresies, because he was known to all as incorrigible and desperate." At his very first interrogation,

his impudence and obstinacy became all the more known. He maintained that the name of the Trinity was only used after the Council of Nicaea, and that none of the earlier doctors and martyrs knew what it was. When obvious evidence was shown against this . . . he broke into other absurdities and calumnies.[12]

It took only eight days for Geneva's anti-Calvinist government to request that a circular letter be sent to neighboring states. A complete dossier was drawn up a month later. The replies were prompt and unanimous in their wish to remove such a plague from the church; Servetus was burned about ten weeks after his arrest. The only issue was *not* Servetus' guilt but his punishment; even Castellio recognized this in his subsequent polemic against the Genevan authorities. Unlike Bolsec, Servetus had no support from Bern or from any of Calvin's refugee friends. Servetus' only followers were a few stubborn Italians who were discovered in the Genevan refugee church in 1558. His case was a serious one, but not critical in the same way as Bolsec's for the inner history of the Church of Geneva.

Bolsec's attack on predestination had served to strengthen elements of opposition to Calvin even inside the Company of Pastors. The clearest proof of such opposition is the curious case of Philippe de Ecclesia. His disputes with his brethren apparently began in February 1549 with some "useless, unedifying, and obscure" remarks to his congregation at Vandoeuvres, for which De Ecclesia was censured. He quickly showed himself rebellious toward any correction, full of hypocrisy and impudence, and indifferent to brotherly admonition in the *grabeau*.[13] After the Bolsec affair, he was again called on the carpet for a variety of offenses including usury, friendship with Bolsec, and preaching on Easter 1552 that Christ's body was not in a certain place but everywhere. The case against him, which included a criminal trial in Genevan courts as well as ecclesiastical censures, dragged on for months. The council tried to get the Company to readmit De Ecclesia if he showed repentance, but the pastors were now anxious to be rid of him once and for all. De Ecclesia admitted to having conversed with Bolsec (who lived in Bernese territory until 1555 and even won a few Bernese rural pastors over to his views) and with Troillet, the other recent public enemy of Calvin's doctrine of predestination; but he said only that he had talked with them, not that he had accepted their doctrine. On the other hand, as his brethren repeatedly pointed out to him, he had not publicly defended the official Genevan doctrine. They agreed that he was showing no sign of repentance. For the magistrates, the whole affair had become one of those nasty problems which ought to be resolved by Christmas, and once again they tried to force a reconciliation — but vainly. The affair dragged on into January 1553, when the Small Council wearily agreed that the Company was right and notified De Ecclesia that he would be removed from his post by Easter.[14] This stubbornly independent preacher, compromised by many failings and not closely connected with Calvin's political opponents, serves as proof that there was very little unanimity of opinion within the Company of Pastors even after Calvin's reorganization of the mid-1540's.

There were other cases of ministers appointed after Calvin's return in 1541 who had to be dismissed for serious professional faults. Nicolas Ferron, who preached in the city at St. Gervais, was accused by two of his maidservants of attempted seduction in the spring of 1549.[15] The matter came up in the Company's *grabeau*, where his colleagues decided that the most prudent solution was to demote Ferron to a rural parish. While he was being censured, Ferron rose against Calvin, calling him

vindictive, a man who hides his secrets against someone until the last moment, and a man who likes to be flattered. He [Ferron] threw himself upon the others, calling them flatterers and slanderers, and claiming that he was every bit as honorable a man as Calvin. Then, carried away by his wrath, he stormed out of the meeting and didn't come back.

Ferron also refused a proposal by Farel, who happened to be visiting Geneva then, to let the churches of Neuchâtel and Lausanne serve as arbiters in this matter. Ferron was accordingly sent to the country, and after a second scandal arose from his chambermaid's complaint, he was called before the magistrates and deposed. He requested a letter of recommendation for a new job, but was refused both by the council and by the Company. Like De Ecclesia, he was deposed by a government generally described as strongly anti-Calvin.

These two cases do not exhaust the evidence of disunity within the Company of Pastors. Traces of deviation from official church policy may be found as late as 1558, when the pastor of the distant rural church of Draillans (in the Bernese *baillage* of Thonon) was admonished for having read Bern's prohibition against preaching about predestination during his regular Sunday sermon. When he was censured in the Company's next *grabeau*, this pastor, "instead of recognizing his fault, answered with many calumnies towards certain magistrates, and spoke to us with unbelievable arrogance, without wishing to correct himself, which is unworthy of a minister of the Word of God."[16] Traces of sympathy for Bolsec's opinions about predestination, mixed in this case with sympathy for Castellio, had to be censured in a certain N., "newly returned from Tübingen where he had studied for several years," as late as 1564. This last troublemaker had even been singing and teaching a song composed by Bolsec while in Geneva's jail![17]

Obviously these signs of opposition should not be exaggerated. Nearly all the time, Calvin was in full control of the Venerable Company of Pastors; and the quietly successful workings of Geneva's ecclesiastical machinery left few traces in the official records. Most of the institutions which Calvin had established in the early 1540's were running smoothly: the Sunday catechism schools, the Friday congregations or scripture exercises for pastors, even the Consistory. Still, it is interesting to note that Calvin could be challenged even within the Genevan church before 1555, as well as by laymen.

✝

While it does not seem exaggerated to say that the principal activity of the Company of Pastors from 1547 to 1555 lay in the purification of its membership and in the great quarrels raised by excommunication and predestination, it is certainly true that such local activities fade into the background soon after the defeat of Perrin. They are replaced by a period when the international affairs of the Church of Geneva fill the major share of the Company's minutes. Missionary preoccupations, the despatch of Genevan-trained pastors to announce the Word of God to mushrooming Reformed congregations in France and elsewhere, became their primary concern. A recent book by Robert M. Kingdon[18] has described the meticulous care with which these pastors were trained and examined, and the secrecy with which they were sent off, sometimes to face a martyr's death. Men were drawn in from France, taught, apprenticed as pedagogues or secretaries or often as apprentice pastors in obscure rural parishes in Switzerland where they learned the collective self-discipline of the *grabeau*. They were also examined in the standard Genevan fashion, by preparing an exegesis of a selected Scriptural verse before the Company of Pastors. The candidate was then given a formal letter of accreditation by the Company. At last, under an assumed name and often posing as a travelling merchant, the Genevan-trained pastor was sent to a French town which had requested a shepherd from Geneva. "The process of placement," noted Kingdon,

seems to have occupied most of the Company's time from 1557 through 1562; practically every page of their registers is devoted to lists of elected men and to various matters pertaining to assignments, or to copies of the subsequent written reports from the men sent out. Though the registers are abbreviated and have long and annoying lacunae, they still provide the impression that the pastors were really absorbed in their supervision of the missionary campaign.[19]

The whole process would have been impossible under an anti-Calvin government, for the magistrates were well aware that the French crown regarded such activities as subversive.

The total number of missions sent out by Geneva's Company of Pastors reached very impressive totals. Their men were sent not only to the Kingdom of France, but also to the survivors of the old Waldenses, or Vaudois, in the valleys of Piedmont, to Turin, Antwerp, and London, and on one occasion to a new French colony in Brazil. Here are the figures, year by year:[20]

1555: 5 (4 to Piedmont)	1559: 32 (all to France)
1556: 5 (2 to Piedmont, 2 to Brazil)	1560: 13 (1 to London)
1557: 16 (4 to Piedmont, 1 to Antwerp)	1561: 12 (all to France)
1558: 23 (1 to Turin)	1562: 12 (all to France)

The grand totals amount to almost 120 missions involving about 100 different men. For a church the size of Geneva's, which included eight urban and ten rural ministers, this was indeed a mammoth enterprise. Yet it was carried off with little visible strain, except once or twice around 1560 when the Church of Geneva was so short of manpower that a few requests had to be refused. Almost all members of the Company except for Calvin himself were loaned out sometime during this missionary thrust.

†

Gradually, in the struggles for solidarity of the late 1540's and early 1550's and then during the missionary campaign of the late 1550's and early 1560's, the church of Calvin developed her institutional maturity. Bit by bit, across the daily problems of Genevan life, it affirmed its duties and its coherence. First and foremost, this was a company of preachers whose duties, said the Ordinances of 1541, were "to announce the Word of God, to indoctrinate, admonish, exhort, and encourage both in public and in private." The Genevan pastorate was a vocation that demanded a solid education, a sturdy voice, a good measure of courage, and an upright character free from a lengthy list of shortcomings for which its members could be, and were, dismissed.

The pastors were the first element in Calvin's church, but they were not the only part in the edifice erected by the 1541 Ordinances, when the "spiritual government demonstrated and instituted by the Word of our Lord" was "reduced in proper form to take place and be observed among us." Calvin's preamble abruptly remarked that there are four orders of offices in the government of the church: pastors, teachers, elders, and deacons. Each was to have its properly delimited sphere of action in Geneva, under the surveillance of the civil authorities and aided by the fraternal admonition of the ministers. Calvin's second order, the teachers, have drawn relatively little attention.[21] They were instituted to "teach sound doctrine to the faithful" and especially to the young, whom they instructed in the catechism at noon on Sundays, and at other times in languages and human wisdom. The doctors or teachers were to "raise up seed for the time to come, in order not to leave the church a desert to our children," and to "prepare youth for the ministry and for civil government." To this end, the existing school system was overhauled. An elementary school, directed by a minister or a catechist, was erected in each of Geneva's four parishes. Above these the 1541 Ordinances strongly desired a superior school or *collège*, "which we hope will soon be established with the Lord's help." But this wish remained unfulfilled, for Geneva's upper school remained in poor repute for a long time after the dismissal of Castellio. Only with the founding of the Academy in 1559 did this part of Geneva's ecclesiastical structure begin to function as Calvin had intended it to.

Calvin's third order, the elders, formed a famous part of the Church of Geneva. A dozen laymen, chosen among the members of the Small Council or the Two Hundred, presided over by a Syndic, met once each week together with the Company of Pastors to form the famous Genevan Consistory. Unlike the *collège*, this institution began functioning smoothly soon after Calvin's return. Its records during Calvin's lifetime fill twenty almost illegible volumes in the archives of Geneva,[22] and its activities have fascinated nearly all students of Calvin and his city.[23] The elders were intended "to keep watch over every man's life, to admonish amiably those whom they see leading a disorderly life, and where necessary to report to the assembly which will be deputized to make fraternal correction." This body, named the Consistory after an old episcopal court that had been primarily concerned with marriage cases, was numerically dominated until 1555 by the laymen; the elders are repeatedly described in the 1541 Ordinances as representatives of the *Seigneurie* rather than ecclesiastical officials, and it is emphatically stated that they are not a court of justice. Calvin himself saw this body as essentially remedial rather than oppressive, as one phase of the care of souls. He stipulated that there be no rigor in the decisions of the elders and that their corrections were "only medecine to turn sinners to the Lord." He also emphasized that the activities of the Consistory should be thorough and its members chosen from all parts of the city, "so that its eyes may be everywhere." No fewer than eight times in the instructions for this body are the elders told how and when they should admonish offenders, but they are never told that they should punish them.

Although the Consistory's powers were sometimes ill-defined, its actions were nonetheless vigorous. Its records exhibit extraordinary minuteness and remarkable variety among the offenses recorded for correction. Penalties for not attending church and for misbehaving during service were common. More serious cases, still not uncommon in the 1550's, of Genevans who could only pray or say a credo in Latin, who still asked the Virgin Mary to forgive their sins, or who kept altars with images in their rooms, were also brought to their attention.[24] Other offenses were more picturesque. They included a widow who said *requiescat in pace* on her husband's grave; a goldsmith who made a Catholic chalice; a barber who tonsured a priest; a man who owned a copy of *Amadis of Gaul*; somebody who said the Pope was a fine man; and a woman who drank from a sacred spring near Geneva.[25] Many of the activities censured by the elders were trivial, but they worked thoroughly and fairly. Nobody was exempt from their jurisdiction. On one memorable occasion in 1546, they even censured the Syndic Amblard Corne (then serving as president of the Consistory) for dancing at a wedding. Corne swallowed his medecine and proved himself a circumspect magistrate and friend of Calvin thereafter. On another occasion, they severely censured Calvin's sister-in-law for adultery and turned her over to the civil authorities for punishment. The incurable François Bonivard appeared frequently before them, as did many lesser figures.

The penalties meted out by Geneva's elders frequently involved humiliating acts of penance, such as kissing the ground after a blasphemy, which were deliberately modeled on those used by Christians of the second and third centuries. The experience was sufficiently strong so that the offender either corrected himself, like Amblard Corne in 1546, or else became a vehement opponent of the Consistory, like Mme. Perrin who was censured at the same time for the same offense.

Except for one vitally important point, there was nothing unique about Geneva's Consistory. Most of its provisions closely resembled those of ecclesiastical tribunals in other Protestant cities, especially Zwingli's Zurich and Bucer's Strasburg. Every case which came before Geneva's elders could also have been punished, sometimes with far greater severity, by a comparable body in Basel, Zurich, or Bern. The originality of Calvin's Consistory lay in its power of excommunication, which was definitively confirmed in 1555; elsewhere in Protestant Europe this remained the prerogative of the civil government.

Gaining the right of excommunication for the Consistory was a vital triumph for Calvin, but it was assured only after the tribunal had been operating for fourteen years. Once, in 1543, Calvin had to threaten resignation in order to prevent the Small Council from claiming full power to excommunicate. A decade later, the magistrates informed the pastors that their original intention had been to reserve for themselves the power to absolve anyone rejected from communion by the Consistory, and this issue remained in doubt until 1555. Only in 1556 did the Consistory win the power to hear witnesses under oath. Amblard Corne, now First Syndic, had steered the matter through; "although Satan had done his best to overturn such a holy and useful order," report the Company's minutes, "Corne reported . . . that God had been victorious."[26] The Consistory's powers were extended still further in February 1560, when the magistrates ruled that the elders might be chosen from all members of the Two Hundred, including the foreign born, and that the Syndic presiding over the Consistory would no longer carry his official baton with him. Upon Calvin's suggestion, they agreed that all sinners would have to make public amends after their excommunication had been removed, but declined Calvin's other suggestion that bits of metal (jetons) be given to all orthodox communicants.[27]

Not much is known about Calvin's fourth office, the deacons. In the 1541 Ordinances they were charged with caring for the sick and administering alms to the poor, while sternly repressing begging. In Geneva these duties were combined in the all-purpose institution known as the hôpital général, which had been founded in 1535.[28] Its management was entrusted to four lay procureurs, one of whom acted as treasurer. They were elected in the same manner as the elders, and were frequently members of the Small Council. The 1541 code seems to have made little change in the running of this hôpital, or of the supplementary plague hospital which had to be set up soon afterwards. Generally, the procureurs supervised the revenues and expenditures of the almshouse, bought food for its inmates and staff, and managed the barber-surgeons. Once, in 1544, the deacons were accused by Geneva's public treasurer (Amblard Corne, again!) of using public funds to speculate in grain. But generally the office of deacon was both time-consuming and underpaid. One of the most experienced procureurs, Jean Chautemps, reported in 1560 that he would never take the job again, especially during a plague like that of the 1540's, even if he were paid a thousand écus.[29]

Calvin's Church of Geneva, subdivided into two ecclesiastical and two lay orders, was an ideal construct. Formal distinctions between spiritual and temporal authority were, however, often blurred in practice. The Company's minutes occasionally equate faith with sovereignty, especially when dealing with Geneva's rural parishes; "the honor of God, the magistrates, and the pastors" was to be strictly preserved in these districts. The magistrates — *Messieurs de l'Estat* — generally preceded the pastors — *Messieurs de l'Eglise* — in these records. The magistrates had the authority and often the inclination to intervene in the business of the Church of Geneva. They confirmed and when necessary dismissed Genevan pastors. They decided when and where sermons would be preached. They ordered the sermon topics for Easter week in 1544.[30] On special occasions, as in the cases of Bolsec or Servetus, they even judged dogmatic questions. In the last analysis, the Church of Geneva, like other Swiss Reformed churches, was under the control of the local magistracy. The Reformed Church's most powerful weapon, excommunication, was less radical than the traditional Catholic variety, for at Geneva the excommunicated were expected to hear the sermon every Sunday except during the four weeks each year when communion was given.

Despite these obvious limitations on its independence of action and the small number of its unique features, the Church of Geneva exercised a truly remarkable attraction in many different places.[31] Her organization was copied by the Reformed churches in France, including Consistories and pastoral synods. Huguenot schools in France copied Genevan regulations *verbatim* in numerous cases. The spirit of the 1541 Ordinances even reappears in such an unlikely place as the Huguenot military code of 1562. Outside France, the Vaudois of Piedmont were heavily indebted to Genevan precedents. When they drew up their ecclesiastical discipline in 1564, they specifically ordered that the Genevan Ordinances be followed, and in doubtful cases they consulted the Genevan Company of Pastors for doctrinal and disciplinary rulings. The farther away from Geneva, the less important was direct imitation of her church; but the indirect influence of Geneva, especially in Old and New England, is a well-known tale which needs no elaboration here. Quite simply, the Church of Geneva was a fact of European civilization.

✝

At last, in 1564, the Company of Pastors suffered its severest
loss while at the pinnacle of its fame and reputation. Calvin
died. What would happen now? Who could replace him? At
the next meeting of the Company these questions were debated.

The brethren decided to elect someone to serve [in Calvin's position
as Moderator], adding that this office (*charge*) was temporary and
should be elected from year to year. In this way no preeminence may
be introduced among those who may afterwards succeed to the service
of this church, under the pretext that the order currently held by the
brethren was not well understood by their successors, as happened
with the ancient church.[32] Also this will prevent churches in France
and elsewhere from falling into the same danger, when ambitious or
imprudent men, claiming to imitate Genevan customs, would wish to
make a perpetual bishop in each assembly of pastors. Such a custom
would be neither good nor useful. One sees from experience that God
sometimes augments and sometimes diminishes his graces to individual
men, so that a man who may sustain such an office today would no
longer be fit for it a year later.

As for the late M. Calvin, he had been like a father to each and every
one of this Company. God had put such grace in him and had given
him such authority with the people, which helped each one of us to
serve his ministry better, that when we chose [moderators] each year,
we could have picked none other. If we had, we would have scorned
God's great gifts in him, which were always accompanied with a
sincerity and good conscience which each of us could notice. In fact,
God had so blessed his conduct that in all business concerning this
ministry, this Company was never deprived of good advice. It was
never observed of him that he sought any profit for himself or his relatives, but that he preserved a fine sense of equality. But now we do
not know if God will choose hereafter to put so many gifts all together into any single one of us.[33]

Across the official history of Geneva's Company of Pastors,
Calvin's personality appears only in silhouette. He was always
primus inter pares among his colleagues. Occasionally his preeminence appears. Sometimes the Company met at his home.
Nearly always, he served as their spokesman before the magistrates. Once, in 1547, he even presided over three sessions of the

Consistory assuming a role belonging to the magistrates.[34] But often he was only one minister among others, fulfilling his normal duties each week, preaching, lecturing, and baptizing in his allotted turn. Calvin's voluminous writings and correspondence took a heavy toll of his time, as his successor discovered. But it is worth noting, as special evidence of Calvin's lifelong struggle against what the twentieth century calls the cult of personality, that neither he nor his successor was dispensed from routine pastoral work in order to fulfill these pan-European responsibilities.

NOTES

1. Here abbreviated *R.C.P.* See the fine appreciation by R. Stauffenegger in *Schweizerische Zeitschrift für Geschichte*, n.s. 15 (1965), pp. 98–106.
2. *C.O.*, XXI, col. 216; G. Fatio, *Céligny* (G., 1949), pp. 64, 69; P.-E. Martin, *Trois cas de pluralisme confessionel* (G., 1961), pp. 37–38.
3. Roget, *HPG*, I, pp. 114 ff, 123.
4. Williston Walker, *Jean Calvin*, trad. Weiss (G., 1909), pp. 308 f, 314 f.
5. *C.O.*, XXI, col. 332. See lists of Genevan pastors in H. Heyer, *L'Eglise de Genève, 1535–1909* (G., 1909), pp. 205–53. Some Genevan pastors served two or three rural parishes. This also seems to have been the case in the Bernese pays de Vaud, where 123 parishes were reduced to 70 in 1540, and gradually increased to 86 by 1574: see Robt. Centlivres, "Les premiers inventaires des paroisses vaudoises," in *Mélanges Charles Gilliard* (Lausanne, 1944), pp. 344–55.
6. I follow François Wendel, *Calvin: sources et evolution de sa pensée religieuse* (Paris, 1950), pp. 47–49. Compare the 1541 text in *R.C.P.*, I, pp. 12–13, with the pastors' interpretation of it in 1553 (*ibid.*, II, pp. 49–51), on the right to excommunicate and absolve.
7. *R.C.P.*, I, p. 82.
8. *Ibid.*, pp. 85, 89, 91, 102.
9. *Ibid.*, pp. 85, 89.
10. *Ibid.*, pp. 97, 98, 102, 103.
11. *Ibid.*, p. 131.
12. *R.C.P.*, II, p. 3.
13. *R.C.P.*, I, pp. 47, 56–57.
14. *Ibid.*, pp. 134, 144–48, 151–52.
15. *Ibid.*, pp. 58–61.
16. *R.C.P.*, II, p. 82.
17. *Ibid.*, p. 112.
18. *Geneva and the Coming of the Wars of Religion in France, 1555–1563* (G., 1956), pp. 14–53.

19. *Ibid.*, p. 31.
20. Chronological list in Kingdon, p. 145, to which the missions to points outside France (Piedmont, Antwerp, London) have been added; see *R.C.P.*, II, pp. 62, 64, 68, 69, 70, 74, 79, 84, 91.
21. See the recent and full treatment by Robert W. Henderson, *The Teaching Office in the Reformed Tradition* (Philadelphia, 1962).
22. AEG, Eglise de Genève, Reg. Cons. 1–20. Excerpts in *C.O.*, XXI, and in vols, II–VII of Roget, *HPG*. Oddly enough, we still lack a thorough study of the workings of the Consistory in Calvin's Geneva, based upon a full examination of these twenty volumes.
23. This interpretation follows principally J. T. McNeill, *The History and Character of Calvinism* (Oxford, 1954), pp. 162 ff, and Ernst Pfisterer, *Calvins Wirken in Genf*, 2 Aufl. (Neukirchen, 1957), pp. 101 ff.
24. Roget, *HPG*, III, pp. 120–21; V, pp. 101–02.
25. Good selection of such examples in Walker, *Jean Calvin*, p. 305.
26. *R.C.P.*, II, pp. 52, 59, 68.
27. *C.O.*, XXI, cols. 726–28; Roget, *HPG*, V, pp. 286–89.
28. See Léon Gautier, *L'Hôpital général de Genève de 1535 à 1545* (G., 1914). Accounts of the hôpitalliers for 1538–40 and after 1556 are in AEG, Arch. hôpitalliers, Fe 1–5 (through 1564). As in the case of Geneva's Consistory, we still lack a truly thorough monograph on this institution.
29. Accusation printed by J.-F. Bergier, "La démission du Trésorier Amblard Corne en 1544," in *Mélanges Paul-E. Martin* (G., 1961), pp. 458–59; Chautemps' defense is in AEG, P.H. 1663.
30. *R.C.P.*, I, pp. 17, 60, 132, 139; *C.O.*, XXI, col. 332.
31. See P. Imbart de la Tour, *Les Origines de la Réforme* (Paris, 1935), IV, pp. 423 ff; Roget, *HPG*, V, p. 274; VI, p. 156; Alain Dufour, *La guerre de 1589–1593* (G., 1958), pp. 24–25; P.-F. Geisendorf, *L'Université de Genève 1559–1959* (G., 1959), p. 34; Giorgio Peyrot, "Influenze franco-ginevrine nella formazione della disciplina ecclesiastiche valdesi alla metà del XVI sec.," in *Ginevra e l'Italia* (Florence, 1959), pp. 215 ff.
32. This is a good example of Geneva's application of the lessons of history. Compare Calvin's account of the rise of Papal power in the *Institutes*, IV, vii, and the pastors' subsequent decision in 1580 to change their moderators every week (*infra*, p. 212).
33. *R.C.P.*, II, pp. 102–03.
34. *R.C.P.*, I, p. 89; II, p. 87; *C.O.*, XXI, col. 396 n.

SIX

The Secular Arm

Calvin's Geneva was indeed a theocracy. This does not imply that she was governed by her clergy; it means rather that Geneva was in theory governed by God through a balance of spiritual and secular powers, through clergy and magistrates acting in harmony. In the sixteenth century, the intimate association of the ecclesiastical and the secular government of a community was generally assumed to be both natural and desirable. Furthermore, the sphere of secular government was almost without exception the wider of the two. Geneva scarcely constitutes an exception to this rule. The share of her Venerable Company of Pastors in the everyday government of the republic was far less than has often been assumed. To a twentieth-century mind, their role seems to have consisted in supplying certain moral checks and balances to the civil government, in tempering the harsh necessities of secular rule with the persuasions of conscience.

During the factional struggles that periodically disturbed Geneva before 1555, the pastors' task was to uphold moderation and to promote civic unity, except on a very few occasions when God's honor was involved. After 1555, they were required to play the role of loyal opposition, to criticize the secular arm, and to remind Geneva's rulers to heed their responsibilities more carefully than they sometimes did. The Company of Pastors made a constant effort to remain "outsiders" in Geneva, to preserve some degree of independence in thought and in action. Sometimes they collaborated with the magistrates, usually as junior partners; but often the secular arm of Calvin's Geneva acted alone. In this chapter we propose to examine the secular part of Calvin's Geneva, the workings of a fledgling government in one of Europe's smallest and newest independent cities.

†

The locus of effective power within the Republic of Geneva is easy to identify. It was the Small Council, a body of twenty-five men headed by the four chiefs of state or syndics, and including the republic's treasurer and two secretaries. It met at least three times each week in the *Maison de Ville* of the Upper City in order to transact the most important of Geneva's public business. The Small Council conducted all foreign affairs, pronounced and executed death sentences, ran the public mint, and in short exercised all the prerogatives of sovereignty. It was the administrative hub of Geneva as well, keeping its regulatory and supervisory eye upon a host of public activities ranging from craft regulation to street sanitation. Before this body came a stream of petitioners, ambassadors, messengers, accused criminals, and sometimes pastors — anybody with a complaint, a warning, or a favor to ask. The Small Council had to protect the people of Geneva against wars, plagues, and famines; it had to dispense justice in a surprisingly large number of civil cases as well as in criminal cases; and it had to supervise the conduct of a large number of ill-paid public officials. *Messieurs de Genève*, as sixteenth-century records call the Small Council, certainly worked very hard in order to keep their tiny state going.

Beneath the Small Council were the Two Hundred, who were assembled at least once a month in order to vote on important legislation, to grant pardon to convicted criminals if they saw fit, and to elect the members of the Small Council each February. Beneath them was the medieval commune, the general assembly of all male citizens, which was usually summoned twice each year: in order to elect the presiding judge of the civil court and fix the price of wine in November, and in order to elect the four syndics each January. Both assemblies had essentially legislative rather than administrative duties, and intervened only sporadically in the daily routine of public business. The Two Hundred and the general assembly did fulfill a democratic political function rarely found in sixteenth-century Europe, but their elections were generally prearranged affairs at which the popular will was powerfully, but indirectly, heard.

In other words, the Small Council was fairly safe from democratic turmoil despite the democratic constitutional structure of Geneva. Bonivard, describing how its members were chosen, noted in 1556 that "in normal times very few magistrates are removed from office unless they have committed some misdemeanor. If they have erred, Geneva usually does not wait until election time to punish them, but puts them immediately into prison."[1] Occasionally schemes were devised to promote a more rapid turnover among the membership of the Small Council. In 1536, a demand was voiced that any member who received as many as ten negative votes in the Two Hundred be deposed, but this was not adopted.[2] The scheme used by Perrin's followers to "pack" the Small Council with his supporters in 1553 has already been noted; this scheme seems to have been abandoned the next year, after it had served its purpose.[3] Basically, Bonivard was correct in stating that few magistrates were removed at elections. Apart from the two cases of 1540–41 and 1556–57, when defeated political factions were being purged, the turnover among Genevan magistrates was slight. Between Calvin's return in 1541 and his death in 1564, apart from the years mentioned above, only twenty-four new magistrates were sworn in, and fourteen of them replaced deceased incumbents.[4]

It is important to note that all magistrates in Calvin's Geneva were native-born, sons of men who had purchased the right of *bourgeoisie*. This had been an unwritten law ever since the Eidguenot revolution of 1526. This fact helps explain some of the antagonism and misunderstandings which separated them from the pastors, who were almost all immigrants from France. In Geneva, such immigrants could be and by 1559 were elected to all other offices, but the Small Council remained closed to them. This also meant that the governing class of Calvin's Geneva was recruited from the city's merchants rather than from the liberal professions, which were a virtual monopoly of the immigrants. It is even probable that none of the sixty-odd men who served on the Small Council during Calvin's lifetime held a university degree. Genevan magistrates were deep-rooted, hard-working, but unlettered men, who were incapable of maintaining a dialogue with their pastors and who often had the practical man's impatience with legal or theological subtleties.

If we examine the membership of the Small Council late in Calvin's career, in 1559, when the Academy was built and Calvin himself was finally made a Genevan *bourgeois,* we discover that the First Syndic was a practicing apothecary.[5] Two other Syndics were notaries, and the fourth, a wholesale merchant. Among the other magistrates were seven merchants, seven notaries, a lawyer, an architect, an artisan who made purses, and four men whose professions are difficult to discover. More than two-thirds were wholesale merchants or notaries, which was also the case when Calvin arrived, or ten years after his death.[6] None of them, so far as we can tell, was especially rich, at least not by the standards of an Italian banker or even a London goldsmith. None possessed a title of nobility, as five Genevan magistrates did in 1605.[7]

The Small Council of 1559 was largely a product of the anti-Perrinist purges. Eighteen of its members had been in office three years or less, and eight members would die or be removed from office in the next three years. Only four members had sons or brothers who would later become Syndics, and only four more had sons who would rise to the same dignity they held. In general, these men did not perpetuate themselves in office or start magisterial dynasties. In many ways, it is easier to discover what they were not than it is to venture positive judgments about them.

Perhaps the best way to shed light on the governing class of Calvin's Geneva is through a single example, for these men were much alike. Let us begin at the top, and examine Geneva's First Syndic in 1559, Henri Aubert. He was then serving his third term as Syndic, and would serve three more times before his death in 1576. Aubert was an elderly man, somewhere in his sixties.[8] He was still a practicing apothecary, to judge from his request in 1558 to remove the heads of two executed criminals from the public gibbet in order to anatomize them. Until his first election as Syndic, Aubert had served as the public apothecary, and he was still making *torches* for the state (at prices his colleagues thought too high) in 1564.[9] Clearly, Geneva's chief of state was still very much the active businessman, running his *boutique* with the aid of his son Jean, who undoubtedly helped him whenever the demands of public business or the illnesses of advanced age bothered him. Henri Aubert's shop was located on the *rues-basses,* in the Poissonnerie, in or near the home which he had purchased in 1544.[10]

He had acquired a modest bit of wealth by 1559. His father was probably poor, but Henri had made a good marriage in the early 1530's, claiming a handsome dowry of 200 écus and 800 Genevan florins. He purchased a few bits of land, sometimes as collateral for large sales of *espicerie* and medicine, but he was not sufficiently affluent to contribute to the huge ransom paid to Bern in 1536. During the next decade, Aubert's wealth increased, and he owned two small houses by 1550. Just before becoming First Syndic in 1559, Aubert acquired a large home, a stable, and several pieces of property by inheritance through his wife.[11] He seems to have made no further acquisitions. Aubert was probably paying the dowries of his three daughters by his second wife, all of whom married in the 1560's and 1570's, and setting up Jean in business; Henri paid him a sizable sum in 1560 (as the other children discovered after their father's death), since he was about to marry and buy a home.[12] We do not know how much property Aubert owned when he died. Probably he had two small houses in town and some scattered pieces of property outside the walls at Chalex and Sécheron. He was sufficiently affluent to hire a French pedagogue for his children,[13] but he was not really rich, especially if we compare him to the wealthiest French or Italian refugees.

Aubert had had long experience in Genevan government. He had first been named to the Council of Two Hundred in the memorable year 1536. He had served briefly on the Small Council in 1537, as a temporary replacement for a magistrate who had died in office. Aubert was then dropped from the Two Hundred in 1539 and 1540, while the *articulants* were in power, but he emerged suddenly in 1541 as a member of the Small Council, where he served continuously for thirty-five years.[14] Aubert's career as a Genevan magistrate involved him in a wide variety of administrative tasks, which was generally the case among such unspecialized rulers. In 1545 we find him, no doubt because of his professional knowledge of drugs and poisons, investigating the first serious outbreak of sorcery in post-Reformation Geneva. We find him as paymaster of the extensive work on Geneva's fortifications in 1547 — a task which proved to be a major headache to Aubert, who was still quarrelling with the republic's auditors in 1552, 1556, and 1557 about clearing his accounts in this business. He was himself named to the auditing board in 1557, but was discharged from it in 1560 because, he said, the work took too much of his time. He was named in 1572 to succeed a deceased colleague as supervisor of the mint.[15] A multitude of such tasks kept Aubert busy. He was a versatile magistrate — the list of his jobs given here does not begin to scratch the surface. He was never sent on a diplomatic mission, nor did he take a prominent part in the great trials of Bolsec or Servetus, but he was a respected colleague among *Messieurs de Genève*.

Aubert was deeply involved in Geneva's factional quarrels. During the famous riot of May 16, 1555, Ami Perrin had seized the silver-tipped Syndic's baton from him to wave before the crowd, on the grounds that Aubert was too short to be seen, which the latter of course vigorously denied. There was considerable ill-will between Aubert and Perrin's clique; Perrin's terrible-tempered wife publicly described Aubert shortly after this riot as "beau buttecul et soufflecul de scindiquat, tenturier de barbes qui les faysoit noyres."[16] François-Daniel Berthelier, one of the four executed *Enfants de Genève*, described him as "a little apothecary who'd never done much and to whom nobody ever paid any attention."[17] If Aubert had taken only verbal abuse, he would have been fortunate. But he probably took some physical abuse as well, if Bonivard was correct, in that same May 15 riot.[18]

[Aubert] commanded them to go home, since the nine o'clock curfew had passed. Balthasar Sept, who was an Auditor of Justice and who was with this band of rioters, said that they would not retire and even commanded the night watch to go home. The watch replied that he had no authority to command them, since they served a higher office than he did. A great storm of verbiage arose. The Syndic [Aubert] then commanded them as the watch had done, but they paid him no attention either. While this argument continued, the candle was extinguished three times and re-lit three times; when it was extinguished, the Syndic received several good fisticuffs in his stomach.

All in the line of duty, of course. The dignity of Genevan rulers was still a somewhat fragile thing, not yet reinforced by Calvin's delineation of the duties and rights of magistrates in his *Institutes.*

                     †

If we shift our attention from who they were to what they did, we find that the magistrates of Calvin's Geneva engaged in a wide range of activities. Probably the most important of these, as for any responsible sixteenth-century government, was the dispensation of quick and cheap justice. Nearly half of the public offices allotted by the Small Council and the Two Hundred in their annual *conseil des offices* each February were judicial offices.[19]

Complete control over both civil and criminal justice had been a critical issue during Geneva's revolution in the 1520's. The struggle had been ended by an edict of November 1529 which created a new civil court, judged by a Lieutenant of Justice who was assisted by four Auditors. They were "responsible for the summary execution of justice . . . according to their consciences, tempering the law with equity, without regard to the estate or condition of the people involved . . . and without taking bribes or any other sinister machinations."[20] The Lieutenant's court, like the Small Council, was to meet three times each week, and to deliver all its judgments within eight days. Appeals from cases involving large sums of money could be made to the Small Council. During Calvin's lifetime, the Lieutenant's court grew in prestige. The chief civil judge was a personage only slightly inferior to the Syndics, and he carried the same staff of office as they did: a black baton with the republic's coat of arms engraved on both sides. It is noteworthy that the *grabeau* system of private and mutual criticism, which had previously been extended from the pastors to the Small Council in 1558, was also adopted by the Lieutenant's court in 1563.

Basically, the Lieutenant's court handled Genevan civil justice while the Small Council, with a few extra men, had cognizance of criminal cases. While we have a good knowledge of the structure and ceremonial of the former court, we have very little information on how it actually operated. There are 1859 *procès criminels* conserved in Geneva's archives for the period 1536–1564, but there is only one register from the Lieutenant's court for the same period.[21] Perhaps many of the cases brought before the Lieutenant in these early years were simple and petty, and it is possible that some of its sentences were oral rather than written.

Representing the public interest in the Lieutenant's court was the *procureur général* of the republic. This office had been created in 1534 to investigate the city's particular interest in any case being tried before civil courts inside or outside Geneva. The Genevan *procureur* was entrusted with multiple responsibilities. He named guardians for Genevan public wards. He, together with the public treasurer, was responsible for the collection of public debts. Sometimes he administered confiscated property. Generally, he acted as legal watchdog. In skillful hands, this position (which was forbidden to members of the Small Council) might serve as a kind of popular tribune, and the Small Council occasionally observed that the *procureur* interfered too much in matters which were not his proper concern. The job was lucrative — an edict of 1554 granted this official one-fourth of all fines levied in the Lieutenant's court — and it was coveted by such ambitious and avaricious Genevans as Perrin's chief aide, Pierre Vandel.[22]

Neither the Lieutenant's court nor the Small Council was a court of last appeal. After 1541, the republic established a review court for civil cases, composed of twelve judges drawn equally from the Small Council, the Sixty, and the Two Hundred. It met monthly and sat until all cases brought before it had been decided. Appeals in criminal cases might be brought before the Two Hundred, who were invested with the right of pardon for Genevan citizens and foreigners alike. But the right of appeal in Geneva definitely stopped at these two points. The republic was extremely severe towards anyone who tried to appeal a decision from a Genevan court to a foreign jurisdiction. The offender was likely to have all his Genevan property confiscated and to be permanently banished, according to a law passed by the *articulants* in 1539 and first invoked against them in 1541.

The rough edifice of Genevan justice was first comprehensively organized in a code of fifty-one articles passed by the councils in the early 1540's. Calvin, who also prepared the republic's ecclesiastical and political codes in the same period, here had an opportunity to utilize his legal training in Bourges under Pierre de l'Estoile.[23] Calvin seems to have proceeded with considerable caution. He apparently made few changes in Geneva's customs, which were based upon the episcopal charter of 1387. Except where he had to weed out some of the impractical features of canon law, such as the prohibition of interest (never enforced at Geneva anyway), Calvin seems only to have pruned the law in order to bring it into harmony with current conditions. He made no attempt to increase the punishments prescribed by canon law or by Genevan tradition. His intention was rather to make punishment *less* severe, while attempting to ensure that all men were equal before the law and that the laws were actually enforced. Changes in the letter of the law were therefore slight; those that were made served to bring Genevan law into closer *rapprochement* with French practice. Calvin's code lasted twenty-five years, and served as the base for the comprehensive Genevan law code of 1568, which was drawn up by his good friend Germain Colladon. This code fills fifty-six large pages in the *Sources du droit du Canton de Genève,* and it remained the foundation of Genevan public law until the end of the republic. Colladon made Genevan law nearly identical with current French practice, especially with the customs of the Duchy of Berry. In the sphere of written law, as in language and many other fields, Calvin's Geneva was slowly and almost imperceptibly changing from a Savoyard capital to a French provincial town.

Thus far we have examined only the outer shell of Genevan justice. It is more interesting to examine justice in action, to see its inner spirit. Here it is worth repeating at the outset that the peculiarity of Genevan justice lay in the fact that the extant laws were fully enforced. Many accounts of Calvin's Geneva, wishing to illustrate the unbelievable severity of her justice, point to a five-year span in which 58 people were executed and 76 banished.[24] Yet all the crimes for which capital sentence was pronounced were also punishable by death in the famous *Con-*

stitutio Criminalis Carolina promulgated earlier in the reign of Charles V by the Diet of Regensburg in 1532. Thirty-eight of Geneva's executions were for witchcraft or for spreading the plague, which the *Carolina* punished with hideous tortures and executions. Among those banished, 27 were tainted with sorcery or with spreading the plague, and 53 were foreigners; banishing foreigners was among the commonest tactics of any European government in this age. No one was ever executed in Geneva for blasphemy (not even Gruet), or for disobedience to his parents — though many historians have said the contrary, and though the laws of Charles V did permit capital punishment for certain forms of blasphemy. Except for those Genevan rural subjects put to death for malign sorcery (45 in 1545 and 12 in 1562), the total number of recorded executions in Calvin's Geneva amounted to 89 for sixteen years (1542–46, 1548–50, 1557–64), or an average of less than six per year. Even with sorcery cases included, Geneva averaged fewer than ten executions per year. It is difficult to say if this is above average for city states of Geneva's size, since the data for a comparative study appear to be lacking in Bern or Zurich or in some of the Imperial Free Cities.[25] The only certain conclusion is that Geneva executed nobody for reasons which sixteenth-century Imperial law (to which Geneva may or may not have been subject) would have considered unusual.

Genevan justice made remarkable efforts to judge cases carefully, yet rapidly. The idea that the judicial process needed speeding up, that lawyers delayed cases for their own purposes in order to benefit the richer and more patient party, was something of a cliché in sixteenth-century Europe. Energetic monarchs occasionally took steps to abbreviate the judicial process; in the territories around Geneva, both the Senate of Savoy and the *Parlement* of Franche-Comté were reformed for this purpose in the 1560's and 1570's.[26] *Messieurs de Genève* also passed lengthy codes for the abbreviation of justice in 1546, 1556, 1574, and 1584.[27] The unusual thing about Geneva's reforms is that they worked. Cases really were expedited quickly, without "superflous proofs and procedures;" the Lieutenant's court passed sentence in over a hundred cases per month by 1600, and the government of Bern complained several times that Geneva judged her criminal cases too quickly. (One such complaint came in 1566, when a Bernese messenger requesting pardon for a condemned man arrived immediately after the execution.)

Geneva also had little trouble with *venalité des offices,* the sale of judicial posts, which was an increasingly common plague in sixteenth-century states. In theory, everybody vigorously condemned the sale of judicial office (ancient writers had strongly opposed it), but in practice many vigorously pursued it. Results were sometimes comic; in France, a judge who had legally purchased his office under Henri IV was required by oath to swear that he had not purchased his office. The Republic of Geneva was in a special quandry, since the dictates of republican virtue and the concept of office as a *charge,* a duty to serve the commonwealth and not a means of private enrichment, here collided violently with the demands of an empty public treasury. Geneva's solution, in 1552, was to sell judicial secretariats, but never judgeships—and to sell them only for a fixed price to men who had already been elected through traditional channels.[28] (When Geneva resumed the sale of legal secretariats in the 1590's, these posts were sold at public auction and then the high bidder was confirmed by the Two Hundred.) Geneva's solution avoided the blatant hypocrisy of some of her neighbors; and she saved the essentials by avoiding the sale of judgeships, while permitting that of lesser offices.

So far as our fragmentary evidence goes, it seems likely that Geneva enforced her laws with commendable impartiality, well above European norms. Before the final triumph of Calvin's supporters in 1555, some accusations of judicial bribery were made against Perrin and Vandel by the not always reliable Bonivard and his secretary Froment.[29] Such charges probably contain the proverbial grain of truth. But generally Genevan judges did precisely what the 1529 edict had demanded of them: "the summary execution of justice . . . tempering the law with equity, without regard to the estates or conditions of the persons involved." A Council of Sixty, unfriendly towards Calvin, ordered Perrin imprisoned on September 20, 1545, "so that justice will be done to the great as well as to the small." The Council of Two Hundred on February 5, 1556, objected to a Syndic's being judged by his brother and ordered that "the Small Council may not have one law for the great and another for the small."[30] Both were voicing a commonplace Genevan opinion. Genevan judges handled their tasks with commendable skill and with a minimum of delays. Justice was done by amateurs and some- times a little too quickly for the fastidious Bernese, but it was generally done. Perhaps the most eloquent commentary on Genevan justice came from its most famous victim, Michael Servetus, who at one point in his trial was asked whether he preferred to be tried in Geneva or be sent back to France. Servetus fell on his knees and implored *Messieurs* to be tried in Geneva.

✝

Next to the prompt and equitable distribution of justice, per- haps the most important responsibility of a sixteenth-century state was to remain solvent. The problem of raising enough revenue to meet their annual expenditure was an especially critical one to *Messieurs,* whose state lacked wealthy clergy, prosperous merchant-bankers, or other easy sources of ready money. Balancing the Genevan budget was a difficult task each year, and financial problems took up a large part of the govern- ment's time and energy.

The financial structure of Calvin's Geneva was very simple. The republic's treasurer, her chief fiscal official, was elected for a three-year term by the general citizen assembly in November, together with the Lieutenant of Justice. The Small Council con- trolled the treasurer through a four- or five-man board of audit, the *Chambre des Comptes,* which was drawn entirely from their own membership. This board had been started in 1538 in order to check the books of Claude Pertemps, a follower of Farel who had served as treasurer during the hectic years 1535 and 1536.[31] It rapidly became a financial clearinghouse for the Re- public of Geneva. It countersigned all *mandements* by which Geneva paid her public debts, and it checked the accounts of all men who handled public moneys: ambassadors, granary supervisors, and fortress engineers, in addition to the official treasurer. This board of audit, which lasted until 1798, met four times each week (as often as the Small Council) and sitting on it was an onerous and ill-paid task, as Henri Aubert had complained to his colleagues in 1560.

Like civil justice, public finance in Geneva had been radically expanded in consequence of the Genevan revolutions. The new city-state had succeeded to all the revenues of her predecessor, the Prince-Bishop and his cathedral chapter. She immediately began to track down all the ancient sources of revenue, the tithes and tolls and annuities, and to collect them herself. Geneva was "secularized" with a vengeance in 1536, and one immediate result was an astronomical increase in municipal revenues. The Republic of Geneva collected all the old "Papist" taxes and used them to pay the Reformed clergy, reaping a handsome annual profit in the bargain. Calvin's annual income was far below that of a well-bred cathedral canon. The Reformed Church of Geneva operated fewer rural churches than had the old regime, and the new *hôpital général* was more economical than the network of quasireligious foundations which had been scattered over pre-Reformation Geneva. For example, in 1544 the Republic of Geneva spent 4000 florins on her ministers and 1500 on the *hôpital*, but took in almost 12,000 florins from tithes and other taxes levied on her rural parishes alone.[32] Secularization was profitable in Geneva, as in many other European states from the tiniest German principality to Henry VIII's England. Of course, Geneva's situation would be modified after 1559 when the foundation of Calvin's Academy added a large annual charge to the budget which could not be balanced by a corresponding increase in revenue.

The ways in which the new republic collected her public revenues left much to be desired.[33] Once, in 1544, Geneva's treasurer publicly denounced the way these taxes were being collected by her revenue farmers or *amoditaires*. The system was hopelessly confused, he said; public taxes were not properly registered and were invariably "paid late and with lots of grumbling." The situation was all the more scandalous because several tax farmers were magistrates or close relatives of magistrates, and these men were among the principal offenders. The Two Hundred passed edicts in 1546 and 1551 which forbade magistrates to collect taxes, but this reform was imperfectly observed. The largest Genevan tax, the *gabelle* on wine, was

GENEVAN BUDGETS, 1536-1566

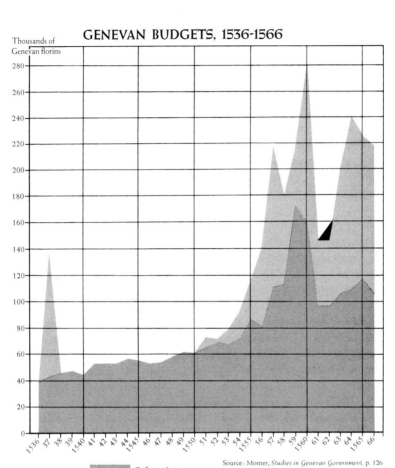

Thousands of Genevan florins

Trésor ordinaire

Trésor de l'Arche

Trésor de guerre

Source: Monter, *Studies in Genevan Government*, p. 126

These budgets (like the official wine prices tabulated in Graph #2) are expressed in Genevan florins, which was a "money of account" rather than a coinage. The value of this "money of account" relative to a stable and undebased coin, the *écu-sol* of Savoy, inflated by exactly 50% between the beginning of the Genevan Revolution in 1526 and the period immediately after Calvin's death. An *écu-sol* was worth 44 Genevan sous (3⅔ florins) in 1526; it was worth 55 Genevan sous from 1536 through 1549; and it was worth 66 Genevan sous (5½ florins) in 1568. (See J.-F. Bergier, *Genève et l'écon. européene de la Renaissance*, pp. 439-40, for an exact table of yearly equivalents.)

farmed in 1552 by a magistrate's son, whose father was his guarantor and actually made the payments to the treasurer.

The slow payment of public debts about which the treasurer complained in 1544 was probably inherent in Geneva's economy. Private debts were paid no more quickly. But the sizable arrears owing to the public treasury remained a public scandal, which was only attacked systematically after the overthrow of Perrin in 1555. Then, a special list of back debts was drawn up, and great pressure was put on the chief offenders (several of them members of the Small Council) to clear their accounts with the treasury. By 1560, those who had not settled these debts were threatened with prison, and *Messieurs* seized the estate of an important *amoditaire* (Jean Philippe's son) in order to liquidate his debt to them. A general code governing *amodiations* was finally passed in 1559. It standardized dates and durations of all public revenues to be auctioned, demanded a single annual payment, and repeatedly insisted that all *amoditaires* be solvent and free of back debts to the treasury. This code, like many other pieces of sixteenth-century legislation, was a counsel of perfection. Seven months after passing it, Geneva's rulers awarded their second largest tax, the *gabelle* on meat, to their largest debtor. They had briefly debated the question in council, but after all he was the high bidder.

While the republic attempted to remove her magistrates from tax farming and to collect back debts in the 1550's, she was also inaugurating a second and secret public treasury. *L'Arche pour se debasler,* reads the title printed on the cover of this privy purse for the years 1551–1568, and it was precisely that: a special account expressly intended to pay off Geneva's onerous foreign debt, principally in Basel.[34] Interest on this debt was the single largest item in the budgets of Calvin's Geneva, amounting to one-fifth or more of her annual income. The secret treasury for "de-Baselling" paid Geneva's interest regularly and even repaid a little of the principal in 1557 and 1558. Like many another secret treasury, the *Arche* soon began paying other expenses as well: diplomatic missions, improvements to fortifications, or public purchases of grain. For anyone who seeks to trace the growth of oligarchy in Calvin's Geneva, and who recognizes the importance of finance to a sixteenth-century state, the

Arche is an institution of the first magnitude. During Calvin's lifetime, however, its importance was less than that of the public treasury.

Genevan public finance, like Genevan justice, was handled fairly successfully by her mercantile magistrates. Corruption existed in both spheres, but it was relatively infrequent, and serious efforts were made to abolish it altogether in the 1550's. Geneva was not an especially rich city, particularly not before the arrival of religious refugees in the 1550's, but she was both financially and judicially autonomous, and her rulers asked for nothing more.

Genevan magistrates had a great many matters other than justice and finance to occupy them. One of these was the public regulation of trade and industry, a function that had been unknown under the Prince-Bishop. Like her downstream neighbor on the Rhone, Lyon, but unlike her powerful ally Bern, Geneva had no craft guilds in the early sixteenth century. And like Lyon, Calvin's Geneva organized only a very few professions before the 1580's. Lyon organized her jewellers, locksmiths, and medical professions under public supervision, while Geneva organized her printers (1560), jewellers and goldsmiths (1566), and her medical professions (1569). The main difference between these lists is Geneva's emphasis on her printing industry, which had become her first and only export trade. Public regulation of this craft had been suggested as early as August 1559 by two pastors, Beza and Des Gallars: "because of the disorders and divisions among the printers, particularly between masters and apprentices, it would be proper for *Messieurs* to create a committee and summon the master printers, who shall declare the order to be established in order to avoid future misunderstandings. Afterwards the journeymen should similarly be heard in their grievances." Within six months, the relevant edicts were drawn up. They showed a strong concern for social justice and represent a moderate approach to relations between master and employee. The preamble provided that a three-man committee, including one magistrate and one minister, should enforce this code by a semiannual inspection of every printer's shop in Geneva.[35] Even in craft regulations, the principle of cooperation between magistrates and clergy was unswervingly followed.

GENEVAN WINE PRICES, 1539-1568

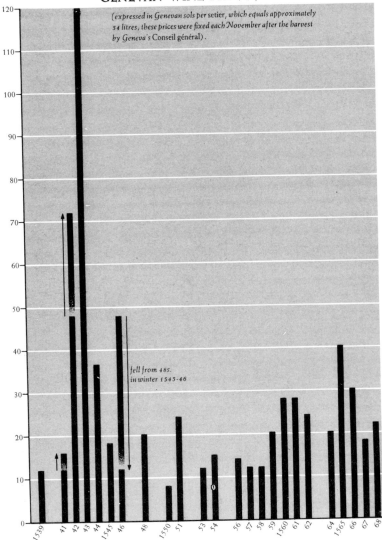

(expressed in Genevan sols per setier, which equals approximately 54 litres, these prices were fixed each November after the harvest by Geneva's Conseil général).

fell from 48s. in winter 1545-46

Prices printed by J.-F. Bergier, *Genève et l'écon. européene de la Renaissance*, pp. 119-20. The especially high prices between 1542 and 1546 were caused by the presence of plague in Geneva as well as by mediocre harvests.

160

Like Lyon, Geneva organized her goldsmiths and jewellers because their activities touched closely upon the public coinage.[36] She organized and supervised her medical professions during the great plague of 1568–1570.[37] Efforts had been made to organize both these professions since 1557, but during Calvin's lifetime Geneva never tried to establish a comprehensive network of craft guilds covering all the city's important trades. The outlines of such a system began to appear after 1580, as nine guilds were set up in the last two decades of the sixteenth century. Basically, Calvin's Geneva remained a city without guilds.

†

If we examine the evolution of the ruling class in Calvin's Geneva from 1536 to 1564, where are the most striking changes? Not in their external qualities, for Geneva was throughout this period governed by amateur magistrates who did not form a professional caste nor have a liberal education. They were simple and straightforward men, capable of few subtleties. But a radical change had come over the secular arm of Geneva in her first generation of independence insofar as her style of government is concerned. It was an abrupt change from the freewheeling attitudes of Jean-Ami Curtet, Lieutenant of Justice in 1536, imprisoned on bread and water for three days for keeping a concubine, but nevertheless elected First Syndic next February; from ex-Syndic Jean Goulaz, then *procureur* or state's attorney, arrested in 1541 for gambling and unspecified "insolences" at the public baths; from Antoine Gerbel, fined heavily and suspended from the magistracy in 1545 for seducing his maid; from Jean Philippin, Syndic in charge of the Consistory four years before, reprimanded by the Consistory in 1548 because he hadn't been to communion in seven years, who responded that he cared no more for their excommunication than for the Pope's.[38]

New styles of behavior prevailed by the time that the Small Council of 1558 (which included Curtet among its members) assembled for the first time to adopt the pastors' system of mutual criticism, the *grabeau*. "With love and charity," read the minutes, "each and every one was censured, from the highest to the lowest, revealing every man's imperfections and vices. May the Lord give us all the power to profit by it!"[39]

It was just as abrupt a change from the traditional Genevan elections, which were tumultuous affairs giving full scope to the questionable talents of factional chiefs such as Jean Philippe's manager, Jean Lullin, who "was wont to prepare entire slates of offices as though they were his to be given" after a series of public banquets and private deals at his tavern.[40] These were replaced by quiet, predestined elections that opened with a speech by a minister, followed by a public prayer read by the republic's secretary. By 1562, these elections had become so dull that the government had to make public cries against citizens who refused to cast their votes;[41] previously, the usual complaint had been that unqualified men were casting votes.

Sometime during Calvin's residence in Geneva, most noticeably after 1555, these men had evolved from carefree demagogues into the grave and painfully honest stereotype of Calvin's ideal magistrate. Their serious descendants governed the Republic for the rest of its long life.

Notes

1. *Ancienne et nouvelle police* (G., 1865), p. 26.
2. *R.C.*, XIII, p. 436.
3. *Supra*, p. 82 f. In 1554, not a single new man was named to the Small Council.
4. Lists of magistrates, by years, appended to Roget, *HPG*, II, pp. 331–34; III, pp. 315–18; IV, pp. 339–40.
5. Information on them compiled from a variety of sources in AEG, such as the corrected copy of Galiffe's *Notices généalogiques,* the biographical dictionary of L. Sordet, and the analysis of notarial records compiled by L. Dufour-Vernes in eight volumes for the period 1536–1700.
6. Compare *Studies,* pp. 91–92, 101–02.
7. *Ibid.,* pp. 95–96.
8. AEG, État-civil, Morts, XII, fol. 142: "X^{bris} 1576 . . . [H.A.] agée entre 80 et 90 ans."
9. AEG, R.C., t. 54, fol. 106; t. 43, fol. 41; t. 59, fol. 112^v.
10. AEG, Notaire Michel Try, V, fols. 69^v–71.
11. Notaire Jean du Verney, VII, fols. 47–48; Not. Claude de Compois, IX, fols. 229–30; X, #t; XII, #q, Ba; Not. Théo. de la Corbière, I, fols. 245–48, 267–70; Not. Michel Try, VI, fols. 59–60; R.C., t. 55, fols. 103^v,

112; t. 54, fols. 297^v, 310, 312; Fin. M 26, fol. 30^v; M 30, fols. 5^v, 94; M 35, fol. 79; M 36, fol. 6. Judging from the *lods* (inheritance tax of one-eighth), Aubert acquired about fifteen hundred florins' worth of property in 1558.

12. Not. B. Neyrod, II, fols. 81–82; Not. Pierre de la Rue, VII, fols. 124 f; XII, fol. 32^v; Not. Michel Dupuis, IV, fol. 10f; R.C. pour des particuliers, t. 19 (Feb. 1577), fols. 92, 93^v.

13. *C.O.*, XXI, col. 736.

14. *R.C.*, XIII, pp. 455, 482; R.C., t. 31, fol. 78; t. 35, fol. 26.

15. R.C., t. 42, *passim;* t. 46, fol. 294; t. 50, fols. 97^v, 99; t. 52, fols. 44^v, 80^v, 243; t. 53, fol. 26^v, 6; t. 67, fol. 118; t. 56, fol. 3.

16. J.-A. Gautier, *Histoire de Genève* (G., 1894 ff), III, p. 618 n. This same phrase about Aubert's dying beards black reappears in the anonymous note found outside the city on Sept. 23, 1555: *C.O.* XV, col. 790.

17. Roget, *HPG*, IV, pp. 316–17.

18. *Ancienne et nouvelle police*, p. 138.

19. Six of ten offices allotted in 1556, for example: R.C., t. 51, fols. 6–9^v; compare *Studies*, pp. 59–69.

20. *Sources du droit*, #635.

21. AEG, Jur. Civ. A 1 (summer 1561). Records of this court are complete only after 1593. The *procès criminels* are not complete either, since in 1553 council minutes state that 79 such *procès* had been handled in the previous year, while surviving records show only 41.

22. *Studies*, pp. 63–64.

23. Josef Bohatec, "Calvin et le code civil à Genève," in *Revue hist. du droit français et étranger*, 4e sér., 17 (1938), pp. 229–303; also Ernst Pfisterer, *Calvins Wirken in Genf* (Neukirchen, 1957), pp. 29–63, esp. 60 ff.

24. Pfisterer, *Calvins Wirken in Genf*, pp. 46–53.

25. The diary of Nürnburg's hangman from 1577 to 1617 shows a total of 361 public executions, or nine per year. For other figures, see J. Janssen, *History of the German People after the Close of the Middle Ages*, rev. by L. Pastor, transl. Middlemore (London, 1910), XVI, pp. 160–68.

26. See L. Chevallier, *Essai sur le souverain Sénat de Savoie* (Annecy, 1953), p. 22; and L. Febvre, *Philippe II et la Franche-Comte* (Paris, 1912), pp. 613 f, 617, 643 ff, 740 ff.

27. *Sources du droit*, #834, 935, 997, 1130, 1148, 1163, 1232, 1235, 1250.

28. *Sources du droit*, #883. By 1562, Geneva was selling six legal secretariats for a total of 190 écus (over half of it for the Lieutenant's court), or about 1% of the republic's total budget: see Fin. S 12.

29. Bonivard, *Ancienne et nouvelle police*, p. 90 f; Froment quoted by André Biéler, *La pensée économique et sociale de Calvin* (G., 1959), p. 112.

30. H. Fazy, "Procédures et documents du XVIe siècle: Favre et le Consistoire," in *MIG*, 16 (1886), p. 26; Pfisterer, *Calvins Wirken in Genf*, p. 55.

31. J.-F. Bergier, "La démission du Trésorier Amblard Corne en 1544," in

Mélanges Paul-E. Martin (G., 1961), pp. 449–51. Records of this board exist only after 1594: AEG, Fin. A.

32. *Studies*, pp. 18–19. Compare Feller, *Geschichte Berns*, II, pp. 314–21, on the profits of secularization in a nearby state.

33. *Studies*, pp. 20–22, 123–25. Compare the even worse situation in Lyon: R. Doucet, *Credit public et finances municipales à Lyon au XVIᵉ siècle* (Lyon, 1937).

34. *Studies*, pp. 22–23; Roget, *HPG*, III, p. 211 n. 1.

35. Paul Chaix, *Recherches sur l'imprimerie à Genève de 1550 à 1564* (G., 1954), pp. 18–26, 30–33.

36. Antony Babel, *Histoire corporative de l'horlogerie, de l'orfèvrerie et des industries annexes* (G., 1916), pp. 11, 14–19.

37. Léon Gautier, "La médecine à Genève jusqu'au début du XVIIIᵉ siècle," in *MDG*, 30 (1906), pp. 13, 26 f, 107–11, 137–87.

38. Roget, *HPG*, I, pp. 6, 24 f; II, p. 183; III, p. 43 (compare *C.O.*, XXI, col. 329).

39. Roget, *HPG*, V, pp. 116–18.

40. *Studies*, pp. 104–05.

41. Roget, *HPG*, V, pp. 283 f; VI, p. 197.

SEVEN

The Refugee Colonies

In November 1557, the Small Council decided that Geneva needed to be put in a state of military preparedness, and accordingly ordered all the city's inhabitants to assemble for a full-dress military review; but they immediately rescinded this order, because the number of foreigners in Geneva was greater than the number of citizens, and such an assembly might give these immigrants cause for excessive pride.[1] This episode provides a small illustration of the important fact that Calvin's Geneva was populated by several thousand refugees of several different nationalities. Sixteenth-century specialists have known this for a long time, but the precise dimensions of this immigration have only begun to emerge since 1957, when Paul-F. Geisendorf published a critical edition of Geneva's *Livre des Habitants* covering the period from 1549 to January 1560.[2] As a registry of foreign residents in Calvin's Geneva, this is obviously incomplete. It omits the scattered early arrivals, mostly priests from France or Italy, whose appearance began to be noted by Genevan chroniclers in 1542, and it also omits the continuing arrivals from France and Italy in the 1560's. But it seems likely that the currents of emigration reached their peak in the 1550's, which is precisely the decade covered by the *Livre des Habitants*. Certainly the very size of this book provides eloquent proof of the numerical strength of this emigration to Calvin's city. It contains more than 5000 entries for its eleven years, which amounts to a tremendous influx into a city whose total population when Calvin came was scarcely 10,000.

Furthermore, the *Livre des Habitants* is incomplete, even for the 1550's. Scattered indications point towards the conclusion that this official register includes about two-thirds, possibly even less, of the total immigration into Geneva. For example, only 8 of the 14 religious refugees recruited in 1556 for the new French colony in Brazil appear in it, though all 14 were then residing in Geneva.[3] About half (43 of 88, by my count) of the Genevan-trained pastors sent to France between 1555 and 1562 can be found in it.[4] The number of immigrant printers and booksellers in Geneva between 1550 and 1559 provides a better example: though only 113 of these 5000 men gave his occupation as printer or bookseller, a careful search of other records has turned up an additional 97 men exercising these professions in Geneva in the 1550's; 39 of them do not appear in the *Livre des Habitants,* while 58 appear there without indicating their profession.[5] None of the famous Genevan printers registered his occupation—neither Conrad Badius, Robert Estienne, Jean Crespin, nor Eustache Vignon.

The *Livre des Habitants* is no more complete so far as "exotic" refugees (those from areas not linguistically French) are concerned. The following table provides a few specific illustrations on this point:[6]

Region	L.H. entries	Total adult men	Dependents
England (1555–59)	86	126	79
Italy (1550–53)	11	38	29
Italy (1554–1555)	38	88	132
Italy (1556–1557)	85	120	89
Italy (1558–1559)	89	135	39

As the third column amply demonstrates, the *Livre des Habitants* falls well short of providing total statistics on immigration because it does not include dependents (wives, children, servants, or close relatives). Although the great majority among its 5000 names were probably bachelors, it is certain that not all of them were. Some of the wealthier and more prominent refugees brought along a great train of dependents. Printer Robert Estienne was preceded by his business agent and accompanied by five sons and a daughter. The widow of the great humanist

Guillaume Budé led three sons and two daughters to Geneva in 1549. Lyon publisher Antoine Vincent (whose name does not appear in the *Livre des Habitants*) brought his whole household in 1559: wife, six children, widowed sister, and nephew. Some of the Marian exiles from England also brought their households. Merchant John Bodley brought his wife, three sons, a daughter, a maid, and two apprentices. Sir William Stafford brought his wife, sister, cousin, son, daughter, and four servants.[7]

A few other pieces of evidence will serve to qualify these conclusions. The most prominent of all these refugees, the Neapolitan marquis Galeazzo Caracciolo, arrived in 1551 accompanied by a single valet, whereas a humble silk-dyer from Verona named Giovanni Pietro Clerici arrived in 1557 with a wife and no fewer than nine children.[8] Such piecemeal indications cannot furnish us with a definitive guide to the question of refugee families, but they do suggest that we should add more than a thousand dependents to the official list, at the very least, in order to approximate the total number of immigrants to Geneva in the 1550's.

It is also worth remembering that in any attempt to calculate the total number of refugees in Calvin's Geneva at any given moment, there are reasons to subtract names from the *Livre des Habitants* as well as to add them. Many refugees did not stay long in Geneva. The city was desperately overcrowded, its economic opportunities were limited, and in some cases the religious climate was unsatisfactory. The government of Geneva expelled some of these newcomers late in 1557 for bigamy, dissolute living, vagrancy, or Anabaptism.[9] Many printers and booksellers returned to their original homes in Lyon after a few years, because it was impossible for them to earn a decent living in Geneva.[10] A "fairly large trickle" of men also went off to fight in the Huguenot armies in the spring of 1562, when the Wars of Religion broke out.[11]

The non-French refugees also left Geneva in fairly large numbers. The English colony began to drift back home immediately after Elizabeth's accession to the throne in 1559, and, after its leaders saw their famous English Bible through Genevan presses in May 1560, the Small Council granted them a general farewell.[12] Geneva's small Spanish colony was decimated in 1561

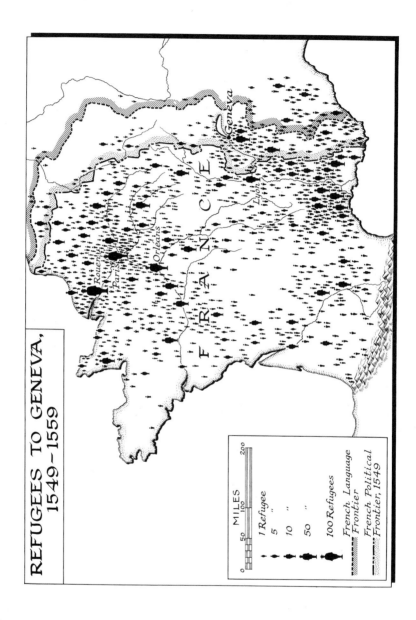

REFUGEES TO GENEVA,
1549–1559

MILES
0   50   100   200

→   1 Refugee
⊷   5   "
⊶   10   "
♦   50   "
♦   100 Refugees

▨▨▨ French Language
     Frontier
░░░ French Political
     Frontier, 1549

when some of its leaders went off to England or Flanders, and the separate Spanish church had to be shut down. Even the Italian colony, which preserved its special church in Geneva until the nineteenth century, suffered from attrition. Individual radicals, disturbed by the burning of Servetus, began leaving Geneva after an anti-Trinitarian scandal broke out in their church in 1558. Mistrust for the iron regime of Calvin led some of them, such as the Sicilian poet and gentleman Giulio Cesare Pascale, to seek a more liberal climate at Basel or points farther east.[13] We do not know how many imitated his example; those who left were less important quantitatively than qualitatively.

The register of Genevan citizenship, or *Livre des Bourgeois,* provides some illuminating information on the depth of these refugees' roots in Calvin's city. Until the defeat of Perrin in 1555, there had been a decided antipathy against admitting these newcomers to citizenship. That year, however, this policy was dramatically reversed, and Geneva began granting citizenship to most refugees who wanted it. By January 1560, they were even trying to force some "rich Italians and other merchants," who had not yet done so, to purchase Genevan *bourgeoisie.*[14] In all, Geneva created 341 new *bourgeois* between 1555 and 1557 (only 50 less than in the preceding eighteen years), and 303 new *bourgeois* between 1558 and 1565.[15] But, when we consider that Geneva probably received at least 7000 immigrants between 1550 and 1562, this is not a very impressive total. It seems clear that only a small minority of these religious refugees ever received Genevan citizenship.

After these speculations about the exact numerical size and Genevan attachments of these refugees, we should once more recognize that, by and large, the official register gives an excellent cross-section of Geneva's new residents. If studied carefully, the *Livre des Habitants* brings out some interesting facts about the special characteristics and qualities of these refugees. Probably the first point that strikes the observer is the sharp distinction between the quality of the earlier refugees and the quantity of the later ones.

Glancing over the first dozen pages of the printed edition, covering the period through August 1551, one encounters an interesting array of names: Laurent de Normandie, Calvin's fellow-townsman and the most important of Geneva's book-sellers; wineseller Didier Rousseau, an ancestor of Jean-Jacques; Philippe de Corguilleray, Burgundian nobleman, later leader of the Genevan contingent to France's colony in Brazil in 1556; five of Calvin's fellow-townsmen, all ordinary artisans; the second son of France's most famous sixteenth-century humanist, *noble Jean Budé, natifz de la ville de Paris, filz de messire Guillaume Budé, conseiller et maistre des Requestes ordinaires de la maison du Roy de France;* the widow of a member of the king's *grand conseil;* Parisian printer Conrad Badius, who had just published the poems of Theodore Beza, Calvin's future successor; a Florentine merchant, Michele Pugliano, who later became a citizen of Strasbourg and who denounced another Italian merchant for heresy in Zurich in the 1560's;[16] brothers Léon and Germain Colladon, renowned jurists from the Duchy of Berry; Guillaume Trie, a rich merchant from Lyon, whom Calvin would later use to denounce Servetus to the French Inquisition; the French royal printer, Robert Estienne; the Neapolitan marquis and courtier of Emperor Charles V, Galeazzo Caracciolo; the learned physician from Lyon, Philibert Sarrasin; Jean Macar, *escollier,* soon a colleague of Calvin's in the Company of Pastors; Claude Baduel, *professeur des bonnes lettres;* Jean Crespin, a lawyer from Artois who had practiced before the *Parlement* of Paris, soon to become famous as the author and printer of a Calvinist martyrology. It would be difficult if not impossible to find so important a collection of names in the remaining 200 pages.

On the other hand, the overwhelming majority of these refugees came to Geneva after Calvin's triumph. Over 1700, more than a third of the entire total, registered in the single year 1559. Over 1600, another third of the total, registered in 1557 and 1558. The vast majority of these names are completely undistinguished. Most of them were artisans, with a solid sprinkling of students drawn to Calvin's new Academy in 1559. It is likely that a sizable proportion of these refugees of 1557–1559 returned to France sometime after 1562, for the reasons already mentioned. The elite of Geneva's refugees, and the permanent base of her French and Italian colonies, were already firmly established in Calvin's city before 1555. After them came the crowds.

✝

The *Livre des Habitants* provides an excellent guide to the geographical composition of Geneva's refugees, since more than nine of every ten of them listed his birthplace. The vast majority among these refugees, of course, came from the kingdom of France. The estimate given in the introduction to the *Livre des Habitants* and repeated elsewhere, that they amounted to two-thirds of the total, is a gross understatement;[18] in reality, the subjects of Henri II of France account for at least three-fourths of these names. Geneva's refugees came from all parts and all provinces of France, although they came in far greater numbers from such populous provinces as Normandy and Languedoc than from Brittany (see p. 168). However, a sizable minority were not French subjects. Over 500 entries came from the French-speaking part of Savoy, and two dozen came from the tiny pocket of land ruled by Geneva herself. These entries do not represent religious refugees, but rather the normal current migrating from the countryside to the city. This was simply a continuation of the perennial process by which Geneva or any other city replenished her urban population.

Three dozen entries came from the Hapsburg territory of Franche-Comté. Sixty-five came from the Duchy of Lorraine, which was in theory part of the Holy Roman Empire. Seventy-two came from the seventeen Hapsburg provinces of the Netherlands. All of these regions were French-speaking political units lying along the eastern frontier of the kingdom of France. But as soon as one crosses the linguistic frontier separating French from German, the number of refugees to Calvin's Geneva declines remarkably. A few cases should make this point clear. Of the 72 names from the Netherlands, exactly half came from Hainault, and only a fifth came from the rich and populous Flemish-speaking regions which included the great city of Antwerp. Only six men came to Geneva from the German-speaking Swiss League, compared to 20 from the French-speaking Bernese territory, the Pays de Vaud. Outside of the French-speaking areas on her western frontier, the entire Holy Roman Empire contributed only 18 names to the total. There were almost 50 refugees in Geneva from the French-speaking Papal enclave at Avignon, compared to only nine from the entire Papal States in Italy.

Furthermore, the intensity of persecution within the French-speaking world does not seem to have played a decisive role in determining the relative size of emigration to Geneva. It may perhaps explain the tiny number of names (six) from Jeanne d'Albert's Huguenot kingdom of Navarre. But there was almost as much emigration to Geneva from Franche-Comté, where few Protestants were persecuted before 1560, as from the southern provinces of the Netherlands, where Charles V's Inquisition had diligently pursued heretics.

Except for France, the only regions well represented in the *Livre des Habitants* are England and Italy. Both had national churches in Geneva during the 1550's, while the Germans did not get theirs for another generation. English and Italian refugees seem to have mingled but little with the native Genevans, although they had frequent contacts with French immigrants. Of the nine marriages celebrated in John Knox's Genevan church, three involved French brides and one an Italian groom;[19] no doubt comparable figures could be adduced for the Italian church. Italian refugees were more important numerically than the English. They were also more important for the history of Geneva, simply because they could not return home safely after 1559. There are more than 200 Italian names in the *Livre des Habitants*, about a fourth of them from Piedmont. This was the region closest to Geneva, and the only part of Italy whose inhabitants had emigrated to Geneva ever since the fifteenth century.[20] Even without Piedmont, the rest of Italy provided more refugees to Geneva than Marian England and the Hapsburg Netherlands combined.

There were several centers of emigration from Italy. The Waldensian villages in Calabria and the humanistic circle around Juan de Valdés in Naples provided most of the prominent refugess from south Italy.[21] Very few came from the Papal States, which had few centers of Evangelical propaganda. Tuscan refugees came overwhelmingly from the independent city-state of Lucca, where Vermigli had converted several prominent families through his preaching.[22] Fifteen names came from the Republic of Genoa, and 32 from the populous Republic of Venice. The

Duchy of Milan contributed 31 names, 22 of them from the city of Cremona, which had been the center of religious concern both to the Spanish governor of Milan and to the Inquisition.[23] United with the Italian church before 1558 and after 1561 was a colony of Spaniards, largely monks fleeing from Seville, who added 22 names to the total.[24]

Only about 350 refugees in all, or one in fifteen, came from regions which spoke languages other than French; only 36 of the 664 *bourgeois* created in Geneva from 1555 to 1564, or one in eighteen, came from this group.

†

To summarize this information, we may note that an overwhelming majority of refugees to Geneva in the 1550's spoke French, though not all were subjects of the King of France. Those who did not speak French tended to go their separate ways in their national churches. It is obvious that this flood of new residents had an enormous impact upon the history of Geneva, both in Calvin's lifetime and later. We propose to offer a few suggestions about the intellectual, economic, and social contribution of these refugees to the life of Calvin's Geneva. We cannot measure very much political influence of these refugees, at least upon the uppermost level of Geneva's government, for the Small Council remained closed to all but native-born Genevans until the fall of the republic in 1798. The most prominent of the refugees — Colladon, Caracciolo, Budé, De Normandie — were admitted to the highest offices legally open to them, the Council of Two Hundred, in 1559;[25] others soon followed them. Although refugees were increasingly appointed to other bodies, especially the Consistory, they did not in general occupy what we would today call the decision-making posts in the Republic of Geneva.

†

The total intellectual impact of the French refugee colony upon the history of Geneva would be difficult to exaggerate, and its impact upon the history of the Reformation in France was nearly as great. Here it is impossible to do more than trace the outline of their impact on Geneva in the light of recent scholarship, but even such a bald summary is eloquent enough. These refugees brought with them a fund of specialized skills which the city desperately needed. With very few exceptions, the representatives of the liberal professions in Calvin's Geneva — particularly doctors, lawyers, and clergymen — were immigrants. All of Calvin's fellow pastors after 1545, and all teachers at his Academy, with one exception, were born outside Geneva.[26] In a sense, this simply continued a trend that began before Calvin's arrival, for Geneva's first Protestant preacher, printer, and schoolteacher had all arrived there from France in 1532 and 1533. Genevan-born men began to enter the faculty of the Academy in 1568 and the Company of Pastors in 1573; and by the end of the century a very high percentage of Geneva's Venerable Company of Pastors and Professors were composed of Genevan-born citizens. But this was emphatically not the case during Calvin's lifetime. The pastors, the professors, the printers, even the doctors and lawyers in Geneva were overwhelmingly religious refugees from France — and the exceptions were more likely to be refugees from Italy or England than natives.

The most famous physician in Calvin's Geneva was Philibert Sarrasin from Lyon, who once took in the twelve-year-old son of John Bodley and future founder of Oxford's Bodleian Library as a boarder. The most notorious physician in Geneva was Giorgio Blandrata from Piedmont, who was expelled in 1558 for his anti-Trinitarian opinions.[27] There were only three physicians in Geneva when Calvin arrived, but eight when he died — and all eight were immigrants.[28] Below the physicians were their auxiliaries, the apothecaries. This profession was a near monopoly of the Piedmontese colony in Geneva, both before and after this great wave of immigration. Between 1536 and 1569, at least 96 Piedmontese apothecaries practiced in Geneva; only 24 French immigrants exercised this profession, and few of them settled permanently in Geneva.[29]

The most famous lawyer in Calvin's Geneva was his good friend Germain Colladon, from the Duchy of Berry. The most notorious lawyer in Geneva was Matteo Gribaldi from Piedmont, who was permanently banished from the city at Calvin's request

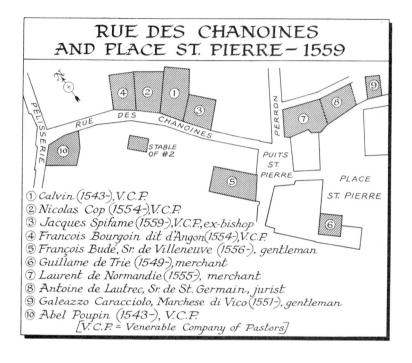

**RUE DES CHANOINES
AND PLACE ST. PIERRE – 1559**

STABLE OF #2

RUE DES CHANOINES

PELISSERIE

PERRON

PUITS ST. PIERRE

PLACE ST. PIERRE

① Calvin (1543-), V.C.P.
② Nicolas Cop (1554-),V.C.P.
③ Jacques Spifame (1559-),V.C.P.,ex-bishop
④ François Bourgoin dit d'Angon(1554-),V.C.P.
⑤ François Budé, Sr. de Villeneuve (1556-), gentleman
⑥ Guillame de Trie (1549-),merchant
⑦ Laurent de Normandie (1555-), merchant
⑧ Antoine de Lautrec, Sr. de St. Germain, jurist
⑨ Galeazzo Caracciolo, Marchese di Vico (1551-), gentleman
⑩ Abel Poupin (1543-), V.C.P.
      [V.C.P. = Venerable Company of Pastors]

in 1555. There were only fourteen jurists in the entire *Livre des Habitants*, nearly all of them French.[30] This seems surprising when one considers the great quantity of lawyers trained in six-teenth-century universities, and when one considers that Calvin himself held a law degree. But when one also remembers that Michael Servetus was a physician and that the Sozzini family, also founders of Unitarianism and occasionally in correspondence with Calvin, were nearly all jurists, then the connections between the liberal professions and radical Protestantism become more apparent. Calvin exercised a considerable degree of prudence in failing to attach any chairs of law or medecine to his Genevan Academy, although his successor tried to introduce both disciplines in order to make the school more attractive to foreign students.

The case of Jean Crespin is also significant here. This Nether-lander, son of a patrician family of Arras, had practiced law in France before the *Parlement* of Paris. However, after he moved to Geneva, Crespin became a publisher of devotional and political tracts in several languages, and the compiler of Calvinism's great *Histoire des Martyrs*.[31] There is no trace of Crespin the lawyer in Geneva. Laurent de Normandie, once mayor of Calvin's native city of Noyon, underwent the same change from lawyer to publisher after his arrival in Geneva. Calvin himself had already set the example by abandoning law for more worthwhile pursuits.

✝

The vital center of these refugee colonies lay in their special churches. We have already seen that, so far as questions of personnel and doctrine are concerned, the established church of Geneva was more the church of French refugees than of the Genevans. After 1560, so was the Consistory. The life of the French colony in Geneva clearly centered around the church and around her foreign propaganda agency, the Geneva printing industry.

The smaller colonies — English, Italian, even Spanish — had their own churches and thus their own nuclei of intellectual activity. It has been said that Calvin's Geneva was an apostolic city where men preached and wrote in many languages. The achievements of these foreign churches in Geneva in the 1550's are similar to each other and generally faithful to the patterns established by the French refugees. For example, the English colony began its activities by printing the form of worship to be used in their church. Then, amidst a number of polemical treatises concerned with current religious and political questions in England, they printed an English New Testament in 1557, an English Book of Psalms in 1559, and finally a complete English Bible (a collaborative effort involving the colony's six best-educated men) in 1560. They brought along their own printer, Rowland Hall, who published many of their works, including the 1560 Bible. Another member of the colony apprenticed himself to Jean Crespin, perhaps to help with the English editions printed on Crespin's presses.[32]

The Italian colony had its church in Geneva two years earlier than the English. Their special printers, Pinerolo and Tudesco, signed the *Livre des Habitants* in 1553 and 1557. The Italians published the form of worship used in their Genevan church, the New Testament, the Psalms, and finally a complete Bible in 1562. They also printed several important polemics, which were directed against Nicodemites and Anabaptists rather than against the more political targets of the English refugees, since the Italians had lost hope of seeing a Reformed state established on their soil by 1550. Their propaganda effort was nevertheless at least as great as that of the English exiles, and they even scored some notable advances over the English by translating Calvin's *Institutes* in 1557 and Beza's *Confession of Faith* in 1560.[33]

The Spanish colony, few in numbers and given a separate church in 1558 partly because of doctrinal heresies revealed that year within the Italian congregation, conformed (as far as its limited strength permitted) to the patterns of the English and Italians. Juan Perez de Pineda, who fled from Seville (probably to Germany) in 1555, translated the New Testament into Castilian in 1556 and the Psalms in 1557. Both editions were printed in Geneva by Crespin, and two barrels of these translations were smuggled into Seville in 1557 in one of the most daring feats of sixteenth-century Protestant propaganda.[34] But the Spaniards had no national printer and never translated a complete Bible, and their special church only lasted for three years.

The intellectual activities of these foreign churches, especially as reflected in their publications, were not intended for consumption in Geneva. They were weapons hurled from a holy fortress back into their own countries, intended either to persuade or to convert. The editions of the form of worship used in their Genevan churches were intended principally as models to be read and copied elsewhere. All these communities were experimenting with what they felt was an ideal form of church, and they enthusiastically publicized their experiments.

The French colony also had a printer whose activities paralleled to some extent the Bible translations and other theological productions of these foreign refugees: Robert Estienne.

The list of his Genevan editions from 1551 to 1559[35] shows a preponderance of scholarly texts of the Bible, both in French and in Latin. The keystone of this arch was Estienne's edition of Beza's somewhat hasty French Bible of 1555, a job which was really no better done than the English or Italian editions; Beza himself overhauled the work in 1565 and remained dissatisfied with the result even afterwards. Estienne did official editions of the Genevan catechism and form of prayers in 1553. He did all of Calvin's Latin writings after 1553, twelve volumes during the next six years, and concluded this task with the great folio edition of the final revision of the *Institutes* in 1559. Estienne printed the treatises of Calvin and Beza defending the burning of Servetus. He did some doctrinal treatises by Viret, and reprinted some neglected commentaries by Bucer. Estienne, who was probably the most famous scholarly printer in Europe in the 1550's, also published books that were not theological. He did Hotman's commentary on Cicero's *Orationes*, a Hebrew edition of the Genevan catechism, and a boys' Greek grammar. He printed other pedagogical aids, including a Latin dictionary, a guide to Greek and Hebrew pronunciation, and a French grammar in 1557. He even produced an edition of Erasmus' *Adages* in 1555, which was almost the only work of that prolific writer to be republished in Calvin's Geneva.

Estienne's work was basically, indeed heavily, theological. The other works he printed, in Latin, directed to the scholarly community of Europe, were humanistic. Here too there is no trace of works in law or medecine, nor even of such famous and profitable practical handbooks as the *Guide des chemins de la France* which his son Charles published in Paris in 1553.

✝

The economic impact of the refugees is more difficult to measure than their intellectual impact. In general, our knowledge of the economic history of Calvin's Geneva is still extremely scanty, and a disproportionate amount of what we do know is confined to a single and somewhat unusual industry, that of Geneva's printers. Only about 200 of the 5000 inscribed refugees were either printers or booksellers, and only 113 said so in the *Livre des Habitants.* Many more (180) registered as merchants, and the vast majority of those indicating a profession (1536) were merely artisans. Among these artisans, almost 700

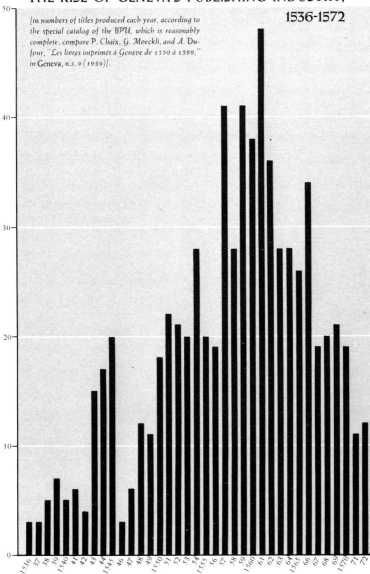

1536-1572

[in numbers of titles produced each year, according to
the special catalog of the BPU, which is reasonably
complete, compare P. Chaix, G. Moeckli, and A. Dufour, "Les livres imprimés à Genève de 1550 à 1599,"
in Geneva, n.s. 9 (1959)].

Source: R. M. Kingdon, Geneva and the Coming
of the Wars of Religion in France,
pp. 98-99.

belonged in some way to the textile trades (carders, weavers, dyers, bleachers, etc.); 264 were leatherworkers, including 181 cobblers; 249 were with the building trades, mostly as carpenters; 228 were metalworkers, about a third of them goldsmiths; and only 93, mostly butchers and bakers, were connected with the food trades.[36] This is an ordinary pattern of trades, not radically different from the pattern that had existed in Geneva in 1536. The refugees represented a great pool of skilled manpower as well as a sizable leavening of merchants and entrepreneurs, and their very numbers made them a vital economic force.

The role of these immigrant merchants in Calvin's Geneva is difficult to trace. None of their *livres de commerce* survive, and very few have post-mortem inventories where their total wealth may be calculated and their investments analyzed. It is extremely difficult to determine how much capital these refugee merchants brought with them to Geneva. For example, the patrician exiles from Lucca were often wealthy merchants when they left home and again when they died, yet their memoirs repeat in chorus that they left home with only a small fraction of their capital assets and were never able to recuperate the rest.[37] The French refugees may have been more fortunate. Robert Estienne fled to Geneva with his working capital virtually intact. Three cases of French refugees who found ingenious ways of evading Henri II's 1551 edict confiscating all French property of his subjects who fled to Geneva have recently come to light. Even Theodore Beza was able to draw an annual revenue from his family property at Vézelay in the 1560's.[38] It should not surprise us if less prominent heretics were also able to conserve their family wealth in Catholic countries.

It seems beyond reasonable doubt that these refugees brought to Geneva sizable amounts of capital and advanced business techniques, both of which helped to spur her commerce from its rather sleepy state in the 1530's to a far more dynamic condition by the end of the sixteenth century. Although the decisive role of the refugees in this development is clear, the precise phases of Geneva's economic evolution are still mysterious, especially during the period of the first refuge.[39]

The only Genevan industry that has thus far been studied, the printing trade, does bear overwhelmingly the mark of refugee leadership. Among the master printers in Geneva from 1550 to 1564, only one of the 35 who signed a book was a native Genevan; that ill-advised man, Jacques Dupan, bought an expensive lot of equipment, but had to abandon his attempt after fourteen months of activity.[40] When her magistrates officially regulated the size of this industry in 1563, they permitted 24 master printers to operate 34 presses. All but two of these printers were immigrants from France, and the exceptions were Italians.[41] The only large publishers in Geneva, each with four presses in 1563, were the house of Estienne and Jean Crespin, the martyrologist. Nearly all Genevan printers handled devotional literature; nearly all printed some works by Calvin, who saw 160 editions of his books come off Geneva's presses between 1550 and 1564.[42] The annual production of book titles in Geneva (see p. 179) rose steadily in the 1550's and reached a peak early in the 1560's.

If we move from the master printer, not necessarily an entrepreneur, to the financiers of Geneva's printing industry, we again discover French refugees. The kingpins of this publishing industry, the men who could promote the really large ventures, were two immigrant *libraires:* Laurent de Normandie and Antoine Vincent. The latter, a wealthy publisher from Lyon who emigrated to Geneva in December 1559, was involved in numerous speculations. By far the most important among them was his leadership of the consortium which printed a massive quantity of Huguenot Psalms, with lyrics by Beza and Clément Marot, in 1561 and 1562.[43] This enterprise has been described as the largest single printing venture to be launched in the sixteenth century. It has left traces of nineteen separate editions in Geneva, seven editions in Paris, and three editions in Lyon. Geneva alone printed at least 27,400 copies of these musical Psalms by 1562, and about a third of the city's presses were being used for this project alone. Copies of these psalms were sold in cities as distant as Antwerp—in fact, wherever there were French Protestants. Antoine Vincent appears as the chief, if not the sole, financier of this entire venture. He bought mountains of paper for it, including the total output of a Genevan magistrate who was obliged to work day and night to fill Vincent's orders, thereby annoying his neighbors and drawing a large fine on himself. Vincent had to hire two extra typecasters who did nothing but prepare the fonts used for these Psalms.[44] Before he died in 1568, Vincent had engaged in many other enterprises, which his biographer describes as important but difficult to identify with certainty.

Our knowledge of Vincent's business activities centers around his most important editorial enterprise; while our knowledge of his chief rival, Laurent de Normandie, is based primarily on his post-mortem inventory of 1570.[45] A boyhood friend of Calvin and once mayor of Noyon, he had fled to Geneva soon after the visit of an Inquisitor in 1547. He renounced his legal career soon after arriving in Geneva, and by 1554 he entered the printing industry in partnership with another refugee. De Normandie worked on a large scale, financing several of Geneva's poorer master printers and selling his books through a network of *colporteurs,* brave peddlars who distributed these forbidden books throughout the Kingdom of France. At least twenty of the *colporteurs* who worked for him ended as Huguenot martyrs.[46] Few of the editions that De Normandie sold were bound; most were small, designed to be slipped hurriedly into one's pocket. The overall size of his operations is quite impressive. His inventory of 1570 lists over 200 accounts due, some of them very large, and a stock of almost 35,000 books on hand. Over 10,000 volumes of his stock represented titles by Calvin, and more than 12,000 volumes were Bibles or parts of Bibles (including 2800 of Vincent's Psalms of 1561).[47] His total stock was worth nearly 20,000 *livres tournois,* a very respecable sum for any European merchant, though not large enough to put him in the topmost rank among sixteenth-century entrepreneurs.[48] De Normandie may have been Geneva's largest publisher, but it is next to impossible to determine how his business volume and total assets compare with those of other Genevan merchants.

The only comparisons, in matters of wealth, would seem to be with other French immigrants such as the Trembley brothers of Lyon, one of whom left a *fonds de draperie* evaluated at 15,000 Genevan florins in 1597, or with the Italian immigrants from Lucca and Cremona who established Geneva's most profitable capitalist enterprise, the *Gran Bottegha,* later in the century. Much scattered information about these refugee enterprises lies buried in the ample records of Genevan notaries, and remains to be unearthed. About all that we can confidently affirm is that the French refugees to Calvin's Geneva successfully established the republic's first export industry, religious propaganda. It also seems certain that these French and Italian refugees carried on larger enterprises, and amassed more wealth, than native-born Genevans did in the sixteenth century. Refugee families made most of the loans to the Republic of Geneva in the 1580's, and were most heavily taxed (on a graduated scale) to support the war effort of 1589.[49]

Finally, it seems clear that in the general evolution of sixteenth-century Genevan commerce, both of the city's great export industries — publishing and later silk — were made possible by the wealth and experience of refugee merchants. It even seems that in both cases, Geneva was simply following the evolution of her downstream neighbor on the Rhone; Lyon had the largest publishing houses in France in the early sixteenth century, and by 1550 she was Europe's leading city north of the Alps in the manufacture and distribution of silks.[50] In both cases, Genevan competitors were manufacturing the same products within a few decades.

✝

The social impact of these refugees upon Geneva is also difficult to quantify or to grasp adequately. It is certain that these new residents altered the shape of Genevan society, chiefly by bringing in a fresh supply of nobility to replace the Savoyard families who had been expelled from Geneva during the municipal revolution of the 1520's. Seventy *nobles gentilshommes* registered in the *Livre des Habitants,* most of them from the lesser nobility. Perhaps not too many among them settled permanently in Geneva, though several were granted Genevan citizenship. On the whole, they were a turbulent lot, and one has the impression that they gave Calvin nearly as much worry as they did service during their residence in Geneva.

For such Huguenot nobles, discontented with their sovereign, intrigue and conspiracy were almost a standard occupation. Many engaged in desultory plotting, and a few were deeply involved in the most spectacular of the many conspiracies that swirled through this troubled period of Valois France, the Conspiracy of Amboise of 1560.[51] The mastermind behind this plot, a young nobleman named La Renaudie, was not a Genevan *habitant*, although his chief lieutenant, M. de Villemongis, was. So were some of their principal associates, including young noblemen from provinces as distant as Brittany and Languedoc. Several of the commoners surprised in the woods at Amboise shortly before the projected kidnapping of the young king and the murder of the Guise regents — for nothing less was at stake in this audacious plot — were Genevan residents. Furthermore, after the plot had been quashed, several of the fleeing survivors were allowed to re-enter Geneva and were given the city's protection. The whole business caused considerable embarrassment, even to Calvin, who had been represented by some of the plotters as favoring this conspiracy.

The dozen or so gently born pastors sent from Geneva into France between 1557 and 1562 were often involved in conspiracies. Theodore Beza, who came from the lesser nobility, clearly gave some encouragement to the Conspiracy of Amboise, while the *bourgeois* Calvin was far more scrupulous about committing himself. Another noble clergyman and Genevan refugee, Jacques Spifame, *seigneur de Passy* and Bishop of Nevers, was embroiled in several different intrigues soon after his arrival in 1559. Some of these were with Catholic moderates, with whom he negotiated to recover his lost bishopric. After a half-dozen hectic years, Spifame's double plotting, plus charges of perjury and adultery, caused Geneva's government to behead him in 1566.[52]

Not all the noblemen in Geneva were incurable plotters or restless adventurers like Philippe de Corguilleray, who embarked for Brazil in 1556. Some resided quietly in Geneva, adding the glamor of their rank to a city starved for social distinction. Outstanding among these noble ornaments was the Neapolitan Galeazzo Caracciolo, known to everybody in Geneva simply as "M. le marquis," whose biography has been written by Benedetto Croce.[53] He had suddenly fled the court of Charles V in the summer of 1551 to settle in Geneva, without his family. He made trips to the neutral territory of Venice in 1553 and Mantua in 1555 to see his father, and he travelled again to Venice in 1558 in a last vain effort to persuade his wife to join him in Geneva. Caracciolo's faithfulness to Calvin and to Calvin's city remained unbroken. Although he had no theological training, he was instinctively orthodox and totally unaffected by the violent dogmatic quarrels within the Italian church he had helped to found. The famous outburst of anti-Trinitarianism erupted during his absence in 1558 and ceased after his return. Caracciolo also became a test case for Calvinism in 1559, when he requested a divorce from his wife on grounds of religious incompatibility. This case had a certain international resonance because he happened to be a grandnephew of the reigning Pope, Paul IV — that archpersecutor of heretics who once said that he would burn his own grandmother if necessary. Caracciolo's divorce was as important an affair as the Servetus trial, and similarly required a justificatory pamphlet by Beza and the advice of such other theologians as Bullinger.

Caracciolo was content to be an elder in the Italian church and a pillar of the Italian community within Geneva. He became a Genevan citizen in 1555 (the first Italian refugee to do so), and by 1559 he was installed on the Consistory and on the Council of Two Hundred. He was given all the honors that Geneva could legally bestow on a foreigner, including a reserved seat in the cathedral and an invitation to all official banquets. He met all prominent Italians, Protestant or not, who passed through Geneva. He lived quite modestly after his re-marriage in 1560 to a widow from Normandy with a small dowry. They had a little home on the square facing the cathedral, a tiny rural summer home just outside Geneva, and only two servants. This was indeed a modest establishment for the godson of an Emperor and the bearer of one of the greatest titles in the Kingdom of Naples.

Except for a poorly documented departure from Geneva between 1572 and 1577, Caracciolo remained in his small home near the cathedral until his death in 1586. His children, together with the rest of his family, remained in Naples. His eldest son inherited his title and fought in several campaigns for Philip II of Spain. Another son fought at Lepanto; a third was an abbot, a fourth a priest. After Galeazzo's death, his close friend, the pastor of the Italian church in Geneva, wrote a biography of him in Italian. It was rapidly translated into Latin, French, and English. This was a signal honor, for until this time only Calvin himself was commemorated at Geneva by a biography; but there was ample reason to propagandize such a "rare and singular example of constancy and perseverance in piety and true religion," as the title of Caracciolo's biography proclaimed him to be.

†

The significance of these refugees for the history of Geneva has many different facets, few of which have been investigated in any depth. This essay is designed only to show the size of the problems facing the truly thorough investigator of Calvin's Geneva. However, the other side of the coin, or the impact of Calvin's Geneva on these refugees, is easier to establish and simpler to describe. For some, Geneva was a point of shelter where they could withdraw from religious persecution in their native land. But for many more, this largely negative feature (which Geneva shared with some Imperial Free Cities and with other Reformed states) was far outweighed by the positive assets of this singularly holy city. In other words, many came less from fear than from hope. John Knox, with his usual talent for bluntness, put the matter simply: "In other places, I confess Christ to be truly preached; but manners and religion so sincerely reformed I have not yet seen in any other place."[54] William Whittingham, a Genevan citizen with a French wife, described Geneva in the preface to the English Bible of 1560 as "the mirror and model of true religion and true piety." The Italians were equally enthusiastic. Vergerio, a former bishop, composed a pamphlet in 1550 which described Geneva as a republic whose only sovereign was God, where only seven ministers preached ten times each Sunday and at least twice every other day, where ecclesiastical discipline was exemplary, and where the entire population were models of piety and concord. Not surprisingly, the French refugees were most enthusiastic of all in their descriptions of Geneva intended for home consumption. The paroxysm of praise was reached by Jean Tagaut, one of the new professors at Calvin's Academy in 1559. Geneva was adorned by this author "with the colors of paradise; her environs, the countryside, lake, and mountains, play a symbolic role in a truly supernatural exaltation. Legions of angels watch from the mountains over the safety of the city. . . . The position of this poem, at the head of the famous collection [Crespin's martyrology] which contributed the most to sustain the faith of the Huguenots, along with reading the Bible and singing the Psalms, is significant."[55] There is an element of humanistic exaggeration in many of these refugee descriptions of Calvin's Geneva, but the hard core of genuine enthusiasm behind every one of them cannot be denied. To these people, Calvin's Geneva was something far more than just a free city; she was a holy city. They came because they were positively attracted to her, and they lived there with the sensations of pilgrims beginning a new life, rather than with the harassed and nostalgic air so common to refugees of our own age.

NOTES

1. Roget, *HPG*, V, p. 82.
2. Here abbreviated *L.H.* A second volume, covering the years 1572–1574 and 1585–1587, appeared in 1963.
3. O. Reverdin, *Quatorze Calvinistes chez les Tompinamous* (G., 1947), p. 26.
4. Kingdon, *Geneva and the Wars of Religion*, pp. 135–43, checked with *L.H.*
5. R. Mandrou, "Les Francais hors de France au XVIᵉ siècle," in *Annales: économies-sociétés-civilisations*, 14 (1959), p. 665; P. Chaix, *Recherches sur l'imprimerie à Genève de 1550 à 1564* (G., 1954), pp. 140–230 *passim*, checked with *L.H.*, omitting printers who came after 1559. In all, there were 300 printers and booksellers plying their trade in Geneva between 1550 and 1564.
6. Figures for England drawn from the *Livre des Anglois*, in Chas. Martin, *Les Protestants anglais réfugiés à Genève au temps de Calvin, 1555–1560* (G., 1915), pp. 331–38; for Italy, from Vincenzo Burlamacchi's "Libro de' Memorie diversi . .", P.H. 1477ᵇⁱˢ at AEG, drawn from the records of the Italian church. There were some Englishmen and some Italians who appear in *L.H.* but not in their church records.
7. See Elizabeth Armstrong, *Robert Estienne, Royal Printer* (Cambridge [Eng.], 1954), pp. 216, 213; Martin, *Réfugiés anglais*, pp. 333, 332; E. Droz, "Antoine Vincent," in *Aspects de la propagande religieuse* (G., 1957), p. 277.

8. See Benedetto Croce, "Il Marchese di Vico," in *Vite di Avventure, di Fede e di Passione*, 3rd ed. (Bari, 1952), p. 211; on Clerici, *L.H.*, p. 93, and P.H. 1477bis.

9. Roget, *HPG*, V, p. 49 n. 1. No doubt the case of Antoine Hue (or Huet), expelled for Anabaptism in 1557, should be joined to these examples; compare *L.H.*, p. 51, and Roget, *HPG*, V, p. 99.

10. I am indebted to N. Z. Davis for this information. See her forthcoming *Strikes and Salvation in Lyon* (Stanford Univ. Press, 1967).

11. Kingdon, *Geneva and the Wars of Religion*, pp. 116–17.

12. Martin, *Réfugiés anglais*, pp. 260–64.

13. On Pascale, see esp. T. R. Castiglione in *Religio*, 12 (1936), p. 28 f.

14. Roget, *HPG*, V, p. 293.

15. A. Covelle, ed., *Le Livre des Bourgeois de l'ancienne République de Genève* (G., 1897), pp. 217–98.

16. Compare *L.H.*, p. 6, and Delio Cantimori, *Eretici Italiani del Cinquecento* (Florence, 1939), pp. 277 ff.

17. See table in *Studies*, p. 24.

18. *L.H.*, p. xv; Mandrou, in *Annales*, 14 (1959), p. 663.

19. Martin, *Réfugiés anglais*, p. 337.

20. Arturo Pascal, "La colonia piemontese a Ginevra nel secolo XVI," in *Ginevra e l'Italia* (Florence, 1959), pp. 65–133. For the entire sixteenth century, about 350 adult males from Piedmont settled in Geneva.

21. T. R. Castiglione, "Il rifugio calabrese a Ginevra nel XVI secolo," in *Archivio Storico per la Calabria e la Lucania*, 6 (1936), pp. 169ff; Croce, "Il Marchese di Vico," p. 248f; S. Caponetto, "Origine e caratteri della Riforma in Sicilia," in *Rinascimento*, 7 (1956), pp. 219–81.

22. A. Pascal, "Da Lucca a Ginevra," in *Rivista Storica Italiana*, 49 (1932), pp. 149–68, 281–303; Marino Berengo, *Nobili e mercanti nella Lucca del Cinquecento* (Turin, 1965), pp. 399–435.

23. There is no special study of the Cremonese colony in Geneva; but see Federico Chabod, *Per la storia religiosa dello Stato di Milano durante il dominio di Carlo V* (Bologna, 1938), pp. 145 ff.

24. Many names in *L.H.*, pp. 91, 137f, may also be found in the list of "frayles hereges . . . les quales todos estan en Geneva," Simancas AGS, Estado 210, printed by Marcel Battailon, *Erasme et l'Espagne* (Paris, 1937), p. 749 n. 4.

25. Roget, *HPG*, V, pp. 203–04.

26. *Studies*, p. 98; P.-F. Geisendorf, *L'Université de Genève, 1559–1959* (G., 1959), p. 42.

27. Delio Cantimori, "Profilo di Giorgio Biandrata Saluzzese," in *Bollettino Storico-bibliografico subalpino*, 38 (1936), pp. 352–402; A. Pascal, "Da Lucca a Ginevra," *RSI*, 51 (1934), pp. 472–82, notes the anti-Trinitarian sympathies of another Italian physician, Rustici, in 1558.

28. Léon Gautier, "La médecine à Genève jusqu'à la fin du XVIIIe siècle," in *MDG*, 30 (1906), pp. 26–27.

29. *Ibid.*, pp. 52ff; Pascal, "Colonia piemontese a Ginevra," pp. 114–15.

30. Mandrou, in *Annales*, 14 (1959), p. 665. Only six of the 472 adult male fugitives from Marian England were lawyers or physicians, and apparently none of them reached Geneva; C. H. Garrett, *The Marian Exiles* (Cambridge, [Eng.], 1938), p. 42.

31. There is no good modern biography of Crespin. The best available profile is in E. Haag, *La France Protestante*, 2e ed. (Paris,1883), IV, cols. 885ff.

32. See bibliography in Martin, *Réfugiés anglais*, pp. 297–330; Chaix, *Imprimerie*, pp. 175, 193 f.

33. Chaix, *Imprimerie*, pp. 213 f, 225. The total size of the Italian propaganda effort is not yet precisely known, since new titles keep appearing from time to time. See J. A. Tedeschi and E. D. Willis, "Two Italian Translations of Beza and Calvin," in *ARG* 55 (1964), pp. 70–74, for a recent example.

34. Ed. Boehmer, *Bibliotheca Wiffeniana* (Strasbourg, 1883), II, pp. 60–65; also John E. Longhurst, "Julian Hernandez, Protestant Martyr," in *BHR*, 12 (1960), pp. 90–118.

35. Armstrong, *Robert Estienne*, pp. 228–35.

36. Mandrou, in *Annales*, 14 (1959), p. 665 f.

37. Pascal, "Da Lucca a Ginevra," *RSI*, 50 (1933), pp. 30–60, 220, 424 ff; *RSI*, 52 (1935), pp. 286 ff.

38. Armstrong, *Robert Estienne*, pp. 213–17, 224 f; H. Meylan, "En dépit des édits royaux," in *Mélanges Antony Babel* (G., 1963), I, pp. 291–302; BPU, Mss. Tronchin, vol. 4, nos. 25–27.

39. Cf. Walter Bodmer, *Der Einfluss der Refugianteneinwanderung von 1550–1700 auf die Schweizerische Wirtschaft* (Zurich, 1946), pp. 42 ff. A fuller study of this subject has been promised by Jean-François Bergier.

40. Chaix, *Imprimerie*, p. 179.

41. R. C., t. 58, fol. 69^v; summarized by Kingdon, *Geneva and the Wars of Religion*, pp. 93–94. Lyon in 1548 mustered 413 master printers for the joyous entry of Henri II: see Kleinclausz, *Lyon*, I, p. 506.

42. Chaix, *Imprimerie*, p. 55.

43. E. Droz, "Antoine Vincent: la propagande protestante par le Psautier," in *Aspects de la propagande religieuse* (G., 1957), pp. 276–93.

44. *Ibid.*, pp. 286 and n. 2, 279.

45. H.-L. Schlaepfer, "Laurent de Normandie," in *Aspects de la propagande religieuse*, pp. 176–230.

46. Complete list in *ibid.*, pp. 181–82.

47. *Ibid.*, p. 208, items 8, 10, 13.

48. De Normandie's assets are somewhat greater than most of the scattered samples of middle-rank merchants from different parts of Europe given by Pierre Jeannin, *Les marchands au XVIe siècle* (Paris, 1957), pp. 49–54.

49. *Studies*, pp. 39–41, 43.

50. A Lucchese Protestant living in Lyon offered in 1554 to establish a state-

run silk factory in Geneva, guaranteeing an annual profit of 15%, but was refused: AEG, P. H. 1558. Lyon employed about 1,650 men in silkmaking in 1548: Kleinclausz, *Lyon*, I, p. 504 f.

51. Henri Naef, "La Conjuration d'Amboise et Genève," in *MDG*, 32 (1922), pp. 325–730; good summary with additional information in Kingdon, *Geneva and the Wars of Religion*, pp. 68–78.

52. A. Delmas, "Le procès et la mort de Jacques Spifame," in *BHR*, 5 (1944), pp. 105–37; Roget, *HPG*, VII, pp. 173–87.

53. "Il Marchese di Vico," *art. cit.*, pp. 187–291.

54. Dated 1556; quoted by Kingdon, p. 21.

55. Alain Dufour, "Le mythe de Genève au temps de Calvin," in *Schweizerische Zeitschrift für Geschichte*, n.s. 9 (1959), pp. 501–04 (quote, 503); reprinted in his *Histoire politique et psychologie historique* (G., 1966), pp. 76–79.

PART C

The Legacy of Calvinism

EIGHT

Geneva after Calvin

After Calvin's death, Genevan history changed in some important ways. After 1567, Geneva was surrounded by a Catholic prince who was far more hostile to her religion and her independence than Bern had ever been. While this historical accident had a tremendous impact upon her external relations, it did not necessarily entail any important changes within Geneva, where Calvin on his deathbed had told the pastors to change nothing. Indeed, his successors made a strenuous attempt to hold to both the letter and the spirit of Calvin's teachings. But in ecclesiastical as in political affairs the changing shape of Europe in the late sixteenth century made it impossible to avoid all changes. Simply by remaining immobile within a fluid environment, Geneva after Calvin occupied a different position in European history.

The Republic of Geneva had no more internal history after 1564. The magistrates of the Small Council, aided by intelligent use of pre-election sermons, maintained themselves in office until they died, untroubled by factions or popular demagoguery. On the only occasion where the Two Hundred demanded certain reforms, such as the addition of nonvoting members to the Small Council and the secret ballot, the Republic's magistrates rapidly quashed these would-be innovators. "No prudent man would ever approve such a pure democracy," ran their answer, "because no such state has ever long survived." Mixed government, as practiced in Polybius' Rome, or in Venice, or in Swiss towns, was their ideal; but such novelties as the Venetian ballot "would only make us ridiculous in the eyes of our neighbors."[1] The very ease with which the magistrates disposed of this attack provides eloquent testimony to Geneva's political stability in the late sixteenth century. No further changes were tried for several generations, while *Messieurs* ruled their tiny state unchallenged from within.

Meanwhile, the external history of the Republic of Geneva was extremely eventful during the forty years after Calvin's death. Isolated geographically from Bern, the city was forced to go farther afield and seek more secure guarantees for her independence. The course of her diplomatic activities became more intense; their goals, more serious. Finally, by the end of the sixteenth century, Geneva had to fight a four-year war with the Duke of Savoy. Even afterwards, no definitive peace was concluded. Only when Geneva repulsed a surprise attack from Savoy (the famous Escalade of December 1602, which is still celebrated annually in Geneva) did she attain some measure of political security. Improved fortifications and a professional garrison were the price she finally paid for continued independence.

The Church of Geneva, like the Republic, had few internal difficulties during the forty years after Calvin's death. Pastors and professors generally worked in harmony, although they were no longer dominated by a single personality as they had been when Calvin was alive. Theodore Beza, who inherited Calvin's post as Moderator, was a prolific writer of tracts, an excellent representative for the Company before the magistrates, a diligent correspondent with leaders in all parts of Reformed Europe, and a superbly successful director of Calvin's Academy. But he only intended to continue Calvin's work, changing nothing in his theology or in his church, and in particular he kept Calvin's intentions by maintaining collective government rather than one-man rule within the Company.[2]

The foreign relations of the Church of Geneva are still imperfectly known during the post-Calvin age, chiefly because Beza's correspondence is only now in course of publication. But it seems likely that the very rigidity of Genevan dogma, coupled with the irreplaceable loss of Calvin himself, caused the influence of her church to decline somewhat. The Vaudois of Piedmont no longer sent extraordinary appeals to Geneva for ecclesiastical decisions after 1564; and the great flood of requests for Genevan-

GENEVA AND HER NEIGHBORS
1536 – 1567

FRANCHE-
COMTÉ

FRIBOURG

B E R N

Morges
Lausanne

Lac de Genève

St. Claude

Nyon

Thonon
Evian

Gex

Geneva

VALAIS

Nantua

Bellegarde

Ternier

Bonneville

S A V O Y

Seyssel

Rhone River

Annecy
Lac
d'Annecy

Chamonix

Baillages of Gex, Ternier,
Thonon, occupied 1536 by
Bern, ceded 1567 to Savoy.

Land occupied 1536 by Valais,
ceded 1569 to Savoy.

(N.B. Savoy under French
occupation 1536 –1559)

0   5   10   20 MILES

trained pastors, the principal theme of the Company's business
since 1555, slowed to a trickle after 1566 — only five men were
sent out over the next six years.[2a] The one part of Geneva that
preserved its attraction undiminished by Calvin's death was his
Academy, which continued to draw students from all parts of
Europe.

In this chapter, we propose only to sketch the history of the
Republic of Geneva and the Church of Geneva from Calvin's
death until the early seventeenth century. Beza's death in 1605,
less than three years after the defeat of the Savoyard Escalade,
marks the end of an epoch which we can adequately name Calvinist (as opposed to Calvin's) Geneva. Its fundamental charac-
teristic was a mixture of uprightness and rigidity, the acute
awareness of being a holy city, which was Calvin's most enduring
legacy to Geneva.

✝

The principal theme of the history of the republic from 1564 to 1603 was her search for political security. After Calvin's death, and after the Savoyard occupation of the *baillages* surrounding the city in 1567, Geneva continued to anchor her hopes to the perpetual alliance with Bern. The increased volume of her diplomatic relations was skillfully handled by Michel Roset, already a seasoned ambassador with two dozen missions behind him in 1564.[3] Roset possessed a mastery of German which was both rare and valuable at Geneva, and he was sent on missions (between two and ten per year) to different parts of the Swiss cantons. He was often despatched to the Swiss Diet, to the permanent French embassy at Soleure, or to the Protestant cantons of Basel and Zurich. Almost invariably, his road passed through Bern, where he stopped over eighty times between 1564 and 1589. (By comparison, Roset made only four trips to the Savoyard court at Turin and none to France.) Michel Roset was a clever negotiator as well as a skilled linguist, and he understood thoroughly the rules of sixteenth-century diplomacy. When he died in 1613, the note on Geneva's mortuary register — *hoc tempore quasi pater patriae* — testified eloquently to his role in preserving the independence of the republic throughout a very troubled period.

The years of Roset's greatest activity correspond to the years of Geneva's greatest peril. The first such year was 1567, when a Spanish army commanded by the Duke of Alva passed within a few miles of the city en route to the Netherlands.[4] Geneva thought, quite wrongly, that she was in danger of attack from these seasoned troops, and hired 400 Huguenot veterans as a special garrison. But there was no plan to storm the famous nest of heresy, and the idea that Alva might try such a thing seems to have occurred to Philip II only when his army was already passing Geneva. However, Alva's passage did have two important consequence for the republic. First, the cost of the special garrison began a series of financial crises at Geneva which continued into the following century. Second, and even more important, Alva's passage provided an excellent occasion for the Duke of Savoy to demand from Bern the execution of the Treaty of Lausanne (signed in 1564), to which the great powers of France and Spain had finally agreed. Accordingly, as soon as Alva's army had passed, Geneva was once again surrounded by Savoy, who regarded the existence of an independent republic as a personal insult, now compounded by heretical obstinacy. The situation of 1535 had returned, except that now a better fortified and Calvinist Geneva faced a more modernized Duchy of Savoy.

For the time being, the distant prudence of Philip II of Spain and the preoccupation of Duke Emmanuel-Philibert with the Italian-speaking part of his lands assured that no Catholic prince would begin military aggression against Geneva. In fact, the republic established an important *mode de vivre* with Savoy in 1570, by which the Duke guaranteed Geneva's liberty of commerce with his possessions for twenty-three years. The agreement simply sidestepped the thornier legal questions of Genevan sovereignty and Savoyard rights within the city. Both Bern and Philip II were well pleased with this arrangement, which noticeably lessened religious tensions and seemed to remove the possibility of a war of religion. Despite the excitement in Geneva when news of the massacre of St. Bartholomew burst upon her on August 23, 1572, local tensions continued to remain low.[5] Although Geneva mounted a special guard for a month and placed an order for 16,500 bullets while the refugees from the massacre poured in — 500 in a fortnight — there was no danger. Emmanuel-Philibert even showed his good intentions in December 1572 by offering to help Geneva in any way possible.

So long as this duke reigned in Savoy, nothing disturbed Genevan security, but the republic did not slacken her diplomatic activity. Finally, in 1579, Michel Roset's efforts bore fruit. The Treaty of Soleure, which was signed that year between France and the Swiss cantons of Bern and Catholic Soleure, did not involve Geneva as a partner; but the treaty was drawn specifically to protect Geneva against Savoyard menaces.[6] As Roset noted, "either we are deceived, or the French are on our side in this business." France (or more exactly her clever ambassador Pomponne de Bellelièvre) had been thinking of such a treaty for eight years, and their embassy had in fact approved of Genevan participation in all negotiations leading up to the final signature. Roset's diplomacy succeeded in modifying the official text in several important clauses, changing nuances to turn Geneva from a protectorate of Bern and France into a weak but sovereign state. This treaty was approved in Geneva, first by the Company of Pastors and then by the general citizen assembly. The republic sent delegates to sign the pact as procurators, rather than as contracting parties. In such fashion Geneva took her first halting step towards the French sphere of influence, and in such fashion Henri III and his diplomats overcame their scruples about the preservation of heretics (as Francis I had overcome his scruples half a century earlier in regard to the Turks). Their official position is admirably sketched in the royal instructions to the Swiss embassy in 1582:[7]

It would have been a good thing if the city of Geneva were long ago reduced to ashes, because of the evil doctrine which has been sown from that city throughout Christendom and which has produced many calamities, most of them in my own kingdom. Nevertheless, because of the city's location, we cannot afford to let it fall into the clutches of any neighboring prince . . . For if this were to happen, and the pass of l'Ecluse to be strongly fortified, then I could not aid the Swiss League, nor [a far more relevant point] could they aid me.

This treaty with its guarantees of French concern for Genevan independence came none too soon. One year later Emmanuel-Philibert died and was succeeded as Duke of Savoy by the young dreamer Charles-Emmanuel. Filled with romantic ambitions, the new ruler was given to spinning grandiose plans which he generally lacked the means to execute. Several such plans involved the recapture of the city which his luckless grandfather had lost in 1536. Much of the history of the Republic of Geneva after 1580, from the brief outbreak of hostilities in 1582 until the Escalade twenty years later, is little more than a continuous series of alarums and excursions to thwart Charles-Emmanuel's projects.

In order to parry these threats, which involved economic as well as military blockades, Geneva had to extend her diplomatic horizons and refine her techniques. The first test of the Treaty of Soleure came in 1582, when Geneva was invested by 1200

French, Piedmontese, and Italian mercenaries.[8] The besiegers'
commander was incompetent, he had no siege artillery, and in
any case his efforts were rapidly checked by diplomatic pressure
from Bern and from the French embassy at Soleure. It was only
a sudden summer thunderstorm for the republic, who had armed
her students at the Academy and requested a garrison from the
Swiss, but it was an authentic sign of things to come.

This affair also left Geneva with a considerable budgetary
deficit. Accordingly, in September 1582, the Small Council

> studied the news that M. Beza had previously heard from England
> and Paris: that if *Messieurs* wrote to the Queen of England and to the
> Mayor of London, and if some of the ministers of our church wrote to
> the bishops, we might obtain some kind of gift to alleviate our recent
> expenses and debts.[9]

The republic despatched an ambassador (a former tutor to the
Scottish Count of Lennox) to the court of Queen Elizabeth, who
had officially heard nothing from Geneva since John Knox had
launched his notorious *First Blast of the Trumpet Against the
Monstrous Regiment of Women* from there twenty-five years before. The ambassador never got a personal interview with the
Queen, but the Privy Council finally agreed that a general collection might be raised throughout the kingdom, under episcopal
supervision, to aid Geneva. John Bodley, a refugee at Geneva in
the 1550's, was named to supervise these collections. After six
months of work, Geneva's ambassador returned in 1583 with
£5,730 sterling (over 100,000 Genevan florins, or a third of the
republic's annual revenue in this age). He also brought back
valuable letters from Elizabeth to the Swiss Protestant cantons,
urging them to form a united front against the House of Savoy;
he had obtained this "not without some difficulty," for Elizabeth
had been on good terms with Savoy for some time. In sum,
Geneva's first attempt to squeeze charity from distant Protestant
rulers was an undeniable success. This mission to England in
1582 set a pattern which the republic would repeat in her later
political crises of the sixteenth century.

The military alert of 1582 also stimulated Genevan diplomacy
in the more traditional areas of Switzerland. Roset achieved his

last great triumph when Geneva signed a triple *combourgeoisie* with Bern and Zurich in 1584 which also permitted the Genevans, by a special loophole in article seven, to treat with the French.[10] Roset narrowly missed adding the other Protestant cantons of Basel and Schaffhausen to this pact. In principle, Zurich had agreed to this treaty as early as January 1583, but could not publicly reveal her decision for a full year because of the delicate state of internal Swiss politics. Geneva hastened to confirm the alliance in April 1583 by sending a pair of joined silver goblets to her allies, and tried earnestly to convince Bern of the usefulness of such a new *combourgeoisie.* This took time and the help of the French at Soleure, but finally Roset won most of the disputed points. When all of Bern's objections had been overcome, Geneva rapidly approved the treaty and confirmed it amidst considerable pomp. The Small Council rented trumpets and tambours, built a statue of Mars on an abandoned boat, staged a patriotic play by local schoolboys, and cleaned Geneva's streets regularly in preparation for the visiting dignitaries. The menu at the public banquet for her visitors went a little beyond the letter of Geneva's sumptuary laws; her government, painfully conscious of the example which it set, preferred to err on the side of hospitality. The price was cheap, for this alliance remained in force until 1798 as the cornerstone of the republic's independence. It even left Geneva free to strike bargains with outside powers, so long as these did not infringe the other provisions of the treaty.

The conclusion of the 1584 triple alliance came none too soon. Sixteen months after the signing, Charles-Emmanuel published an edict which forbade the export of grain from his lands to the rebellious city of Geneva. For almost two years, Geneva was subjected to an economic blockade which nearly starved her.[11] The republic could not even collect tithes in grain from the rural parishes which her pastors served. The Duke's enforcement agents patrolled the countryside so well that peasants in the enclaves belonging to Geneva were forced to eat grass. Within the walls, prime wheat tripled in price, and the government was forced to buy grain in regions as distant as Alsace and the Palatinate. Tensions ran high. The Academy even had to be closed down for a time because all the law students from Germany had fled Geneva.[12] Once again, as in 1582, the city sent a cycle of letters to all Protestant powers, including England.[13] Another flood of refugees, mostly from the rural lands near Geneva, poured into the city, while a new register of *habitants* was opened; special collections had to be raised, starting in January 1587, to provide them with adequate rations of food. Geneva's situation was indeed tense. In a speech before the Small Council in December 1586, magistrate-professor Jacques Lect explained that a solution by force of arms would be both necessary and just.[14] But Geneva's allies, especially Bern, did not envisage an offensive war, because any aggression might trigger a general European holocaust. For the moment, Geneva had no choice but to suffer.

Tensions lifted only slightly during the next few years. The blockade was slackened, the Academy reopened, but tiny incidents with Savoy continued to furnish pretexts for a general war. Once the international situation had turned to the advantage of the Protestants, after the defeat of the Spanish Armada in 1588, Geneva had no hesitations about beginning a preventive war.[15] Local conditions were also very favorable in the winter of 1588–1589. Bern was thoroughly alarmed by the discovery of a Savoyard plot to seize the pays de Vaud. The King of France was also annoyed with the Duke of Savoy, who had seized the Marquisate of Saluces from him late in 1588. Philip II of Spain, chief protector of Charles-Emmanuel, was preoccupied by the loss of his Armada. If Geneva were to begin a war in midwinter, the Duke of Savoy would be at a disadvantage because the passes between the two halves of his lands, Savoy and Piedmont, were blocked by snow, while Geneva's Swiss allies would be centrally located and possess a safe, walled base of operations. So reasoned Michel Roset, in a famous speech before the Small Council in January 1589. The only missing ingredient was Swiss soldiers, and a French embassy was busily gathering them. Accordingly, Geneva declared war against Savoy in March 1589, even rushing forward to attack before all the necessary treaties had been signed.

Roset and Geneva expected a short war, as in 1536. They knew that prolonged fighting was ruinously expensive (although this worry had been solved, at least on paper, by the treaty which Geneva signed in April 1589, whereby the French promised to pay the entire cost of the war). In the beginning, things went exactly as planned. The clever promises of French ambassador Harlay de Sancy succeeded in raising an army of 12,000 Swiss, principally Bernese, who intended to recover the lands ceded to Savoy in 1567. Just as in 1536, all military objectives were rapidly achieved by Bern and the French against a nearly unarmed enemy. Geneva contributed 1500 mercenaries to the war effort, men whom she was trying hard to control through an idealistic military code which the French Huguenots had abandoned after two months of warfare in 1562.[16] At first there were few problems. The Savoyard nobility put up little resistance. Great chunks of booty were distributed among the allies, with Geneva reserving one *baillage* for herself and garrisoning all the castles there.

Then, catastrophe struck. Harlay de Sancy, master architect of the 1589 alliance, took his army into Savoy, captured the places he had promised to capture, then turned this army into France in mid-May. It was a magnificent sleight-of-hand which later delighted Voltaire:[17]

The King gave him posthaste a commission and no money, and he left for Switzerland. Never was there such a series of negotiations. First he persuaded the Swiss and the Genevans to make war jointly with France. He promised them cavalry which he could not deliver. He raised ten thousand infantry and made the Swiss pay them a hundred thousand écus. Once at the head of this army, he took a few places from the Duke of Savoy, then he persuaded the Swiss to march to the aid of his king. Thus, for the first time, the Swiss donated both men and money to France.

Geneva's problem, as Roset saw at the time, was that Sancy had failed to conclude a truce with Savoy. Bern and Geneva were left to continue the war alone, while Charles-Emmanuel was being reinforced by the invincible Spanish infantry of his father-in-law, Philip II. Geneva had been thoroughly duped by Sancy. She had helped to sow the wind and was now about to reap the whirlwind.

The war between Savoy and Geneva continued for four years,

sometimes hot and sometimes cold. Effective Swiss aid vanished with Sancy's army, while the enemy now disposed of more than 7000 troops, including 1500 Spaniards. Geneva kept about 900 men scattered in her rural garrisons, while Bern had about 2000. Savoy now recaptured her countryside just as easily as the other side had captured it a few months before. By mid-August, the war between Bern and Savoy had slackened into a series of truces, since both sides were waiting for favorable news from France. One by one the Genevan garrisons fell, until the last body of 300 men surrendered at Bonne in Faucigny on August 22, 1589. Contrary to the terms of its capitulation, this garrison was all massacred. The reason was that Savoyard troops, bent on pillage, explored the Genevan headquarters and powder depot with lighted matches; 50 soldiers, including a Spanish captain, were killed by the resulting blast, and the enraged Spaniards immediately revenged this "treachery" on the disarmed garrison.

Nothing, certainly not atrocity stories like the Bonne massacre, could persuade Bern to continue the war. The Bernese signed a treaty with Charles-Emmanuel which restored all their conquests to Savoy, and they provisionally agreed not to aid Geneva if she were attacked by Savoy. The Duke proceeded to move his major military effort into France and left his bastard brother as Governor of Savoy, entrusted with the task of reducing Geneva. Beyond this point, Geneva's war became local rather than international. It was fought on one side by inefficient Savoyard militia and highly efficient Spanish professionals, whose instructions forbade their use for any offensive purposes; and on the other by a far smaller army, paid in copper slugs and pious promises, defending a superbly walled city which could be provisioned along its lake from Bernese soil.

A rather strange sort of siege warfare and campaign of attrition was required under these circumstances. The Governor of Savoy built a ring of forts around Geneva, of which the most important stood within two miles of the city's walls. Another pair of forts girdled the lake at its narrowest point. Galleys were constructed to control the lake and bring the blockade of Geneva to perfection. These operations took over 3000 men, or about four times the number Geneva could afford to keep armed. The Genevan fighters spent their energies in a series of sorties, never lasting more than two days, in which they surprised and usually captured isolated garrisons, razed the fortresses, and then retired with whatever booty they could collect. At one point, they even captured one of the pincer forts on the lake, at Versoix, which was garrisoned by 600 men. Geneva cut them off from their water supply, threatened them with artillery, and forced them to surrender before reinforcements could arrive, thereby breaking the blockade. By similar methods, Geneva captured all enemy forts in the *baillage* of Gex, and the republic was sufficiently brave or confident to name a military governor for the region in January 1590. Much of the rest of this war was fought in the same manner, with Geneva pursuing her policy of rapid sorties and castle-snatching, while the Savoyards and their Spanish auxiliaries concentrated their efforts on devastating the lands around Geneva, pursuing the same sort of scorched-earth policy as the Spanish army in Flanders. Despite all their efforts, the siege of Geneva remained imperfect, and the Spaniards' orders not to invade Genevan soil remained unchanged, to the immense annoyance of their Savoyard commander.

In most wars, this would be a good time to begin negotiations for a truce. The Swiss worked incessantly for one. So did many local Savoyard nobles, who failed to see the need to continue a war in which their lands were systematically plundered by the Spaniards and in which they were likely to be captured and ransomed by the Genevans. Neither of the principals, however, cared to negotiate, although both were desperately short of the all-important nerve of warfare, money. The French embassy in Switzerland did its best to help the Genevans (to whom they remained allied), even robbing a Spanish pay caravan on the highway near Basel in December 1590, and using their haul to send a final expedition of Swiss mercenaries into Savoy. These troops destroyed the galleys on Lake Geneva, fought one indecisive battle, then marched off into France like Sancy's army in 1589. Venice, another enemy of Savoy, even hired some Moslem mercenaries in Albania and sent them to fight with the Genevan Calvinists; most of them deserted. Somehow Geneva struggled through, paying for her war largely by levying contributions on the surrounding countryside, until a general truce was signed between France and Savoy in August 1593. Hostilities

were quickly ended on the Genevan front by the Savoyard commander and by the French commander in Geneva. This truce
was renewed regularly until the general peace treaty was signed
at Vervins in 1598. This treaty settled all the great international
questions, but there was some confusion as to whether or not
Geneva was included in it. Henri IV of France said she was,
along with his other allies, while Savoy denied this, since it
would imply recognition of Genevan sovereignty.

Politically and diplomatically, the war between Geneva and
Savoy had settled very little. Geneva had not gotten the help
she expected from Bern, or the full scale of help she needed
from France, and the republic still lacked a really firm guarantee
for her independence. Diplomatically, the importance of the
war was that it marked a decisive turn away from Bern and
towards France in the republic's endless search for a reliable
protector against Savoy. From a more general point of view, the
importance of this war was simply that Geneva somehow survived it and kept her independence. As the historian of this war
has remarked,

this independence was menaced, with the arrival of the century of
absolutism, by the general movement of the times, which favored the
growth of large states at the expense of small ones, sacrificing whatever remained of medieval particularism. Municipalities were in the
front rank of the obsolete institutions which modern history reduced
to souvenirs . . . and, complicating matters further, this struggle between a sovereign smitten with absolutism and a commune become
a republic was at the same time a war of religion.[18]

Geneva had waged war in the name of France, and her su-
preme commander had always been provided by the French
crown. After the truce of 1593, Geneva continued to gravitate
politically within the French orbit, basing her policy on the
premise that Henri IV would eventually reimburse her enormous wartime expenses, as France had promised to do in the
Sancy treaty of 1589. Consequently, her major activity for the
rest of Henri IV's reign was centered on the French court rather
than on the Swiss League. Geneva went so far as to establish
a resident embassy at the French court after 1594, an event

without parallel in the history of the republic and rarely dupli-
cated in the history of any state her size.[19] The war had given
an enormous thrust to her other diplomatic activities as well.
By the time of the 1593 truce, Geneva had sent missions to the
seven United Provinces of the Netherlands, to Elizabeth of England, to the Elector-Palatine and other Protestant princes of the
Empire as far east as Danzig or Transylvania. All these missions
were designed simply to raise money from foreign rulers, in the
manner of the 1582 embassy to England. In general these missions were very successful, since Geneva raised over one-fourth
of her income during the last two years of war from these
sources.[20]

Because nothing had been settled by the truce of 1593 or the
treaty of 1598, Geneva remained on the alert, and her council
minutes frequently record rumors of impending "enterprises"
against the city by Savoy. Yet the one time such an attack really
was attempted, the republic was caught unprepared and was
very nearly captured. The famous Escalade on the night of 11/12
December, 1602 was, militarily speaking, far less important than
the Genevan war effort of 1589 through 1593; yet the anniversary
of the Escalade is still celebrated at Geneva as the culmination
of the republic's successful defense of her liberty, while the war
of 1589 has been forgotten. In patriotic myth, if not in history,
the failure of the Escalade marks an epoch for Geneva.

The Escalade was attempted in winter, on the longest night
of the year, by the governor of Savoy with a force of 300 picked
men, many of them nobles. The Duke of Savoy was not far behind with a larger body of men, ready to consolidate the capture
of Geneva once a breach had been made. The advance guard
got over the outer wall by using scaling ladders, but then a
sentinel gave the alarm at the cost of his life. Trapped between
the outer and inner walls, with their ladders cut and their blast-
ing expert (*pétardier*) killed by well-aimed Genevan cannon-
balls, the Savoyards were forced into pell-mell retreat. After
three hours of confused fighting in the darkness, about 60 at-
tackers were killed and many more wounded, against only 17
Genevan dead. Thirteen prisoners, all noblemen, were captured
and summarily hanged as thieves by the Republic of Geneva,
since no war had been declared. All told, it was a noteworthy

success by a lot of proverbially unwarlike bourgeois against a corps of picked troops. As the Duke of Bouillon remarked a few weeks later while passing through Geneva, "if this had happened in France, gentlemen, you'd all be made cardinals by now."[21]

In its European context, the Escalade can best be understood as part of a series of plots directed against Henri IV in 1601–1602 by the Pope, "under the pretext of religion" (as the French ambassador claimed). After it had failed, Henri IV's reaction dominated the situation: he pushed Savoy out of the Spanish orbit and into the French; he prevented another civil war; and he preserved Geneva as an integral part of the Huguenot sub-state and thus as part of the still unstable French state.[22] The Escalade also alarmed Europe's Protestant rulers in countries as distant as England. The Swiss were very disturbed, and once more pressed for peace talks between Geneva and Savoy. This time, perhaps because of the change in European politics, they were successful. Hostilities were ended and most of the outstanding disputes between Gevena and Savoy were settled, at least on paper, when the treaty of St.-Julien was signed and sealed in July 1603.[23] The Duke of Savoy had grudgingly capitulated and at last had implicitly recognized Genevan independence. This treaty did not settle all the points at issue between Geneva and Savoy; probably nothing could. But it did provide a solid foundation for a long period of peace by ironing out the economic and legal relationships between them in a far more satisfactory fashion than had the *mode de vivre* of 1570.

By the time the treaty of St.-Julien was signed, Geneva was drawing a regular monthly pension of 6000 *livres tournois* from Henri IV. Ever since the signing of the Treaty of Soleure in 1579, and especially since the outbreak of war in 1589, Geneva had been drawing steadily closer to France. By 1605, she could reasonably be considered a French, rather than a Swiss, satellite. Her dependence on France was to lessen somewhat after the death of Henri IV and the abolition of the French royal pension in 1617. The republic gradually established a new balance of diplomatic protectors, including England, in the course of the seventeenth century. But her political and commercial ties remained stronger with France than with the Swiss, and more often than not it was French influence which predominated in

Geneva.[24] When the Republic of Geneva finally fell in 1798, she was annexed by revolutionary France, who ultimately lost Geneva to the Swiss at the Congress of Vienna.

†

While the republic was pursuing her difficult search for a reliable foreign protector who would not subvert her independence, her internal history was at an apparent standstill. Some important changes were happening within the state of Geneva during the forty years after Calvin's death, although their importance seldom appeared on the city's constitutional surface. After 1564, the oligarchic nature of the republic was affirmed and stabilized in a number of ways. We shall try to suggest a few of the more important among them.

One vital way in which the oligarchy of Calvinist Geneva established itself was in the domain of public finance. Most public revenues were increasingly absorbed by the secret treasury of the Syndics, the *Arche*.[25] After 1567, this treasury always handled more money than the official public treasury; but unlike the public treasury, its annual audits were never made public or even revealed to the Two Hundred. The republic's needs of course increased radically in wartime, and the economic blockades of the 1580's, coupled with the war effort after 1589, added considerably to the secrecy of Genevan public finance. The peak of this trend occurred during the war, when three members of the Small Council formed a secret committee, the *conseil de guerre,* to find money to finance this struggle. Somehow they did find it, using a variety of expedients including copper coins; but they left no records whatsoever, and a fair share of the republic's income in 1590 is listed only as coming from the *conseil de guerre,* with no indication of the means whereby it was raised, borrowed, or extorted.[26] Perhaps the most eloquent sign of the times came in 1570, when the Small Council summoned the general assembly and proposed to them that new taxes could be set in the future by the Small Council alone, without ratification by the citizenry. The proposal passed.[27] By the time of the Escalade, and in contrast to conditions which had prevailed in the age of Calvin, the ordinary citizen of Geneva knew nothing about the financial condition of his state.

Even more interesting, because more unusual in a sixteenth-century state, was the manner in which the republic integrated her leading refugee families. Men not born in Geneva were forbidden to sit on the Small Council, but there were no legal restrictions on their sons. The process of absorbing these newcomers into Geneva's political system, begun in 1559 when four of the most prominent refugees were given seats on the Council of Two Hundred, proceeded uninterruptedly after Calvin's death. The process was abetted by frequent intermarriage between refugee and old native families. The first son of a Calvinist refugee to sit on the Small Council of Geneva was elected in 1594. Three of the eight men elected to this body in the next decade had refugee parents. By 1605, there were 10 refugees among the 40 names on the Council of Sixty, while there were 67 refugees among the 138 names on the Council of Two Hundred — all near the bottom of the seniority list, of course.[28] The important point is that the Republic of Geneva had succeeded in integrating her refugees as few other European states had done with comparable groups of foreigners, without clamor and without major changes in the fabric of government.

Quiet, orderly, but decidedly more oligarchic, the Republic of Geneva steered her difficult course through the late sixteenth century. In the 1570's the magistrates decided to wear uniform dress in order to increase their dignity; by the 1580's, they were called "excellencies" or "princes," and ordinary citizens doffed their hats to them in the street.[29] That Geneva was increasingly oligarchic, that the Two Hundred were summoned less and less often, and that absenteeism at the general citizen assembly (noted by the secretary during the 1570 tax proposal) was a chronic problem — all these owe little or nothing to the entrenchment of Calvinism. They were fully a trend of the times. What few city-states survived the sixteenth century invariably did so at the price of sacrificing whatever remained of their communal spirit, by narrowing the base of government. Whether we look at an Italian city-state or at the Imperial Free Cities, the picture is essentially the same as at Geneva.[30]

†

The Church of Geneva in the age of Theodore Beza was subtly different from the Church in the age of Calvin. Much of this difference is due to the changed international circumstances of Reformed Protestantism during the long and tumultous French Wars of Religion.[31] Part of the difference is probably due to Beza himself, who was a different personality from Calvin. Beza was of the lesser nobility, whereas Calvin had a bourgeois background, as did most of the other pastors; this meant that Beza had a nobleman's suppleness and ease of manner which few of his colleagues could match. In his youth, Beza had been a poet. He never completely lost his taste for poetry, even after his impetuous conversion to the Reformation. He was also the disciple of Calvin (though only ten years younger than his master) and represented the second generation of the Reformation at Geneva. Beza's duty was to conserve rather than to create. It is possible that the greatest service which he rendered to Geneva was simply to survive until the early seventeenth century, acting as a physical link to the great age of Calvin.

Basically, Beza continued Calvin's work, and tried to mold his conduct as Moderator of the Company of Pastors along the guidelines sketched out by his predecessor. But there were a few cases where he departed, perhaps without fully realizing it, from the career and even from the teachings of Calvin. Such differences stemmed mainly from Beza's more "activist" temperament, which he dramatically demonstrated during the first War of Religion, by acting as Condé's secretary and by drafting the justificatory memoir for the rebels. Beza, rather than Calvin himself, was the real author of the Calvinist doctrine of political resistance, which he sketched out as early as 1553 and developed to its fullest extent in his famous hundred-page treatise on the rights of inferior magistrates after the St. Bartholomew's massacre in 1572.[32] Beza was always slightly imprudent in his political conduct. The republic's leading magistrate, Michel Roset, had to advise against the publication of Beza's *Du droit des magistrats sur leurs subjets* at Geneva "because it would be very scandalous and could cause a lot of troubles for which the city would be blamed"; Roset also had to reprimand Beza as late as 1576 for supporting a harebrained Huguenot scheme to seize Macon or Châlons—"he shouldn't consent to such things, much less get involved in them." Unlike Calvin, Beza remained on excellent terms with the Huguenot military commanders and was the Genevan agent for Henri of Navarre (later Henri IV) after 1571.[33]

Beza was less austere in his personal relationships than Calvin had been, and was even given to nepotism in his appointments at the Academy. He showed personal pique when his niece was imprisoned for adultery in 1571; his conduct and chagrin were less private than Calvin's had been when his sister-in-law had been convicted of the same crime not long before.[34] In general, however, Beza successfully sublimated his personal interests and carried out his duties as Moderator with considerable success. In some cases his conduct was at least as exemplary as Calvin's had been. Beza and his colleagues protested against the Council's decree exempting him from the lottery to decide which minister should serve the plague hospital during the outbreaks of 1564 and 1567, and when the same exemption was decreed a third time in 1570, Beza successfully persuaded the government not to exclude him from the lottery.[35] (Calvin, by contrast, accepted his exemption from this duty.)

His political role within Geneva was more modest than Calvin's had been. Beza never corrected diplomatic instructions or made entries in the official minutes, as Calvin had sometimes done. He confined himself to giving information and advice, and he gave it, significantly enough, from a bench at the foot of the council table — for so the magistrates had ruled immediately after Calvin's death in 1564.[36]

In certain other domains, Beza simply carried on Calvin's work to the best of his ability. He inherited a large number of polemical quarrels with both Lutheran and Catholic opponents, and pursued them in a vigorous, if somewhat pedestrian, style. He inherited and maintained Calvin's huge network of international correspondents, stretching from Scotland to Poland, and he even extended it in a few new directions such as Transylvania. Finally, Beza inherited Calvin's role as guiding light of the

Academy, of which he had been the first rector in 1559. Beza's record here was particularly excellent. He preserved the Academy throughout a very difficult period, filled with war, plague, and famine, and he extended its offerings by adding a chair in law after 1572. Beza had a special fondness for the Academy, where he maintained his chair in theology long after he had abandoned the annual presidency of the Company of Pastors, and even after he gave up preaching in 1598.[37]

Above all, perhaps, Beza continued Calvin's work by his struggle against the cult of personality. He was directing the work of a Church, not of a man, and like Calvin he saw great danger in any step towards episcopacy. The annual presidency of the Company was a burden which he had reluctantly assumed in 1564, and from which he demanded to be relieved in 1573, 1576, 1577, and 1578. Once, Beza and his colleagues asked the magistrates three times in succession that the pastors be allowed to change Moderators every year or every three years, but they were thrice refused. Ultimately, in March 1580, the council agreed to a more radical proposal whereby the Company changed Moderators every week, and Beza finally stepped down. He had recently been suffering from a severe pulmonary infection which had prevented him from reading or writing for seven weeks, and his recovery (at age 61) had not been complete. After 1580, Beza's writing began to tremble, his hearing worsened, he suffered from insomnia and from general physical debilitation.[38] Clearly, he could no longer sustain the work necessary to direct the Church of Geneva. A sharply defined epoch had ended, not with Beza's death — that came a quarter of a century later — but with his partial retirement. Beza had modestly chosen to abandon the reins of power while remaining as a figurehead on the prow of Calvinist Geneva. It was surely time enough to retire, for by 1582 Beza had lived longer than Calvin, Luther, Zwingli, Melanchthon, or most of the lesser reformers.

After Calvin's death, especially after the outbreak of war in 1589, the government of Geneva began to resume control over her church.[39] Operating in community affairs as a benevolently paternal force, the magistrates of the Small Council became more and more both princes and bishops, as had their predecessor. Trained in Calvin's Sunday school, weaned on cate-

chisms and sermons, they possessed a considerable amount of
theological knowledge and were able to conduct skillfully the
public examination of new candidates for the ministry. Their
encroachments into the proper domain of the pastors reached
such levels that in March 1605, they discussed the possibility
of having one of their members present at each meeting of the
Company of Pastors; the ministers did, however, block this
move.[40] Geneva's magistrates were not acting merely from a lust
for power. In theory, they were fully committed to Calvin's idea
of theocracy and to the privileges of the pastors, and they were
all self-effacing men who never used the first person pronoun
even in their memoirs. But after Beza's retirement in 1580 and
the magistrates' subsequent failure to find a truly prominent man
like Duplessis-Mornay (whom they briefly tried to hire) to replace him, there was no pastor who was equal in abilities or
eloquence to the best of the magistrates, men like Michel Roset.
There would seem to be no reason to quarrel with Eugène Choisy's
judgment that the true successor to Theodore Beza in the Church
of Geneva was Jacques Lect, a magistrate who doubled as professor of jurisprudence at the Academy. But there also seems to
be no reason to doubt another judgment of the same author,
that even in the early seventeenth century Geneva's Church was
never subjugated to her state so deeply as in other Swiss Protestant lands.[41]

Of course, the magistrates' interference in the pastors' activities
did not begin suddenly with Beza's partial retirement. Soon
after Calvin's death, there were numerous cases where the magistrates rudely reprimanded the Company, which apparently did
not keep order within its own ranks quite so tightly as it had
done during Calvin's lifetime. In 1564, Geneva's rulers were compelled to dismiss an urban pastor freshly returned from an important mission to the Queen of Navarre. Jean Merlin had been
bitterly critical of the magistrates' high-handed — "tyrannous,"
he called it — action in exempting Beza from the lottery to determine who should serve at the plague hospital. The Company
tried to bring him to heel, and succeeded to the extent that
Merlin apologized from the pulpit for his intemperate language.
He would not, however, make a promise of absolute obedience
to the magistracy in the future, so out he went.[42] His was the first

case of dismissal of a pastor for insubordination to the civil government since the exile of Farel and Calvin in 1538.

Two other cases soon followed Merlin's. Nicholas Colladon, nephew of Geneva's most famous jurist and secretary of the Company, quarrelled with the magistrates in 1568 over a new law on physical punishment, and again in 1570 over the secrecy of confession to a minister. When he began a third quarrel during Beza's absence in 1571, the storm broke. Immediately upon his return, Beza informed the Council that Colladon and his colleague Jean Le Gagneux (who supported Colladon's every move) were "completely intractable and beyond hope of ever changing." He added that it was impossible for him to exercise his calling with such colleagues. Le Gagneux understood, and left Geneva two days later without asking permission. Colladon stayed for three months, then began a new quarrel with Beza over the legal rate of interest. Beza, noting that he had supported the recent increase in the rate of interest from the pulpit while Colladon had condemned it, told the government that one of them must be a false prophet. This time Colladon left Geneva permanently, taking with him some of the official minutes of the Company of Pastors, which Geneva had a very difficult time getting back.[43]

There were other occasions later when Genevan ministers threatened resignation unless the Council changed an unsatisfactory decision; Goulart once did this in a famous case in 1595. But it was more a sign of the times when the Council called in the pastors in the summer of 1575 for a general censure.[44] The ministers, with Beza in the lead, had condemned the Council for showing too much leniency to the wife of the republic's secretary after the Consistory had condemned her for favoring a clandestine marriage. From the pulpit they unanimously accused the magistrates of weakness and injustice. The irate Council then summoned the ministers for a special sort of *grabeau*. First they forced Beza and his colleagues to admit their indiscretions and to make public apologies, then they summoned them back for special, private censures, reproaching them one by one for their imprudence, indiscretion, or arrogance. Beza in particular was upbraided for "not having properly followed the example of his predecessor" and for his "too great *facilité*." The Company humbly accepted these remonstrances, and Beza repeated his conviction that he was incapable of fulfilling his duty. The government then dismissed the Company, assuring them that the incident was closed.

If such incidents as the dismissal of Merlin or the government censure of 1575 provide useful illustrations of the ways in which the Church of Geneva was being subtly dislodged from the full independence and equality with the secular arm which it had won under Calvin, they do not give the whole story of the Church of Geneva after 1564. In many ways, the years *after* Calvin's death mark a pinnacle in the ministers' activities. Especially noteworthy is the thoroughness and vigor with which they fulfilled their duties as watchdogs of the community's morals.[45]

Very few social activities escaped the notice, and frequently the censure, of Geneva's pastors in the age of Calvinism. Their mandate, as they saw it, was a sweeping one, and it embraced giant responsibilities. The preamble to the revised Ecclesiastical Ordinances of 1576 expresses their position well.

Having considered that it is a thing worthy of commendation above all others that the doctrine of the Holy Gospel of our Lord Jesus Christ shall be preserved in its purity, and the Christian Church duly maintained by good government and policy, and also that in the future the youth be well and faithfully instructed, and the almshouse well ordered — for the support of the poor: which things can only be done if there be established a certain rule and order of living, by which each man may be able to understand the duties of his position.[46]

Establishing this certain rule and order of living was a complicated task which required eternal vigilance. From Calvin's death until Beza's death in 1605, scarcely a year passed at Geneva without some new demand by the clergy for legislation. Sometimes these requests were to remedy fairly trivial abuses, sometimes more serious ones. From time to time, as in June 1574 and again in 1579, Geneva's pastors would stitch together a whole bundle of grievances into a sort of ecclesiastical Grand Remonstrance. They complained that sermons were poorly attended, that the youth of Geneva had become debauched, that justice was not dispensed with sufficient speed, that overly luxurious clothes were being worn in public, that usurers abounded, that the price of grain was too high, and that there was entirely too much cursing in the marketplace.[47] Complementing the remonstrance came their proposals for sweeping reform, which might take the form of a house-by-house investigation of the orthodoxy, occupation, and morals of every person then living in the city.

It was only *after* Calvin's death that the moral and religious legislation inspired by his influence was finally codified into law. The sumptuary codes, regulating excesses in clothing and in eating, were begun by Calvinist (not Calvin's) Geneva. The bulk of this Genevan moral legislation is quite imposing; but then, so is a lot of other European legislation — particularly the sumptuary codes, whose origins go back to fourteenth-century Italy. It is more interesting and more valuable, especially in view of the reputation of Calvinist Geneva, to see how well this legislation was enforced.

Fortunately, we are in a good position to answer these questions with regard to two of the most intriguing moral problems of sixteenth-century Geneva: the repression of luxury and of usury. In Calvin's lifetime, as far back as 1558, the ministers had requested a remedy for needless luxury in clothes, but only a few scattered edicts were promulgated and a few offenders punished. However, the guilty included a magistrate's wife and the daughter of Amblard Corne, perhaps the most prominent magistrate in Geneva at that time.[48] The patterns set in 1558 were repeated when Geneva's sumptuary codes were decreed and publicly printed, those on clothing in 1564 and those on meals in 1566. Punishment fell on rich and poor alike. A poor widow was fined in 1567 for deliberately repeating her offense of wearing an expensive silk kerchief; she also spent four days in prison. In 1569, the wife of magistrate Antoine Liffort bought a very expensive shirtwaist, for which both she and her seamstress paid the statutory fine. In 1575, the wife of magistrate Ami Varro was warned by the Consistory for overdressing. The pastors asked for more stringent restrictions in 1577, largely because only five offenders had been punished for superfluous luxuries during the previous year. Accordingly, the sumptuary codes grew longer.

Men were forbidden to have long hair, women to have curled hair. Class distinctions were sharpened (another sign of Geneva's burgeoning aristocracy) so that, for example, an artisan's wife was forbidden to have a jewel in her ring. Infractions were fairly numerous, about a dozen cases each year under normal conditions. Offenders came from all steps of the social ladder. Ami Varro's wife was fined in 1595 for owning a silk dress, and some of the other offenders of the 1590's have a decidedly aristocratic cast. The daughter of Sicilian nobleman Guilio Cesare Pascale, Mmes. Pellissari and De Normandie, Mme. Jacob Anjorrant, Mlle. Burlamacchi — all members of the élite of the French, and especially the Italian, refugees — were among those punished, both for being overdressed and for being underdressed (a Mlle. Lullin was fined for excessive décolletage). But many of the offenders were artisans, especially valets who often dressed in their masters' or mistresses' clothes. Things had in fact reached the point where a deputation of Genevan tailors appeared before the Small Council in 1599, and some of them confessed that they were obliged to disobey the sumptuary codes in order to make a living.[49]

The important thing to remember about Geneva's sumptuary codes, like all other pieces of Calvinist legislation, is not that the codes were especially severe (Savonarola could do worse), but that they were diligently and fairly enforced. In the late sixteenth century, Geneva seemed to be a poor and plain city to most seasoned travelers, but not to her ministers.

The repression of usury was a constant problem at Geneva, although the city had been ahead of the times in permitting the taking of interest ever since the great Charter of Liberties of 1387. Geneva fixed her legal rate of interest at 5% in 1538 (the year when Calvin was expelled), and maintained it at that level until 1557, when it was raised to 1/15, which in practice meant 7%. All this was done with Calvin's full knowledge and grudging approval.[50] His successors, faithful to his wish to change nothing, grumbled and then acquiesced when the interest rate was raised to 1/12 in 1572. The only scandal that disturbed the ministers came after 1568, when Geneva's magistrates established a public bank from which they were empowered to make loans at 10% interest. Beza and his colleagues felt that this was excessive usury, especially if the loans were made to the poor rather than to merchants, and they warned that "at Geneva, all scandals soon become as big as mountains."[51] They agreed that the threat of scandal had vanished after the legal interest rate was lowered to a less dangerous 8 1/3%.

In this sphere, the pastors seldom complained about existing legislation, but often complained about its enforcement. Unlike offenses against the sumptuary code, usury was not committed in public. Loans were registered with a public notary, who seldom stipulated the precise rate of interest, substituting instead some vague formula like "with the interest permitted by law." Notaries did not wish to inscribe a patently usurious contract, since they too would be incriminated by it. They resorted to a variety of clever ruses, such as inscribing the loan for a value larger than had actually been given.[52] Despite these and other dodges, Calvinist Geneva did catch and punish a fairly large number of usurers, although the exact figures are not known. Here too, as with the violators of the sumptuary codes, we find both the prominent and the less prominent among those condemned. In 1558, a goldsmith was fined for taking 30% on a small loan, and an armorer for charging 8% per month. In 1566 and 1567, two wealthy merchants were condemned for charging 40% and 48%, respectively. Many usurers had infringed the law less flagrantly, having taken only between 10% and 15%. Those who were punished included some of Geneva's leading political figures. The son of Jean-Ami Curtet was condemned in 1564 for charging 15% interest to peasants in the pays de Vaud on small loans, which were made orally and by mutual consent. The most famous case came in 1582, when Ami Varro heard certain unnamed usurers denounced from the cathedral pulpit as dogs, tigers, and thieves. Feeling personally implicated, Varro demanded a hearing before the Council. He was found guilty and condemned to forfeit 50 écus which he had loaned at 10% interest.[53]

Yet after all has been said, these punishments do not add up to very much. Certainly Beza did not think that the magistrates were doing all that they could to punish usurers. In 1568, for example, he asserted that the plague had returned because of the "great usuries which reign in our midst." Later, during the

Varro affair of 1582, he returned to the same problem. "For the last two years," he said, "there has been unceasing talk of usury, and for all that only three or four usurers have been punished . . . it is notorious everywhere that the city is full of usurers, and that the normal rate is ten per cent or more.[54] Yet one should reject the idea that Beza and his colleagues were not economic realists. Once, in 1565, Beza objected to some proposed statutes against usurers because in his opinion they were too severe; he remarked that, if such a law were to be enforced, many men who lived from their capital would be forced to leave and go elsewhere.[55] Many other examples might be adduced of the pastors' acute awareness of the hard facts of capitalist life, and recently one case has been discovered where a minister was himself a mild usurer.[56]

In their struggle to keep Geneva free from excessive usury, the ministers won a qualified victory. This was all that they expected. They knew that greed was as real and as ineradicable a part of corrupt human nature as was vanity; and they only tried to keep both within the smallest feasible limits. At least some of the guilty were punished in Geneva, no matter what their political or social status, and this is more than can be said for the laws against usury in nearly every other part of sixteenth-century Europe.

Only a small part of the energies of the Church were expended in the fight against luxury and greed. Other matters that occupied the ministers of Calvinist Geneva included "disorders in the sale of wine" which caused murmurings among the lower classes in 1577; the preachers warned that such disorders might lead to popular insurrections such as other republics had known. In 1592, noting that the Old Testament made looting a mortal offense, the ministers severely protested the recent pardons granted to a few mercenaries convicted of pillaging; this protest, however, was so ill received that two prominent magistrates deliberately missed Easter Communion that year. In 1580, the ministers complained to the government about frauds which were being committed in the manufacture of silk. During some house-by-house investigations in the 1590's, the pastors found numerous abuses which they protested to the civil power, including the excessive punishment of children and the death of a four-year-old child from malnutrition. The pastors made certain that no women were allowed to keep taverns in Geneva, and they also attempted to keep the streets clean.[57]

Occasionally, their investigative activities led to a serious quarrel with the civil government. Such a case occurred in 1584, when the pastors uncovered some serious abuses in the administration of Geneva's *hôpital général,* and demanded that truly effective remedies be applied. They suggested that all Genevan *bourgeois,* not merely the members of the ruling councils, be made eligible for the office of deacon (as was already the case for Geneva's elders). They also suggested that pastors be allowed to inspect the almshouse at regular intervals, and that they be present when the accounts of the *hôpitalier* were verified and signed. The Small Council refused most of these demands, permitting only that one minister might be present at each of their four annual inspections of the almshouse.[58] Calvin's fourth order, the deacons, remained a body of magistrates instead of simple laymen, and the pastors had gained only limited rights of supervision over Genevan public charity.

By assuming the roles of Old Testament prophets, the ministers of Calvinist Geneva erected a structure that has been called an omnicompetent church. Few fields of investigation were closed to them, and there is a measure of truth in the cliché. The multiple activities of these sixteenth-century versions of the Old Testament prophets, however, seemed also to carry in their train the Old Testament rigidity of doctrine. The clergy of Geneva saw themselves as an immovable rock of orthodoxy. They opposed nearly all intellectual innovations, and they easily slipped into a posture of total doctrinal rigidity. When Gregory XIII's calendar reform came to their notice in 1582, they discussed the matter earnestly with Geneva's government. "Although," noted a Genevan chronicler, "such a reformation was not altogether undesirable, nevertheless, it was decided that we should not yield to the Pope, even in indifferent matters."[59] By the time of Beza's death in 1605, the Church of Geneva was fully dedicated to the principle of immobilism. The most archconservative Protestant theologians of the seventeenth century (who in general have not fared well at the hands of modern historians) came from the Church and the Academy of Geneva.[60]

The reasons for this rigid conformism within the Church of Geneva are not far to seek. The very environment within which the Church had been placed after 1567, as a Protestant rock in a Catholic sea, and as the center of a doctrine that her nearest Protestant neighbor (Bern) regarded with serious misgivings, provides the heart of the explanation. Isolated by religious geography, Geneva saw herself as a beleaguered fortress, and surrounded herself by doctrinal walls as thick and as high as the fortifications that girdled the city. The eternally vigilant Genevan Church fought to maintain her religious orthodoxy, just as the Genevan Republic fought to maintain her independence. This city, as the youthful traveler Thomas Platter noted in 1595, was not beautiful, but she was strong.

City and church, partners in a mutual struggle to preserve their separate identities in an alien world, gradually ceased their mutual conflicts in the early seventeenth century. Little by little, the pastors ceased their eternal investigations of scandals, their petty opposition to the secular arm. Little by little, they became part of the Genevan Establishment, harmonizing their views with those of the civil rulers. They abandoned their attempt to transcend local Genevan conditions, which they had done so well in the age of Calvin. Their attitudes changed partly because of their gradual awareness of Geneva's place as a beleaguered fortress, and partly for the more mundane reason that they were no longer *déracinés*. By the early 1600's, three or four of Geneva's urban pastors were native-born, while the rural parishes were similarly being occupied by Genevan-born citizens instead of French immigrants.[61] Just as the principal refugee families were absorbed into the Genevan magistracy, so the important local families were finally absorbed into the Genevan Church.

NOTES

1. A. Roget, "Les propositions de Jacques Boutillier, ou discussion constitutionelle à Genève en 1578," in *MDG*, 17 (1872), pp. 58–76.
2. The best available biography is Paul-F. Geisendorf, *Théodore de Bèze* (G., 1949). The publication of Beza's *Correspondance*, by H. Meylan and A. Dufour, was begun in 1961; four volumes have thus far ap-

peared, covering the period up to 1564, and the entire project will require twenty more volumes. See also F. Gardy, *Bibliographie des Oeuvres de Théodore de Bèze* (G., 1946), which lists over ninety titles.

2a. See R. M. Kingdon's forthcoming *Geneva and the Consolidation of the French Protestant Movement, 1564-1572*, Chap. 2.

3. Roset badly needs a biography. His diplomatic activities can be followed by using the index to him for vols. 4-6 of J.-A. Gautier's *Histoire de Genève*. Unfortunately, Marguerite Maire, "Introduction à la correspondance diplomatique de M. Roset" (mss. at AEG, 86/Ad/1: Prix Ador, 1925) is incomplete, since it failed to calendar his letters in the archives of Zurich or Bern. Additional information about Roset's other activities—he was poet, historian, military engineer, and wealthy speculator—lies scattered through various parts of Geneva's archives.

4. Roget, *HPG*, VII, pp. 207-33.

5. Henri Fazy, "Genève et la Saint-Barthélemy, 1572-1574," in *MIG*, 14 (1879), esp. pp. 10f, 25; Eugène Choisy, *L'État Chrétien calviniste à Genève au temps de Théodore de Bèze* (G.-Paris, 1902), pp. 81-88.

6. H. Fazy, "Genève, le parti Huguenot, et le Traitè de Soleure, 1574-1579," in *MIG*, 15 (1883). See also Ed. Rott, *Histoire de la representation diplomatique de la France auprès des cantons suisses* (Bern, 1902), II, pp. 95 f, 103ff. Negotiations described in tedious detail by L. Cramer, *La Seigneurie de Genève et la Maison de Savoie de 1559 à 1593* (G., 1912), I, chs. 14-16, and by Peter Stadler, *Genf, die grossen mächte und die Eidgenossischen Glaubensparteien, 1571-1584* (Zurich, 1952), pp. 131-83.

7. Quoted by Fazy, "Genève et le Traité de Soleure," p. 122 f.

8. Negotiations in Cramer, *Genève et Savoie* (G., 1950), III, chs.1-2, and in Stadler, *op. cit.*, pp. 184-212.

9. See L. Cramer, "La mission du conseiller Jean Malliet en Angleterre, 1582-1583," in *BHG*, 3 (1912), pp. 385-404 (quote, p. 391).

10. H. Fazy, "L'alliance de 1584 entre Berne, Zurich, et Genève," in *BIG*, 31 (1892), pp. 277-399; Stadler, *op. cit.*, pp. 215-51.

11. *Studies*, pp. 40-42; M. Bruchet, in *Revue Savoisienne*, 43 (1902), pp. 244 ff.

12. Chas. Borgeaud, *Histoire de l'Université de Genève* (G., 1900), I, p. 235 f; Choisy, *L'Etat Chrètien calviniste*, pp. 243-48, 256 ff.

13. See *Calendar of State Papers, Foreign, Reign of Elizabeth* [June 1586-June 1588], p. 165.

14. Printed by J.-A. Gautier, *Histoire de Genève*, V, pp. 575-87.

15. See the introductory chapter in Alain Dufour's excellent *La guerre de 1589-1593* (G., 1958: vol. 4 of Cramer, *Genève et Savoie*). Unless indicated otherwise, all information in the next seven paragraphs is taken from M. Dufour's book.

16. Dufour, p. 24 f.

17. Voltaire, *La Henriade,* note to Chanson VI; quoted by Dufour, p. 54.

18. Dufour, p. 251 f.

19. François de Crue, "Henri IV et les députés de Genève, Chevalier et

Chapeaurouge," in *MDG*, 25 (1901), describes the workings of this Genevan resident embassy in considerable detail.

20. Indications about these missions in Dufour, pp. 191–93, and about their financial success in *Studies*, pp. 46–48. Documents on one such mission, to the Netherlands, printed by H. de Vries de Heekelingen, *Genève pépinière du calvinisme hollandais* (The Hague, 1924), II, pp. 345–404.

21. See P.-F. Geisendorf, in *L'Escalade de Genève, 1602–1952: Histoire et tradition* (G., 1952), pp. 147–96. The bibliography on the Escalade fills a whole drawer of the BPU card catalog.

22. Henri Naef, "L'escalade de Genève, un événement européen," in *BHR*, 17 (1955), pp. 320–28; R. P. Lajeunie, "Henri IV, Clément VIII, et Genève, 1601–1603" (mss. at AEG, 86/Ea/8, dated 1952).

23. Text of treaty in *Sources du droit*, #1322.

24. B. Gagnebin, "Le XVIIᵉ siècle: la politique extérieure," in *Histoire de Genève . . à 1798*, pp. 365–88, and works cited there. Henri IV's subsidy is described in *Studies*, pp. 52 ff, and its continuation may be traced through AEG, Fin. A 3.

25. *Supra*, p. 158.

26. Dufour, *La guerre de 1589*, pp. 187 n. 3, 190–96; *Studies*, p. 44 f.

27. *Studies*, p. 32.

28. *Ibid.*, p. 98.

29. *Ibid.*, p. 100; Choisy, *L'Etat Chrétien calviniste*, p. 238 f.

30. Compare Marino Berengo, *Nobili e mercanti nella Lucca del Cinquecento* (Turin, 1965), pp. 235 ff., with E. Naujoks, "Obrigkeitsgedanke, Zunftverfassung und Reformation," in *Veroff. der Kommission für Landeskunde in Baden-Württemburg*, 3 (1958).

31. On this subject, see the forthcoming important study by Robert M. Kingdon, *Geneva and the Consolidation of the French Protestant Movement, 1564–1572*.

32. See R. M. Kingdon, "The First Expression of Theodore Beza's Political Ideas," in *ARG*, 46 (1955), pp. 88–100; J. W. Allen, *A History of Political Thought in the Sixteenth Century* (N. Y., paper ed., 1960), pp. 306 ff, 314 ff.

33. Geisendorf, *Théodore de Bèze*, p. 312; Fazy, "Genève et le Traité de Soleure," p. 21; Chas. Dartigue, "Henri de Navarre et 'Messieurs de Genève', 1570–1589," in *BSHPF*, 95 (1948), pp. 1–18.

34. Geisendorf, *Bèze*, pp. 256 ff. esp. 257 n. 3.

35. *Ibid.*, pp. 251–55.

36. *Ibid.*, p. 249.

37. See *ibid.*, pp. 261 ff, 266–70, 290 ff, on these activities. The current publication of Beza's correspondence will further illuminate his influence, which extended even to Scotland (unmentioned in Geisendorf's biography): cf. John Knox, *Works*, ed. Laing, VI, pp. 544 ff, 562, 613 ff; G. Donaldson, "Lord Chancellor Glamis and Beza," in *Miscellany, 8th Vol.* [vol. 43, 3rd ser.], *Pub. of Scottish Hist. Soc.* (1951), pp. 76 ff.

38. Geisendorf, *Bèze*, pp. 321–24.
39. On the beginnings of this reassertion, see R. M. Kingdon's forthcoming *Geneva and the Consolidation of the French Protestant Movement, 1564–1572*, Chap. 1.
40. Choisy, *L'Etat Chrétien calviniste*, p. 369.
41. *Ibid.*, pp. 412, 451 ff; Geisendorf, *Bèze*, p. 323 n. 5.
42. Choisy, *L'Etat Chrétien calviniste*, pp. 20–23; Roget, *HPG*, VII, pp. 100 ff.
43. See H.-V. Aubert in *BHG*, 2 (1899), pp. 138–63; Geisendorf, *Bèze*, pp. 258 ff; Choisy, *L'Etat Chrétien calviniste*, pp. 51 ff.
44. Geisendorf, *Bèze*, p. 319 f; Choisy, pp. 121–25.
45. Choisy, *L'Etat Chrétien calviniste*, p. 473.
46. *Ibid.*, p. 145.
47. *Ibid.*, pp. 106 f, 144 f. Compare Perry Miller, *Errand Into the Wilderness* (Cambridge [Mass.], 1956), p. 7 f, for a similar general remonstrance by the New England clergy a century later.
48. M.-L. de Gallatin, "Les ordonnances somptuaires à Genève au XVI⁰ siècle," in *MDG*, 36 (1938), pp. 213–18.
49. *Ibid.*, pp. 227, 229, 237, 239, 243–48, 259 ff, 269.
50. See the excellent discussion by André Biéler, *La pensée économique et sociale de Calvin* (G., 1959). It is often forgotten that Geneva's adoption of the 5% interest rate in 1538 was just one more example of bringing her laws into line with Bern's: see Feller, *Geschichte Berns*, II, p. 336.
51. See my "Change public à Genève, 1568–1581," in *Mélanges Antony Babel* (G., 1963), I, pp. 271 f, 274.
52. J.-F. Bergier, "Taux de l'intérêt et crédit à court terme à Genève dans la seconde moitié du XVI⁰ siècle," in *Studi in Onore di Amintore Fanfani* (Milan, 1962), IV, p. 114 f.
53. *Ibid.*, pp. 101–04 and notes.
54. *Ibid*, p. 101 n. 39; Choisy, *L'Etat Chrétien calviniste*, pp. 187 ff.
55. Bergier, *art. cit.*, p. 107 n. 58.
56. R. M. Kingdon, "The Economic Behaviour of Ministers in Geneva in the Middle of the Sixteenth Century," in *ARG*, 50 (1959), pp. 33–39.
57. Choisy, "*L'Etat Chrétien calviniste,* pp. 154, 299 f, 463, 441 f.
58. *Ibid.*, pp. 235 ff.
59. Printed by P.-F. Geisendorf, *Les annalistes genevois du début du XVII⁰ siècle* (G., 1942), p. 523.
60. A notable exception is Jacques Courvoisier, "L'Eglise de Genève de Théodore de Bèze à Jean-Alphonse Turrettini," in *Receuil de la faculté de théologie protestante de Genève*, 8 (1942), pp. 23–47.
61. See the biographies of Genevan pastors in H. Heyer, *L'Eglise de Genève, 1535–1909* (G., 1909), pp. 417–530, and the dates of their installations, pp. 199–234.

NINE

The Greatness of Geneva

The historical importance of Calvin's Geneva lay primarily in her value as a model to zealous Protestants in other parts of Christendom, including the British colonies of North America. To them, Geneva was a city set on a hill; she represented a nearly perfect model of Christian discipline. This is why there are seven Genevas in the United States today, as compared with only one Zurich and eight Parises. Calvin's city has preserved her fame into the twentieth century almost exclusively in these moralistic terms. To most scholars and to nearly all laymen, Geneva has come to be recognized as the soil where Puritanism first took root.

But there was another important way in which Calvin's Geneva was unique, and for which she merits a certain amount of the historian's attention. Geneva was almost the only city in Europe both to become and to remain independent in the sixteenth century. She swam very strongly against the political tides of this age, and she swam successfully.

The very decade in which Geneva achieved her independence, the 1530's, was a particularly grim time for Europe's autonomous cities. Late in this decade, the most privileged town of the seventeen provinces of the Netherlands was crushed after an ill-advised rebellion against the regency of the Emperor Charles V.[1] The uprising of Ghent in 1539, which was the last struggle for municipal autonomy in the Netherlands, had a brief and troubled period of success. But on February 14, 1540, Charles V, accompanied by his court and by 5000 mercenaries, made a public entry into the militarily defenceless city. He resided in Ghent for three months before pronouncing a general sentence on the rebellious city. The Emperor found her guilty of disobedience and sedition, and condemned her to forfeit her municipal charters, her artillery, and even the great municipal bell which had so often summoned her citizens together. The *échevins* of Ghent, together with 30 prominent burghers, 10 deputies from each guild, 50 weavers, and 50 foreigners, were ordered to make public penance, bareheaded and in shirtsleeves, before their sovereign. The moat was filled in. Ghent now had to pay an annual tribute to the Emperor. A new constitution was decreed, wherein the prince named the city's *échevins*, abolished the general citizen assembly (*collace*), eliminated the political power of the guilds, and named a new municipal council from deputies chosen by each parish. Ghent lost all control over her rural environs. Last but not least, the Emperor built a new castle within her walls to use as his administrative capital.

Earlier in that same decade, an even larger and far more famous city suffered a political crisis. The Republic of Florence, formerly the capital of Renaissance humanism, also fell to Imperial troops after a prolonged siege in August, 1530.[2] Unlike Ghent, Florence remained independent after her military failure in the struggle for communal autonomy; but like Ghent, she slowly shed her republican tendencies after 1530 and exchanged them for the habits of a princely capital. The last Florentine Republic had produced a remarkable resurgence of civic patriotism. She drew talents as diverse as those of Machiavelli and Michelangelo to work on her defences. She revived the spirit of Savonarola, punishing blasphemers, opening her *Consiglio Grande* with a Mass, and electing Christ as King of Florence by 1100 votes against 18. Yet this final great and nostalgic restoration of her communal spirit failed; it was ultimately crushed beneath the weight of mercenary troops more numerous and more capable than those which the Republic could recruit. The returning Medici treated the rebels more with pity than with fear. Only six republicans were executed, and most of the exiles who had fled in 1530 gradually returned to work under Medici princes. The restored rulers returned to Florence as hereditary *Capo di Stato*, and planned to build a fortress within the walls. The city's aristocrats, well represented by the famous historian

Francesco Guicciardini, had lost both the habit of opposing the Medici and the custom of a republican form of government. They would neither create a Medici prince themselves, nor oppose his creation. Finally, in April 1532, Pope Clement VII rigged a citizen assembly (*balià*) which abolished the basic institutions of the old Florentine Republic, the *gonfalionere* and the rotating *signoria*. Henceforth the city was governed by two councils, both elected for life, and by an executive appointed by the chief of state or "Duke of the Florentine Republic." A few of the old republican trappings remained, but they too withered away during the next decades; the last were removed after the Medici had recaptured rebellious Siena in 1560. Republican and communal traits died a lingering death in Florence, instead of being abruptly cancelled out as in Ghent. But in either case the results were the same. Both cities were put under the control of princes in the 1530's.

In both Florence and Ghent, the effective military force behind these civic transformations had been supplied by the armies of Charles V. This ruler, who dominated sixteenth-century politics much as his difficult subject Martin Luther dominated sixteenth-century religious history, was a consistent and vigorous opponent of rebellious cities. He learned his lesson after the revolt of the Spanish *communeros* in 1519, much as Louis XIV was later to learn his lesson from the Fronde. Charles V tried to uproot the remnants of communal spirit and municipal republicanism not only in Flanders and Italy, but also within the heart of his Empire. After the Schmalkaldic War of 1547, when his armies overcame (at least temporarily) the rebellious Protestant princes and cities, the Emperor made drastic constitutional changes in no fewer than 28 Free Cities of southern Germany.[3] Even Catholic cities and a few Protestant cities which had remained neutral during the war were now subjected to Imperial purification. Charles' primary purpose was to remove the guilds from all positions of importance, and to put municipal government into the hands of a patrician Small Council whose members were chosen for life and who filled their own vacancies. Officially, these changes were made in order to free poor artisans from public chores, thereby enabling them to rear their children properly. In fact, there were artisan councilmen in South German towns who were totally illiterate. Some guild-dominated town councils were excessively large. "My God," said the Emperor when all 72 members of the Small Council of Ulm appeared before him, "what can such a crowd do in a council? How can such dull, simple folk understand important matters?" There were very real abuses in municipal self-government which the Emperor rectified, and few of his reforms were overturned even when some of these same cities again rose in rebellion a few years later.

The only South German city that offered prolonged resistance to Charles V after his victory in the Schmalkaldic War suffered a special fate.[4] The citizens of Constance were put under the Imperial ban, or declared outlaws, in the summer of 1548. Spanish infantry advanced on the city, burning everything in their path, and seized it by storm. The desperate city had vainly tried to give her keys to the nearest Swiss official, the *bailli* of Thurgau. Finally, she had to effect a reconciliation with Charles V. Constance belatedly accepted his religious settlement, the *Interim*, long after it had been imposed on other Imperial Free Cities. This was insufficient. On October 15, 1548, Constance was degraded from the rank of Imperial Free City and her citizens were forced to swear an oath of homage to the House of Austria. She was thus shorn of all degree of political autonomy and became a simple piece of the Hapsburgs' personal domain. Several important citizens, including the leaders of the Reformed church in Constance, fled to safety in Switzerland. "Thus," said a chronicler of Constance, "day changed into night, and light gave way to darkness." It was the exact reverse of the proud motto that the city of Geneva had adopted only five years earlier: *post tenebras lux.*

The case of Constance, a city that was politically allied to the Swiss Confederation, was too close for comfort so far as Geneva was concerned. The weakness, or rather the absence, of Swiss aid to a hard-pressed city,[5] coupled with the exceptionally severe punishment meted out to her by the Emperor, made a deep impression on Geneva. (Apparently Geneva neither noticed nor cared about what had happened in the other 27 Free Cities or in Ghent.) The case of Constance seemed to offer an especially ominous example to Geneva. "There, but for the grace of God, go we." This thought, a cliché in today's Anglo-Saxon world, applies in its most literal sense to Genevan sentiment in 1549. Somehow, they had been spared.

†

What had preserved Geneva? For most of her historians, still infatuated in the twentieth century by the heady liquors of predestination, the answer seems clear. It was the will of God, nothing else. Dispensed thereby from a search for duller and more secular causes for the preservation of the Republic of Geneva, they have let the matter rest. By noting only the successful outcome of their history, they have tended to underrate or ignore some of the dangers that beset their odd little state. The possibility that Bernese protection might change into Bernese domination, as had already happened at Lausanne, or that Savoy might have captured Calvin's city with the Escalade of 1602 or with any of a dozen other schemes — these ideas seem never to have penetrated to the deeper levels of Geneva's historical consciousness. Her historians have generally gone their way with the confidence of sleepwalkers, just as their ancestors tended to do, secure in the conviction that they will be saved. The drama of Geneva's survival is seen at its very sharpest with the passage of Alva's army in 1567 or after the accession of Charles-Emmanuel as Duke of Savoy in 1580. The Genevans themselves, while recognizing the fact of such dangers, could not appreciate them at their true worth, precisely because of this conviction that they were somehow destined to be preserved. The attitude of her magistrates exasperated the hardheaded French diplomats who were trying in the 1590's to preserve Geneva despite her heresy; one diplomat reported that seldom if ever had he encountered such "particularism and unconcern with matters of importance."[6] Many of these same attitudes pervade Genevan historiography, with the result that their portraits of the city's enemies are never quite real. Genevan villains resemble the *marmites* used to symbolize Savoyard soldiers on the city's annual Fête of the Escalade. Children break them, crying "thus perish all the enemies of the Republic!" and out tumbles a mound of candy.

However, sixteenth-century Geneva faced real enemies and

real dangers. Perhaps she overcame them during the age of Charles V simply because she was isolated from the Hapsburg-Valois wars and because she was a jealously guarded satellite of Bern, whom nobody wished to disturb. Perhaps Geneva continued to conserve her Calvinism and her independence in the second half of the century, an age of bitter religious warfare, partly because she developed an aristocratic and efficient government. Few of the remaining autonomous European cities were disturbed in their privileges between 1555 and 1605, although those that had survived into this period had invariably done so at the price of stifling all internal quarrels and eliminating nearly all democratic influences. Geneva's dangers were far greater after 1555 than before, but she was far better equipped to surmount them, for she now possessed both an aristocratic and a Calvinist government.

Geneva's weapons of defense were neatly combined in a phrase that we have already noted[7] when the republic first scented danger from the reviving Duchy of Savoy in 1559: "trust in God and keep a sharp watch." The success of the Republic of Geneva in thwarting repeated threats to her independence was a notable one in the late sixteenth century. On the one hand, her success was a triumph of sheer will power, of the ability to resist even when resistance seemed hopeless (for example, after the withdrawal of Bernese troops in 1589 and during the subsequent siege by Savoyard and Spanish troops). On the other hand, her success was the result of her very practical precaution in building a system of fortifications that had few rivals among contemporary European cities. Geneva was a Holy City, a city set on a hill, but she was also a mighty fortress. Both these reasons must be invoked in order to explain how Geneva managed to survive so many crises.

Sixteenth-century Geneva was a peculiarly successful city. The single most obvious reason for her success was Calvin's residence within her walls for almost three decades. However, this explanation is not so obvious as it appears to be at first glance. Geneva most certainly could never have preserved her precarious independence in this century without having experienced John Calvin; the spirit of civic independence that had overthrown the old regime by 1536 could not preserve the new regime without outside help. Geneva received such help, but only indirectly from Calvin himself. The additional reinforcements that Geneva needed in order to survive the pressures of a revived Savoyard state after 1560 came from the discipline instilled by Calvin and especially from the talented masses of disciples who had come to live in his adopted city.

The fame of Calvin and of his city was extremely widespread in Europe by 1550. The *Livre des Habitants* recorded men who arrived from lands as distant as Crete, Malta, and Tunis in the 1550's. The earliest students at Calvin's Academy came from such places as Catalonia, Scotland, Gelderland, Calabria, and Venice. By 1560, Calvin was corresponding with a Lithuanian prince and had even received a request for trained personnel from the *Superintendus* of the Reformed Church in Russia.[8] His disciples, who were flooding Europe with propaganda from Geneva's mushrooming printing industry, had emphatically put this city on the map. Few princes or scholars had heard of Geneva when Calvin first arrived in 1536, but everyone knew of it now. John Knox told his fellow countrymen that Geneva was the most sincerely reformed place he had ever seen; the ex-bishop Vergerio told much the same thing to the Italians; a whole chorus repeated it to the French. Even a humble Sicilian knew about Geneva, "where people lived well and where the pastors were good men."[9] To Calvin's admirers, the place where he settled had become a wondrous city, which they liked to compare to Jerusalem. Book-peddlers (*colporteurs*) walked through scores of French towns and uncounted miles of French countryside, delivering this message clandestinely and helping to attract thousands of hopeful refugees to Geneva. Calvin's city was known to a surprisingly large number of people (many of whom never came within a hundred miles of it) as a citadel of holiness.

The converse of Geneva's international fame in the age of Calvin was her international notoriety. It has been noted that attacks on Calvin's city began exactly with the defeat of his enemies in 1555.[10] Catholic hostility towards Geneva, which was virtually unknown in the time of Cardinal Sadoleto's 1539 letter, now merged with local conditions to create a very different portrait of Geneva from that distributed by the refugees. Geneva was described as a den of iniquity; the French negotiator at

Cateau-Cambrésis in 1559 even compared her to a cesspool upon the face of Europe. According to this counter-propaganda, Geneva was a licentious city where the dregs of France and other lands had taken refuge in order to indulge their lascivious tastes. After all, argued the Catholic propagandists, why else would so many ex-monks and ex-nuns have gone there? The town was filled with plebeians, peddlars, and other riffraff, most of whom were simply fleeing from the king's justice. Poets soon entered the lists against Geneva, adding their voices to the Catholic chorus of denunciation. The great Ronsard composed an ode, the *Discours sur les misères de ce temps,* during the first French war on religion. The second part, or continuation, of the *Discours* contained a passage about Geneva which began:[11]

> *Une ville est assise és champs Savoysiens,*
> *Qui par fraude a chassé ses seigneurs anciens,*
> *Miserable sejour de toute apostasie,*
> *D'opiniastreté, d'orgeuil, & d'heresie.*
>
> *Laquelle (en ce pendant que les Roys augmentoit*
> *Mes bornes, & bien loing pour l'honneur combatoient)*
> *Apellant les banis en sa secte damnable*
> *m'a fait comme tu vois chetive & miserable.*
>
> *Or mes Roys voyans bien qu'une telle cité*
> *Leur seroit quelque jour une infelicité,*
> *Deliberoient assés de la ruer par terre,*
> *Mais contre elle jamais n'ont entrepris la guerre,*
> *Ou soit par negligence, ou soit par le destin*
> *Entiere ils l'ont liassée: & de là vient ma fin.*

This counter-image of Geneva, which depicted her as a hell instead of a heaven, as the least Christian instead of the most Christian of communities, was every bit as widespread as the first. Though this propaganda, which was most assiduously manufactured in Savoy after 1580, never did whip up a crusade against Geneva, it sometimes produced unexpected results. During the passage of Alva's army in 1567, for example, a Neapolitan temporarily deserted in order to see for himself the wonders of this modern Sodom. He attended an evening sermon and waited in vain for the lights to be extinguished and the general orgy to begin. Bitterly disappointed, he went off to tell his troubles to the local innkeeper. This man corrected his impressions of Geneva's godliness and reportedly persuaded the soldier to settle in the city.[12]

✝

These positive and negative propaganda campaigns spread the fame of Geneva throughout Europe, but they were scarcely noticed by native-born Genevans. Even such educated and articulate supporters of Calvin as Bonivard or Michel Roset seem to have had no inkling of Geneva's international reputation.[13] The interests of these native Genevans remained unwaveringly local, while those of the refugees were international. Only the latter were interested in producing propaganda for Geneva and for Genevan righteousness.

The fame of Calvin's Geneva probably diminished slightly after his death, but it continued to hold a certain attraction during the following decades. Sometimes the rewards of Geneva's fame were reaped in hard cash by the Republic's diplomats, who followed the same paths that had been trodden a few decades earlier by Genevan-trained pastors. Consider the Netherlands, where Calvin's church had sent a pastor to Antwerp in 1557 and later sent the famous publisher Jean Crespin on a mysterious mission to Antwerp and Valenciennes when a Protestant rebellion broke out there in 1566.[14] Apparently the Church of Geneva sent no more official representatives to the Netherlands until the famous Synod of Dordrecht in 1619, but the Republic of Geneva often sent embassies there after 1586. Sympathy for Geneva was converted into money and sent back along the route by which pastors and students had already come. During the war with Savoy, Geneva sent an embassy which brought 39,388 florins into her treasury in 1591. Another Dutch donation netted 58,909 florins in 1593, which were nearly one-fourth of Geneva's total receipts that year. In 1594, another 35,814 florins entered Geneva's coffers.[15] Without these sums, Geneva could scarcely have avoided bankruptcy during the ruinously expensive struggle with her far larger enemy.

The Dutch were not the only region so to aid Geneva. During

the war of 1589, donations for the Republic were raised in places as distant as Danzig and Transylvania. Immediately after the Escalade of 1602, Geneva received gifts from Neuchâtel (4,162 florins), Hanover (312 florins), and the Elector-Palatine (22,748 florins).[16] Charitable collections for Geneva were raised in England in 1583 and 1603, and in French Huguenot Churches in 1567 and 1595. Sympathy for Geneva, converted into charity, was a necessary factor in the financial and thus in the political survival of Geneva. She could be described without much exaggeration as a Church that had a city, in the same way that eighteenth-century Prussia was an army that had a country.

The refugees' activity in spreading Geneva's fame was not their only service to the Republic. We have already noticed that they virtually monopolized the medical and legal professions in Geneva. We have noticed that refugee businessmen, working with refugee capital, laid the foundations for Geneva's remarkable prosperity in the seventeenth century. The complete assimilation of these refugees with the old Genevan ruling class made both the Republic and the Church into homogeneous native organizations by the time Beza died. The talents, the wealth, and the moral fervor that these refugees had brought to Calvin's Geneva continued to serve the city for centuries after Calvin's death. Without them, Geneva would surely have remained a city of mediocre importance.

Native-born Genevans absorbed these refugees into their social and political structure, just as they absorbed Calvin's doctrines. After both of these had taken effect, Geneva produced a new kind of aristocracy, men who eschewed personal glory and who were imbued with a profound sense of responsibility.[17] Genevan rulers, such as Michel Roset's brother-in-law Jean-François Bernard, willed up to half of their estates to the public. Such Calvinist magistrates were well aware that public office, like the ministry, was a *charge*, a responsibility under God to serve the community, and not a means of personal advancement.

†

Thus far we have discreetly avoided the delicate question of Calvin's personal contribution to the greatness of sixteenth-century Geneva. We have suggested that his role was indispensable, but also indirect. To begin with, it is probable that Calvin had no special love for Geneva; if he had a *patrie*, it was France.[18] Despite his residence in Geneva for several decades, Calvin still looked upon himself as an outsider on his deathbed in 1564. To him, Geneva was merely the location in which God had chosen that he exercise his vocation. No doubt any other place would have done just as well, and no doubt some places would have left him with more pleasant memories.

Although Calvin had no great admiration for Geneva, he was nonetheless the greatest benefactor the city could possibly have obtained. His basic achievement, upon which his numerous biographers agree, was to instill Christian discipline upon a refractory and even revolutionary population that had just uprooted her traditional spiritual leader. Discipline, as Calvin remarked in chapter twelve of book four of the *Institutes,* is the nerve of religion. He believed in discipline almost as strongly as Luther believed in faith. As a famous historian has remarked in a slightly exaggerated passage,

the essence of [Calvin's] system was not preaching or propaganda, though it was prolific of both, but the attempt to crystallize a moral ideal in the daily life of a visible society, which should be at once a Church and a State. Having overthrown monasticism, its aim was to turn the secular world into a giant monastery, and at Geneva, for a short time, it almost succeeded.[19]

What Calvin tried to do in Geneva was to repeat, for a city of over 10,000 inhabitants, the same miraculous transformation that God had previously worked in him: to reduce the heart to docility (or to teachability; the Latin which Calvin used when describing his conversion is ambiguous). It was, as Calvin frequently affirmed in his letters, a harrowing task that sometimes seemed beyond his powers. But particular historical circumstances did favor him. If Geneva had not been an independent city, Calvin would probably have encountered even more difficulty; one cannot imagine him exercising his duties in the same fashion under a prince, no matter how pious. If Geneva had been an old and proud free city like the Swiss or Hanseatic towns, he would have met even more resistance from the civil authority. However, Geneva was pliable material which Calvin gradually shaped into a disciplined and educated community. It was the triumph of a superior mind and an inflexible will over a disorganized opposition.

The price Geneva paid for Calvin's triumph was heavy. Many of her leading mercantile families, men who had carried out the successful revolution against the Prince-Bishop, were angered by the prospect of a new independent spiritual authority setting itself up in a reformed city. Although some of these merchant revolutionaries (like Amblard Corne) were won over to Calvin's point of view, many others (of whom Jean Philippe and Ami Perrin are the two most famous examples) moved into opposition to him. They were permanently overthrown in 1555, partly by a younger generation trained in Calvin's Sunday schools. Foreigners who had come to the liberated city of Geneva after 1536 also suffered from the rigors of Calvin's program. Such curious and argumentative spirits as the former French monk, Bolsec; the schoolteacher from Savoy, Castellio; the Sicilian nobleman and poet Pascale; and the Piedmontese physician Blandrata — all were expunged from the Christian body of Geneva. These men reluctantly discovered that Calvin's community was not a forum for discussion, but a closed society. The revolutionaries of 1536 and the unsatisfied minds seeking debate were the principal sufferers in Calvin's Geneva.

But if Geneva paid a high price for Calvinism, she also reaped high rewards. Without the discipline and sense of mission instilled by Calvin, it is difficult to imagine how so many men and so many talents could have been attracted to Geneva by the 1550's. Without this discipline, Geneva could not have managed her unique achievement as a sixteenth-century revolutionary commune that maintained her independence until the French Revolution. Without Calvin, Geneva would have been nothing more than an economically decaying Alpine town that revolted against the House of Savoy. In all probability, she would have been recaptured by her former rulers either before or during the age of St. Francis de Sales. Geneva would exist as a footnote in the history of the Catholic Reformation, and nobody except the natives would have any cause to think her important. With

Calvin, Geneva has earned her share of attention in world history.

NOTES

1. Henri Pirenne, *Histoire de Belgique* (Brussels, 1923), III, pp. 117–28; also Karl Brandi, *The Emperor Charles V*, trans. C. V. Wedgwood (London, 1939), pp. 246–50.

2. Best narrative by Cecil Roth, *The Last Florentine Republic* (N.Y., 1930). My discussion based on the brilliant synthesis by Rudolf von Albertini, *Das Florentinische Staatsbewusstsein im Ubergang von der Republik zur Principat* (Bern, 1955).

3. Bernd Moeller, *Reichstadt und Reformation* (Gutersloh, 1962), pp. 70–74.

4. A. Maurer, "Der Ubergang der Stadt Konstanz an das Haus Osterreich nach dem Schmalkaldischen Kriege," in *Schriften des Vereins für Geschichte des Bodensees und seiner Umgebung*, 33 (1904), pp. 1–86; good summary in Johannes Dierauer, *Histoire de la Confederation Suisse*, trans. Reymond (Lausanne, 1910), III, pp. 338–43.

5. For example, Swiss Protestants gave rapid and effective military aid when the allied city of Mulhouse was about to fall into Catholic hands in 1587; see Dierauer, *Hist. de la Confed. Suisse*, III, pp. 451–56.

6. A. Dufour, *La guerre de 1589* (G., 1958), p. 147.

7. *Supra*, p. 118.

8. *L.H.*, pp. 31, 118, 144, 190; Stelling-Michaud, ed., *Le Livre du Recteur*, pp. 81–84 (#11, 15, 42, 66, 68, 101, 117, 136, 137); *C.O.*, XVII, #3000, 3014; XVIII, #3217, 3232.

9. Quoted by Alain Dufour, "Le mythe de Genève au temps de Calvin," in *Schweizerische Zeitschrift für Geschichte*, n.s. 9 (1959), p. 504.

10. *Ibid.*, pp. 509 ff; reprinted, with additional texts, in Dufour's *Histoire politique et psychologie historique* (G., 1966), pp. 85–94, 97–130.

11. Ronsard, *Oeuvres Complètes*, ed. Laumonier, XI, p. 55, lines 337–50. The following is an approximate translation; the voice here is that of France herself.

In Savoyard fields sits a town
Who by fraud has expelled her ancient lords,
A miserable dwelling-place of every apostasy,
Of stubbornness, pride, and of heresy.

Who (while kings were enlarging my boundaries
And were fighting for honor far afield);
Calling banished men to her damnable sect
Has made me, as you see, puny and wretched.

My kings, understanding that such a city
Would be a sorrow to them one day,
Were quite considering flattening her,
But they never began war against her;
Whether by negligence, or by destiny
They left her whole: and thence comes my downfall.

12. P.-F. Geisendorf, *Les annalistes genevois du début du XVII° siècle* (G., 1942), p. 507 f.
13. Dufour, "Le mythe de Genève," p. 504 f.
14. *R.C.P.*, II, p. 74; Chas. Paillard, "Note sur Jean Crespin," in *BSHPF*, 27 (1878), pp. 380–83; De Vries, *Genève pépinière du Calvinisme hollandais*, II, pp. 162 ff; Crespin, *Histoire des Martyrs*, ed. Benoit (Toulouse, 1887), I, xvi; III, p. 529 f.
15. *Studies*, pp. 46–48.
16. *Ibid.*, p. 53.
17. See the excellent profile by André-E. Sayous, "La haute bourgeoisie de Genève entre le début du XVII° siècle et le milieu du XIX° siècle," in *Revue historique*, 180 (1937), pp. 31–57.
18. Good discussion by Dufour, "Le mythe de Genève," p. 498 f.
19. R. H. Tawney, *Religion and the Rise of Capitalism* (Mentor paper ed., N.Y., 1959), p. 101.

APPENDIX

Calvin's Farewell Address to the Pastors (April 28, 1564)

There are two extant versions of Calvin's final address to the Geneva Company of Pastors on April 28, 1564. The longer and more polished version drawn from the notes of pastor Jean Pinault was printed in *C.O.*, IX, cols. 891–94, and has been reproduced elsewhere, for example in Bernard Gagnebin's *À la rencontre de Jean Calvin* (G., 1964). We have fully translated it on pp. 95–97. The second version, taken from the notes of "B. B. dit Corneille," who was the pastor Bonaventure Bertram, later husband of Beza's niece and professor of Hebrew at the Academy, has to the best of our knowledge remained unpublished. This version exists in BPU, Mss. Tronchin, vol. I, fols. 16^v–17^v, immediately following Pinault's. The variations between them are slight. Bertram's version touches on nearly all the same points as Pinault's, although not quite in the same order and often in a more abridged manner; Bertram's style is somewhat cruder, and it is possible that his account was simply jotted down hastily and never retouched. The text which follows has been established by M. Louis Binz, *sous-archiviste* at Geneva's Archives d'Etat.

✝

"Touchant ce qu'il a demandé de parler aux frères, qu'il avoit bien autrefois esté affligé, mais non pas tant que maintenant il sent sa faiblesse augmenter. Quant aux sens, qu'il les a fort entiers et subtilz plus que iamais, mais que la nature est defaillante. Quant à la nature substantive, qu'il s'eslourdit bien, mais que nonobstant il est tout rassis tousiours. Ne le dit par ambition, mais d'autant que la verité est telle! Dieu veut faire en lui tout au contraire de tous les hommes, à qui tout defaut de sens et de l'entendement; qu'il a souvent predit qu'ils per-droit la parolle quelques iours devant que mourir et qu'il le croyoit encores.

"Touchant sa vie, quant vinst en ceste ville, chassé pour ne vouloir laisser Farel qui n'avoit qu'un aveugle qu'il avoit amené, a tout trouvé sans moeurs et sans discipline, ne vie. Il y avoit bien des presches, d'un Me Froment. A reglé, mais qu'il luy a bon cousté; qu'il a beaucoup travaillé après les meschans, et à les dompter, s'y opposer en assmblées grandes et y venir avec son bonet. 'Tuez-moi,' 'Tuez-moi,' bien qu'on dist qu'on ne m'en vouloit; a eu des obades de 50 ou 60 coups d'arquebutes; a resisté aux complots secrets et a plus de 500 fois veillé que les autres dormoyent.

"Que ceste ville auroit des assaulx de dehors, mais que Dieu s'en vouloit servir, qui nous devoit estre un rocher invincible pour ne la poinct quitter. Que ceux de [Bern] trahirent ceste Eglise à son banissement à cause de l'Eucharistie et encores le craignent plus qu'ils ne l'aiment, veut qu'ils scachent qu'il est décédé de ce monde avec telle opinion d'eux.

"Touchant ses escripts et presches, c'est qu'il n'y a rien de ce qu'il désireroit de perfection telle qu'il luy souhaiteroit mais tant y a qu'il a suivy une simplicité et sens naif tel qu'il luy a esté cognu: n'a usé de subtilitez, n'y allegories encores qu'il le peust et n'a voulu se faire valoir pour quelque nouveau intellec forgé à sa poste, n'a usé de sophisterie, veut vivre et mourir en la doctrine qu'il a eue. Prie les frères d'y preserver et de l'enseigner de la sorte, de ne s'y faire valoir, ne cercher leur ambition ny profit, mais suivre la vraye et naifve sentence de l'esprit de Dieu.

"Touchant l'amitié entre nous et comment nous devons estre vigilans en nostre charge. De la nation meschante qu'à ceste heure qu'il s'en va mourir, ils ont besoing de ouspiller plus que jamais, qu'il n'a point cognu telle amour et humanité entre nous qu'il eust voulu mais plustost des picques couvertes et brocards, que le tout y doit mieux estre que cy devant. Aimez vous l'un l'autre, supportez-vous l'un l'autre, qu'il n'y ait point d'envie.

"Touchant que sommes obligez au ministere et promesses de vivre et mourir en ceste Eglise, qu'y avisons; il scait bien qu'on cerchera force occasions et moyens par dessous, mais tant y a que ce sera pour se monstrer desloyaux à Dieu et aux promesses par nous faictes.

"Touchant de n'innover rien et des prières et catechisme. Quant aux prières qu'elles sont prinses, surtout celles du dimanche, de celles de l'Eglise de Strasbourg. A fait le formulaire du baptesme à la haste pour les enfans de quelques anabaptistes apportez de 10 ou 12 lieux. Quant au catechisme, qu'il a faict à la haste à cause qu'estant rappellé

ne vouloist demeurer icy que Messieurs ne luy eussent accordé la discipline et un catechisme, qu'il leur monstra quant il le faisoit, qu'il y a
bien eu Viret, mais qu'il ne luy servoit de rien; a souvent pensé de le
refaire, mais Dieu ne l'a voulu. Est d'avis de n'innover. Prie les frères
qu'ils luy pardonnent d'avoir esté si impatient, colere et soudain, qu'ils
prient Dieu pour luy. Pour ce faict, recognoist que si Dieu ne l'avoit
soustenu, il seroit reprouvé, mais Dieu luy a tousiours assisté et croit
qu'il le fera et s'il luy plaist le soulager en ses maux et allonger sa vie.

"Touchant Mr de Bèze, puisque les frères l'ont eslue pour estre en
sa place, qu'ils advisent de le susporter et lui bailler courage à lui de
s'efforcer et faire valoir les graces que Dieu y a mises. Item se preparer
aux combats.

"Puis a touché la main de tous priant qu'on priast Dieu pour luy afin
que le Seigneur le fortifiast."

Bibliographical Note

I have attempted to make the notes accompanying each chapter sufficiently complete so that an annotated topical bibliography would be superfluous. Readers interested in investigating any special point in the history of sixteenth-century Geneva are accordingly referred to the footnotes and to the copious bibliographical guides in the collaborative *Histoire de Genève des Origines à 1798* (G., 1951), pp. 185 f, 214 ff, 228 f, 254 f, 280 f, 312 ff, 333 f.

Most of the information used in this book has been obtained from the works of local Genevan historians. There is a sizable mountain of such information today, since conscientious and accurate work has been done on this subject for over a century. The *Mémoires et documents publiés par la Société d'histoire et d'archéologie de Genève*, begun in 1841, and the *Bulletin* of the same society have been veritable models of accuracy and precision throughout their fifty-odd volumes. So have nearly all other monographs published by Genevan historians since the mid-nineteenth century. And those who choose to go beyond this printed work into the Genevan archives soon discover that a pleasant surprise awaits them. Geneva's records, public and private, are among the most complete, best indexed, and best preserved to be found in Europe. Most of their invaluable indices (to notarial records, to criminal trials, sometimes to official minutes) were made by nineteenth-century Genevan archivists, a diligent and tireless breed.

In both their published work and their archival organization, one can see the famous Genevan love of precision at work. Whether this is a product of Calvinist discipline or of Geneva's long and honorable affiliation with the watchmaking industry need not concern us here. My point is, simply, that both in her archival resources and in her printed materials, the city of Geneva has reached a standard of technical perfection as admirable as its utilization is pedestrian. Put the facts on the table, spell all the names correctly, and the story will speak for itself. So runs the credo of what might be called (with apologies to the eighteenth century) the watchmaker-historian, a species with numerous representatives at Geneva. Savor for a moment the following morsel, culled from a monograph published in 1927:[1]

"Will it thus be permitted to us to extract a synthetic notion from the events which we have analyzed here, to place them more exactly in the general co-ordination of history? We do not think so. It is permissible to search out the precise sense of the facts studied, by placing each one in the chain of those which precede and those which follow it; it is even an evident duty, because the facts will not have received their full value except through such a comparative *rapprochement*. It suffices to acquit such a task with prudence, and within the limits still imposed by the unknown."

In other words, Geneva has suffered severely from the type of gap once noted by Marc Bloch, between the technical precision of her research facilities and the primitive, two-dimensional fashion in which historical synthesis is carried on, "with prudence, and within the limits still imposed by the unknown."

Sometimes, of course, these standards of rigid accuracy and precision were broken in Geneva. Perhaps the most perplexing task of the outsider who investigates Geneva lies in his evaluation of the flourishing nineteenth-century school of anti-Calvin Genevan historians which centered around the Galiffe family and around Henri Fazy. These men waged memorable wars against the orthodox Genevan Calvinists, pitting their *Institut national genevois* against the enemy's *Société de l'histoire du protestantisme français*, battling over such subjects as the size of Calvin's income. Their work was dedicated to the proposition that Geneva suffered a sort of expulsion from Eden after the triumph of Calvinism in 1555. The Galiffes in particular carried on their crusade by underhanded methods. They did not hesitate to steal large numbers of official documents from the Genevan archives, and it was no easy task to get them back from their twentieth-century heirs. But now that the dust raised by Fazy and the Galiffes has settled, we can see that these rebels were only Protestant *frondeurs* who shared with their orthodox opponents a certain self-satisfied attitude towards their common fatherland, Geneva, which after all had survived even the nefarious influence of Calvin to emerge honorably into the broad daylight of the nineteenth century.

The last word has seemed to lie with their opponents, who smothered them under the 59 volumes of the *Opera Calvini* and subsequently exorcised their ghosts with the publication of Emile Doumergue's seven gigantic volumes on *Jean Calvin: les hommes et les choses de son temps* between 1899 and 1927. However, both these monuments of erudition

have flaws for anyone whose interest lies primarily in the history of
Geneva rather than in the personality of Calvin. The texts in the *Opera
Calvini,* especially volume XXI, are weighted in favor of the latter at
the expense of the former, as is only fair given their subject. Doumergue,
whose works are seldom cited here, tried in 4000 oversized pages to
refute every detractor of Calvin's work and personality. Doumergue
could see no wrong in his hero, who generally appears as a giant amidst
a background of dwarfs. Geneva was to him one of the more important
among *les choses de son temps,* and a full volume (III), plus parts of
two other volumes (IV and V), was devoted to her. Numerous errors
are inherent in Doumergue's approach. He has little or no notion of
the development of the free city of Geneva, and his treatment of Calvin's
role in Geneva is a gigantic and systematic perversion of the reformer's
own opinions on human greatness ("but still I say that all I have done
is worth nothing and that I am a miserable creature," as he said in his
final speech to the pastors). It would indeed be an amusing spectacle
to have Calvin review Doumergue's biography.

One work I have found immensely valuable—chapters three and four
were quarried from it, and its traces spill over elsewhere — is Amédée
Roget's seven-volume *Histoire du peuple de Genève depuis la Réforme
jusqu'à l'Escalade.* This work, begun in 1870, reached the period right
after Calvin's death when its author died in 1887. Roget was a prominent Genevan, an independent conservative who opposed James Fazy's
Radicals in local politics, and a somewhat shy professor of *histoire
nationale* at the University of Geneva who, reported his colleague,
gave interesting lectures but tended to get lost in detail.[2] He was one
of those gentleman-amateurs who produced some of the finest history
of the nineteenth century. He was very closely wedded to the texts
(which he read accurately, but whose spellings he modernized), yet
capable of seeing a broader panomara from time to time. Roget in fact
stuck so closely to the texts that he seems to me to have avoided a major
sin of his age, which was to read back nineteenth-century parliamentary
parties into sixteenth-century factions. (The "Old-Catholic" historians
of Calvin's Geneva, Kampschulte and Cornelius, are especially guilty
of this.) His year-by-year approach seems at times too detailed, but
at least he is accurate wherever I have checked him, and above all he
is not systematically prejudiced either for or against Calvin. Roget has
technical shortcomings such as paraphrases and modernized spellings,
and there is a slight misshapenness about his work which results from
an overuse of criminal trials and Consistory minutes (he makes Calvin's
Geneva seem even cruder and more unruly than she actually was, since
law-abiding people have so little public history). Roget utterly ignored

the existence of economic history, but so did all other Genevan historians until the last few decades. All in all, Amédée Roget merited the handsome tribute bestowed on him by Lord Acton, who named him in his 1896 inaugural lecture at Cambridge among four examples of "a more robust impartiality than I can provide."[3] His work has stood up well under the pressure of time, and is still indispensable to any serious and fair-minded investigator of Calvin's Geneva.

NOTES

1. Henri Naef, *Fribourg au secours de Genève, 1525–1526* (Fribourg, 1927), pp. 276–77.
2. See Chas. Borgeaud, *Histoire de l'Université de Genève*, III, 426; IV, 145–47. Traces of his political activities lie scattered through F. Ruchon, *Histoire politique de la République de Genève . . . de 1813 à 1907* (G., 1953), vol. II.
3. Printed in Acton's *Lectures on Modern History* (Meridian paper ed., N.Y., 1961), p. 32. There is a good appreciation of the first four volumes in the *Revue historique*, 8 (1878), pp. 197–205. For a grudging modern tribute by a warm admirer of Calvin, see Ernst Pfisterer, *Calvins Wirken in Genf*, p. 10 ("liberaller, aber ehrlicher liberaller").

Index

Academy, Genevan: 3, 93, 110–14, 156, 174, 199, 200–01, 212, 220, 231
Agrippa, Cornelius: 49
Almshouse (*see Charity, public*)
Amadeus VIII of Savoy: 32
Amboise, Conspiracy of: 115, 183–84
Ameaux, Pierre: 74–75
Antwerp: 135, 181, 233
Arche (*see Treasury, secret*)
Articulants: 66–69, 74, 148, 151
Aubert, Henri: 147–50, 156
Augustine, St.: 129–30

✝

Badius, Conrad: 166, 170
Balard, Jean: 9–12, 40, 43, 46, 49, 57, 65, 66, 70, 102
Basel: 31, 47, 73, 109, 113, 117, 138, 158, 169, 196, 200, 204
Bern: 2, 9, 16, 19–20, 31, 35, 39–43, 45–56, 64–89 *passim*, 97, 99–100, 108–09, 115, 117–18, 126–27, 138, 153–54, 194, 196–97, 200, 202–03, 205, 229, 240
Bernard, Jean-François: 234
Berthelier family: 36–38, 80, 84–85, 102, 149
Besançon: 33, 38
Beza, Theodore: 84, 96, 111, 112, 115, 159, 170, 177, 178, 180, 181, 184, 185, 210–15, 217–19, 241
Blandrata, Giorgio: 174, 236
Bodley, John: 113, 167, 174, 199
Bolsec, Jerome: 80, 87, 98, 128–32, 134, 140, 236
Bonivard, François: 2, 15–19, 36, 38, 48, 85–87, 138, 146, 154, 233
Brazil: 135, 166, 170, 184
Bribery, judicial: 154
Budé family: 167, 170, 173, 175
Bullinger, Henry: 89, 100, 108, 128, 129, 185

✝

Calvin, John: 17, 56, 66–67, 70–89 *passim*, 93–120 *passim*, 125–42 *passim*, 147, 152, 154, 156, 170, 174–75, 177–78, 181–82, 184, 186, 194, 210–212, 234–37, 239–41
Captain-General, of Geneva: 34, 48, 88
Caracciolo, Galeazzo: 167, 170, 173, 175, 184–86
Castellio, Sebastien: 84, 126, 133, 136, 237
Cateau-Cambrésis, Treaty of: 114, 117
Catechism, Genevan: 97, 102–07, 178, 240–41

247

Cathedral chapter, Genevan: 12, 13, 34–36, 45, 54

Chambéry: 34, 37, 39, 40

Chambre des comptes: 155–56

Chapuys, Eustache: 37–38, 43

Charles III of Savoy: 16, 35–44, 46–47, 49, 53–55

Charles V, Emperor: 36, 38, 64, 81, 128, 153, 225–28, 230

Charles IX of France: 114

Charles-Emmanuel I of Savoy: 198, 200–01, 203, 229

Charity, public: 14, 139, 156, 220

Chautemps, Jean: 139

Chrestien, Florent: 113

Clement VIII, Pope: 46, 227

Colladon, Germain: 152, 170, 173, 174

Colladon, Nicolas: 214

Combourgeoisie: 16, 33, 36, 41–43, 46, 52, 81–82, 108–09, 200

Condé, Prince of: 115, 117

Consistory, Genevan: 11, 16, 17, 71, 75, 82, 84, 88, 101, 102, 136–39, 142, 185

Constance: 81, 228

Corne, Amblard: 86, 102, 138, 139, 216, 236

Council of 200, Genevan: 11, 55–56, 66, 72, 79, 84, 88, 96, 139, 146, 151, 154, 156, 193, 209

Crespin, Jean: 166, 170, 175–77, 181, 187, 233

Curtet, Jean-Antoine: 161, 218

†

Davity, Pierre: 15

Deacons (*see Charity, public*)

De Ecclesia, Philippe: 132, 133

De l'Estoile, Pierre: 152

De la Baume, Pierre: 32, 38–39, 41–43, 44–46, 48, 51, 57, 58

De la Maisonneuve, Baudichon: 49–50, 52

De la Rive, Girardin: 102

De Normandie, Laurent: 169, 173, 175, 176, 182

Descartes, René: 99

Des Gallars, Nicolas: 96, 159

Diplomacy, Genevan: 73–74, 196–202, 205–08

Duplessis-Mornay, Philippe: 213

Dürer, Albrecht: 8

†

Ecclesiastical Ordinances, Genevan: 127, 136

Education, Genevan (*see Academy*)

Eidguenots: 9, 35–44, 86, 102

Elders (*see Consistory*)

Elizabeth I of England: 199, 206

Emmanuel-Philibert of Savoy: 109, 117–19, 197, 198

Enfants de Genève: 11, 82–87, 102, 119, 149

English refugees: 22, 166, 167, 172, 176

Erasmus: 18, 178

Escalade, Genevan: 194, 206–07, 229

Estienne, Robert: 166, 170, 177–78, 180,181

Eucharist: 97, 104, 106, 240

Excommunication: 84–85, 106, 127, 138–39

†

Farel, Guillaume: 10, 49–54, 56, 70, 71, 79, 95, 125, 126, 214, 239

Favre family: 55, 75, 77, 80, 85, 86, 102

Febvre, Lucien: 100

Ferron, Nicolas: 133

Florence: 226–27

Francis I of France: 19, 54, 56, 68, 74, 198

François de Sales, St.: 58, 236

Fribourg: 16, 21, 35–36, 39–43, 46–48, 50–52

Froment, Antoine: 95, 154, 240

†

Geisendorf, P.-F.: 165

Ghent: 225–26

Gingins, Aymon de: 35, 38, 45
Grabeau: 134, 150, 161 214
Gruet, Jacques: 75–77, 101, 153
Guilds, craft, in Geneva: 21, 159–60
Guillermins: 66–70, 74

†

Henri II of France: 22, 100, 109, 114
Henri III of France: 198
Henri IV of France: 58, 113, 154, 205, 207, 211
Hugues, Besançon: 37, 42–43, 45, 48, 50, 58

†

Institutes of the Christian Religion: 100, 104, 107, 109, 177, 178
Interest in Geneva (*see Usury*)
Italian refugees: 131–32, 166, 169, 172–73, 176–77

†

James I of England: 59
Jews, Genevan: 33
Jussie, Jeanne de: 15
Justice, Genevan: 31, 45, 150–55, 216–19

†

Kingdon, R. M.: 116, 134, 135
Kleberger, Johann: 8
Knox, John: 172, 186, 199, 231

†

Lausanne: 16, 22, 32, 41, 55, 56, 112, 133, 229
Lausanne, Treaty of: 19, 120
Lect, Jacques: 201, 213
Le Gagneux, Jean: 214
Leo X, Pope: 16, 35
Levrier, Aimé: 39, 40, 49
Libertines (*see Enfants de Genève*)
Livre des Habitants: 2, 82, 165–73, 183, 231
London: 135

Lower City, Genevan: 6–9
Louis XI of France: 30
Lucca: 172, 180, 182
Lullin, Jean: 67–68, 162
Luther, Martin: 18, 49, 103, 212, 227
Lyon: 2, 8, 30, 31, 33, 79, 83, 115, 117, 159, 167, 170, 181, 182, 183

†

Mammelukes: 9, 36–44, 46, 53
Marcourt, Antoine: 126
Marot, Clément: 17, 18, 181
Marnix van Sint-Aldegonde, Philippe: 113
Medici Bank: 21, 30, 33
Medicine in Geneva: 113, 174–75
Meigret, *le magnifique:* 54, 77–80
Melanchthon, Philip: 100, 128, 129, 211, 212
Merlin, Jean: 213–14
Missionaries, Genevan: 114–15, 134–35, 194–95, 233
Morand, Jean: 126

†

Naef, Henri: 44
Nägeli, H.-F.: 78, 80, 82, 87–88, 109
Navarre, Kingdom of: 172, 213
Netherlands: 171, 172, 206, 233
Neuchâtel: 33, 67, 70, 126, 133
Nobility, in Geneva: 3, 5, 34, 183–86
Nürnberg: 8, 49

†

Olevianus, Gaspard: 113

†

Palatine, Elector: 206, 234
Paris: 8, 126, 170, 178, 181, 225
Pascale, Julio Cesare: 169, 217, 236
Paul IV, Pope: 185
Perez, Juan: 177
Perrin, Ami: 9, 11, 20, 70, 74–75, 77–83, 85–88, 98, 108–09, 113, 138, 146, 149, 154, 158, 236

Pertemps, Claude: 74, 155
Philip II of Spain: 185, 196, 197, 201, 202
Philippe, Jean: 9, 66, 68–69, 88, 158, 162, 236
Piedmont: 4, 135, 140, 172, 174
Pinault, Jean: 95, 239
Plague in Geneva 72 (*see also Witch-craft*)
Population, Genevan: 2
Predestination: 104, 107, 128–31, 132
Printing industry in Geneva: 32–33, 166, 176–78, 180–83

†

Rabelais, François: 18
Ramus, Pierre: 18
Reformation, Genevan: 9, 49–54
Regular clergy, Genevan: 32, 54
Revenues, public, Genevan: 31, 155–59, 208–09
Ronsard, Pierre: 232
Roset, Michel: 1, 19, 85, 102, 109, 112–14, 196–98, 200–01, 213, 234

†

St. Julien, Treaty of: 207
Sancy, Harlay de: 202
Savoy, Duchy of: 19–21, 26–59 *passim*, 69, 109, 117–19, 194, 196–207, 232
Sept, Michel: 66, 69, 74, 85
Servetus, Michael: 83–84, 98, 101, 131, 140, 155, 169, 170, 175, 178
Seville: 173, 177
Seyssel, Claude de: 15
Soleure, Treaty of: 197–98, 200, 207
Spanish refugees: 167–68, 173, 177
Spifame, Jacques: 175, 184

Strasbourg: 22, 48, 67, 71, 95, 97, 110, 138, 240
Sumptuary codes, Genevan: 216–17

†

Tagaut, Jean: 186–87
Treasury, secret: 158–59, 208
Troillet, Jean: 80–81, 132
Tübingen: 133

†

Unitarianism: 131–32, 175, 185
Upper City, Genevan: 6, 12–15
Usury, in Geneva: 217–19

†

Valdes, Juan de: 172
Valla, Lorenzo: 129
Vandel, Pierre: 85, 86, 87, 151, 154
Varro, Ami: 216, 217, 218
Vaud, Pays de: 4, 33, 35, 89, 119, 128, 171, 218
Venice: 172, 184, 193, 204, 231
Vergerio, Paolo: 186, 231
Vermigli, Peter Martyr: 172
Vincent, Antoine: 167, 181–82
Vingle, Pierre de: 50
Viret, Pierre: 52–53, 79, 89, 97, 178, 241
Voltaire: 46, 202

†

Wars, Genevan: 55–56, 202–07
Whittingham, William: 186
Witchcraft in Geneva: 33, 72, 148–49, 153

†

Zurich: 67, 81, 84, 100, 108, 131, 138, 153, 170, 196, 200, 225
Zwingli, Ulrich: 47, 49, 107, 129, 213